# ELUSIVE EQUALITY

Pitt Series in Russian and East European Studies

*Jonathan Harris, Editor*

# ELUSIVE
# EQUALITY

Gender, Citizenship, and the Limits of Democracy
in Czechoslovakia, 1918–1950

Melissa Feinberg

UNIVERSITY OF PITTSBURGH PRESS

Published by the University of Pittsburgh Press, Pittsburgh PA 15260
Copyright © 2006, University of Pittsburgh Press
Manufactured in the United States of America
Printed on acid-free paper
10 9 8 7 6 5 4 3 2 1


Library of Congress Cataloging-in-Publication Data
Feinberg, Melissa.
  Elusive equality : gender, citizenship, and the limits of democracy in
Czechoslovakia, 1918-1950 / Melissa Feinberg.
    p. cm. — (Pitt series in Russian and East European studies)
  Includes bibliographical references and index.
  ISBN 0-8229-4281-X (cloth : alk. paper)
    1. Women—Czechoslovakia—Social conditions. 2. Women's rights—
Czechoslovakia. I. Title. II. Series.
  HQ1610.3.F44 2006
  323.3'40943709041—dc22
                            2005034018

# CONTENTS

# ACKNOWLEDGMENTS

This book was first conceived inside a remarkable intellectual community at the University of Chicago. More than anything else, this community helped to shape my sense of what it means to be a historian, and I am grateful for that. I must particularly thank Leora Auslander, Sheila Fitzpatrick, and most of all, Michael Geyer, for providing me with incredible models of critically engaged scholarship and encouraging me to always think as boldly as possible. I am also indebted to the members of the University of Chicago's modern European history workshop for their friendship, constructive criticism, and for forcing me to always place Czechoslovakia in its broader European context.

A wide array of institutions and individuals assisted me during the years of research and writing that went into this project. I would particularly like to thank the Czech Fulbright Commission, the Andrew J. Mellon Foundation, the Dwight D. Eisenhower Foundation, the Woodrow Wilson International Center for Scholars, and the University of North Carolina at Charlotte for their financial support. The Center for Gender Studies at the University of Chicago gave me an office for a year, without which this book might never have been written. I would like to acknowledge the assistance I received from the staffs at the many archives and libraries at which I worked in the Czech Republic, especially the State Central Archives and the National Library in Prague, where I spent many, many hours. I am also grateful to Mrs. Jana Kanská, who allowed me to see the interrogation records of her mother, Milada Horáková. Horáková was an inspiring figure to research and the opportunity to read through these papers was a real gift.

This book would certainly never have reached its final state without the excellent feedback I received from the fellow members of the Kennebunkport Circle: Eagle Glassheim, Cynthia Paces, and Paul Hanebrink. May we have many future symposia together! Benjamin Frommer and Andrea Orzoff also helped me enormously as historians and friends. Nancy Wingfield read the entire manuscript twice, and was a constant source of advice and encouragement. Jindřich Toman invited me to present work at several of the Michigan Czech Cultural Studies workshops, which led to many fruitful discussions with the participants. I am grateful to Kathleen Canning, Belinda Davis, Alena Heitlinger, Claire Nolte, and Bonnie Smith for their extremely helpful comments on the penultimate draft. My colleagues from the history department at the University of North Carolina at Charlotte read chapters, helped me negotiate the publishing process, and provided a supportive working environment. Through it all, I could always count on Melanie Feinberg, my twin and my friend, to keep me from despair, make me laugh, or even give me a kick in the pants when I needed it. Paul Hanebrink has been there since the very beginning, and over the years has cheerfully read through so many drafts that he can make the arguments better than I can. Even when circumstances have forced us to be apart, he has always been there for me, and has provided the core of stability, sanity, and love that has made everything possible.

ELUSIVE EQUALITY

# INTRODUCTION

*Gender, Rights, and the Limits of Equality in Czechoslovakia*

> Democracy is not only a form of government, it is not only what is
> written in constitutions; democracy is a view of life, which rests on
> faith in men, in humanity and human nature . . . real democracy is
> only possible where men trust one another, and honestly seek the
> truth. Democracy is a conversation among equals.
>
> Tomáš Garrigue Masaryk, president of Czechoslovakia, 1918–1935,
> quoted in Karel Čapek, *Masaryk on Thought and Life*

IN THE SUMMER and fall of 1989, the world was transfixed by the "carnival of revolution" wending its way through Central and Eastern Europe.[1] It was a season in which the impossible became real: the Hungarians rolled back the barbed wire on their western border, Poles elected Solidarity candidates to the Sejm, and Berliners celebrated under the Brandenburg Gate. Equally dramatic was the scene in Prague, where hundreds of thousands of people gathered in Wenceslas Square, shook their keys, and peacefully brought about a democratic revolution. Czechoslovakia's Communist government melted away, leaving former dissident Václav Havel as the country's new president. Seeing the Communist regimes of Eastern Europe collapse so suddenly and so completely, most observers predicted that Eastern Europe would have a quick and easy transition from Communism to democracy. Local leaders, as well as the Western academics, politicians, and investors who rushed in to help them develop new political and economic systems, generally assumed that their task was straightforward. They would write new constitutions and hold regular elections, and democracy would result. What they failed to see, however, was that even with a man like Václav Havel as the symbolic head of the state, creating a political culture capable of sustaining those democratic institutions was a far more difficult task.[2] As most scholars of the region now realize, changing laws and electing new leaders was only the beginning of a long and difficult process.

A similar moment in Czechoslovakia's past occurred in 1918. In the aftermath of the First World War, empires collapsed across Central and Eastern Europe. Germany's emperor was forced to flee, and his realm became a republic. The Habsburg Monarchy was carved into several independent states, including Hungary, Yugoslavia, and the Czechoslovak Republic. As in 1989, Czech crowds filled Prague's squares to celebrate the change of regime. Many did so because they assumed that this revolutionary shift in government had brought them democracy. Czech nationalists had been craving democracy for decades. The Czechs, they believed, were a nation especially suited to democracy, and, in fact, required it to be truly free. With the sudden departure of the Habsburg emperor, many thought that the Czech transition to democracy was complete. But aside from being something good for the Czech nation, what exactly was this democracy? What were its values, its priorities, its morals, and ethics? What kind of laws would it mandate, what social policies would it foster? What kind of community would it inspire?

For decades, Czechs debated these questions, which became struggles over the meaning of the Czechoslovak state, the nature of the Czech nation, and the value of individual equality and freedom, Conflicts over the meaning of women's citizenship were at the heart of these struggles. Gender equality, far from being a peripheral matter that concerned only a few women's activists, was central to Czech politics. Women's citizenship was a privileged arena in which uncertainties about democracy, and especially democracy's more radical potential, could be vocalized and enacted. Between 1918 and 1950, the Czech love of democracy remained ostensibly strong. But this attachment to democracy increasingly became a tie to a name, rather than to any specific set of political ideals. The reality, as manifested in government policies and programs, was far more ambivalent. By the end, "democracy" could be used to legitimize regimes that were in fact not particularly free, including the rightist authoritarian regime that succeeded the First Czechoslovak Republic in 1938 under the label of "authoritarian democracy," and the repressive Communist government that ruled Czechoslovakia after 1948 under the mantle of the "people's democracy."

## The Peculiar Threat of Women's Equality

My analysis of the problem of democracy in Czech political culture begins with what was known in the early twentieth century as the "woman question." The basic issue behind this term was whether women were equal to men and deserving of the same legal rights and responsibilities. Many Czech women and men believed that democracy and women's equality were inseparably linked. As a result of this feeling, the framers of the Czechoslovak Republic of 1918 proposed granting women suffrage and new access to education and employment. The Czech public responded with applause. Yet this easy acceptance of what Czechs explicitly called "women's equality" belied the true complexity of the woman question. Like democracy itself, women's equality was a term that was open to debate.

Czech feminists, who were perhaps the most utopian of Czech democrats, had a very expansive idea of what women's equality should be. In their version of democracy, all citizens were equal and had the same rights, regardless of gender. In concrete terms, this meant that the rights women had gained shortly after 1918 were not enough. There were still many instances of Czechoslovak law—particularly regulations directed at the family—that did not treat men and women as equals. Statutes spoke of husbands and wives rather than citizens or spouses, and used gender difference as the very basis of policy. Czech feminists made it their mission to see that such laws were changed, even if the results went against widely held beliefs about the distribution of power within the family. In their opinion, tradition was never a good reason for standing in the way of democratic progress. They believed that limiting the reach of the democratic ethic of equality did more than simply curtail women's freedom. Such acts represented an attack on their vision of the Czech nation itself.

These women hoped that all good Czech democrats would share their views, but they discovered that Czechs held widely divergent beliefs about how gender should function in a democratic society. Most Czechs, to varying degrees, did not see "democracy" as a barrier to laws that distinguished between citizens on the basis of their gender. This was not an issue that mapped easily onto partisan divisions. Czech feminists (men and women) belonged to a wide range of political parties. The only party they did not belong to was the Catholic-oriented People's Party. Those who articulated any of a range of nonfeminist positions on women's equality belonged to every Czech political party. While I have generally identified the party membership of individuals, as far as it was known, this information is never a reliable predictor of a person's position on women's citizenship.

Those Czechs who wanted their government to adopt a more limited view of women's equality generally made a much greater distinction between the public and private sphere than the feminists did, relying more on the traditional tenets of bourgeois democratic liberalism. Nineteenth-century advocates of liberal democracy, as Carole Pateman has theorized, essentially worked toward establishing a male fraternity of citizens that would collectively share public power, leaving women marooned in a private sphere that was supposed to exist outside the realm of the state, with each household ruled absolutely by the male citizen at its head.[3] For the most part, twentieth-century Czechs agreed this model was out-of-date and supported opening up the public sphere to women as well as men. But, while the feminists argued that the private sphere also needed to be democratized, their opponents wanted to retain the distinction between domestic and public worlds, with equality stopping at the front door. Inside the walls of the home, citizens would revert to being husbands and wives, and a man would still be the head of his household.

In this version of democracy, man's arbitrary laws could not challenge nature's dictates about gender. As citizens, women might now have an expanded public role, but this did not take away their natural functions within the domestic sphere. Many Czechs firmly believed that women's unique role in the family was not something they could choose: it was their social duty, and their responsibility to the nation. Thus, Czech law would need to endorse that role, primarily by making distinctions between different kinds of rights in different situations, at times allowing social functions to determine which rights a citizen could claim. Far from being irrelevant, gender would be a necessary legal category, and a perfectly acceptable element in policy decisions and government practices.

The struggle to balance individual freedom with the collective needs of society is a characteristic feature of modern democracies, all of which need to make decisions about how to achieve a workable balance between these occasionally competing interests. Modern democratic governments, however, generally have a set of guidelines for achieving this balance: this is their constitution. The Constitution of 1920 gave Czechoslovakia a very progressive rulebook for its future laws. One of its most striking features was Article 106, which essentially forbade discrimination on the basis of gender or class. This section of the constitution gave a concrete content to the model of "women's equality" that many found unsettling. It also gave a sense of mission to Czech feminists, who made implementing Article 106 the foundation of their work, arguing that they were simply pushing their government to adhere to its own rules. Their constant use of Article 106 put their opponents in an awkward position. Those who argued for a more gendered model of citizenship claimed that they were loyal citizens of the republic. Indeed, they believed that their attitude toward rights was the one best suited to the needs of the country. But, unable to deal directly with the legal obstacle of Article 106, this group of democrats began to urge lawmakers to ignore the constitution and its mandate of gender equality. Rather than attempt to revise or amend the article in question, they hoped to simply dismiss the constitution as a relevant factor. Gradually, they found themselves adopting a political methodology that helped to hollow out the Czechoslovak Constitution, turning its rules into mere guidelines that suggested rather than mandated the shape of the law.

Those who attacked the idea of women's equality as a threat to family values and national stability certainly did not see themselves as against democracy. But, although they did not put it that way, they were trying to refashion democracy in order to neutralize the potential danger they believed it posed to established patterns of family life. They wanted to place definite limits on the concept of equality, making it above all subordinate to the national interest. If expanding women's freedom undermined the family as a social institution, and thereby weakened the nation, then it would need to be curtailed for the sake of the greater good.

This need to stabilize the family at all costs was characteristic of Europe during the decades after the First World War. In the aftermath of an incredibly brutal war, postwar revolutions, and economic devastation, Europeans across the continent hoped to restore order by restoring the family. As historians of various Western European nations have shown, Europeans watched women's efforts to free themselves—either via party politics, through cutting their hair and shortening their skirts, or by achieving economic independence—with a mixture of excitement, fascination, and revulsion. They feared the possibility of a world where gender difference no longer existed, or, as historian Mary Louise Roberts puts it, a "civilization that no longer had sexes." Across Europe, the desire to fix gender by grounding it ever more firmly in the traditional family was a strong factor drawing people toward fascism and other forms of authoritarianism. The European Right claimed that it could put society back on track by getting men back to work and placing women back in the home. This appealing message found adherents all over the continent, including Czechoslovakia.[4]

## Czechoslovakia: The Home of Czech Democracy?

The part of Europe that this book refers to as the "Czech lands" contained a complicated mix of peoples in the first half of the twentieth century.[5] Located right in the center of the European continent, the provinces of Bohemia and Moravia had communities that spoke both Czech and German (often interchangeably), and a smattering of other languages as well. The state of Czechoslovakia was constructed by adding the regions of Slovakia and Ruthenia to the Czech lands, creating an intensely multinational republic, in which people identified themselves as Czechs, Slovaks, Germans, Hungarians, Poles, Jews, and Ruthenians, and other nationalities, as well. Much of the most recent scholarship on Czechoslovakia has been concerned with the conflicts between the country's many national or ethnic groups, especially between the Czechs and Germans. In just the past five years, there has been an explosion of excellent research on the process of becoming national in the provinces of Bohemia and Moravia. This literature has examined the intense pressure people felt to pick sides in these struggles, to become either "German" or "Czech."[6]

This book takes a different focus. While not denying the importance of research into conflicts between ethnic groups, I look at the conflicts within one group: the Czechs. In October of 1918, Czechs cheered the prospect of a democratic Czechoslovakia because they believed it would bring them equality and freedom, both as individual citizens and as a nation. For many Czechs, "democracy" always carried within it this double meaning. It was a set of political ideals that would help create a just system of governance for all, and, at the same time, it was the form of government that would best enable the Czech nation to flourish. It was both egalitarian and ethno-nationalist. Therefore, when Czechs debated democracy, they were not just arguing over political ideals—they were also arguing over the way they defined their nation. It is because of this curious tie that Czechs made between democracy and their nation that I believe it makes sense to limit my analysis of democratic discourse in Czechoslovakia to this one national group.

Before 1918, Czechs did not need to be terribly specific about what they meant when they talked about democracy. However, after 1918, it became apparent that there was no single vision of democracy within the Czech nation. In fact, instead of subscribing to one view, Czech politics harbored many different opinions of what democracy should actually look like. While some seemed to favor a liberal state with republican government, others envisioned an egalitarian community of citizens, or a state dedicated to social justice and equality of economic opportunity, or something else entirely. This ambiguity over the meaning of democracy could never be definitively resolved, for to do so might have shattered the political community that had constituted itself around the idea of a Czech democracy. So the term remained open and contested, and debate over democracy became and remained a crucial element in Czech political life.

Turning from a more exclusive focus on minority politics to gender politics gives us a new way of examining democracy in Czechoslovakia. This approach helps us to see that the difficulty of creating stable democracies in interwar Europe cannot be reduced to disputes over who would speak which language or which group would have access to what land. There is something deeper lurking behind these issues: the problem of dealing with difference. The Czechs hoped that the democracy they created within the Czechoslovak Republic would serve them as a sort of political and spiritual home, a place described by Bonnie Honig as "free of power, conflict and struggle, a place—an identity, a form of life, a group vision—unmarked or unriven by difference."[7] National minorities like the Germans, Hungarians, or even the Slovaks, each of which also had its own designs on a mythical political unity, openly resisted being subsumed into a Czech state and therefore posed the most visible threat to this dream for "home." The conflict that resulted certainly did have an impact on Czech politics, as the rise of Konrad Henlein's openly antistate Sudeten German Party and the postwar expulsions of German and Hungarian citizens from Czechoslovakia attest. However, the Czech struggle to deal with the different nationalities in their midst only served to cover up the more fundamental problem: that the home they hoped to find did not exist. Battles over the meaning of women's citizenship reveal that conflict and struggle actually lived at the very heart of the Czech political community. This was an uncomfortable reality to deal with. To safely navigate it, Czechs would need to realize that "democracy" could not be a place of refuge in sameness, but in fact would always be hard work.

This analysis suggests that the strength of the Czech democracy was also its Achilles heel. As has been so often noted, the Czechoslovak Republic was exceptional in Central and Eastern Europe for being the one place where democracy seemed to work. As the typical narrative goes, the Czechs "had" democracy, and when they lost it, after Munich in 1938 and again in 1948, it was not their fault. They merely succumbed to the enormous geopolitical pressures brought against them by the worst totalitarian regimes of Europe. My work, however, complicates this picture by showing that while Czechs wanted to believe that they had achieved democracy, and did in fact establish democratic institutions, their inability to come to terms with the problem of difference rendered them incapable of creating the kind of political culture that would support those institutions in times of true crisis. When dissent threatened the ability of democracy to serve as the national home, Czech politicians tried to stifle it and legislate away the differences instead of working to build a new coalition of citizens. Their attempts to still the conflict in order to save democracy ironically led them away from it.

In essence, although the Czechs were emotionally attached to the idea of democracy, they were not able to deal with the perils of a system that counted equality as one of its primary political values. The arena of women's rights was one place in which this came through most forcefully. The potential of women's equality to destabilize a perceived model of happy domesticity triggered a whole series of parallel fears, reverberating through their hopes for the nation, and the democratic state that stood behind it. As it began to appear that women's rights might pose a threat to the "national home," politicians and the public eventually moved to curtail them, not caring that doing so might go against both the laws and ideals of their democratic government.

Thinking about the Czech case in this way gives us a new means of conceptualizing the crisis of democracy in interwar Europe. Historians frequently concentrate on how democracies were attacked from without by the forces of fascism and communism, and pay less attention to the conflicts that fractured European democracies from within. Rather than assuming that Europeans wanted democracy, we should think about how and why they feared it, and its potential to bring more change into already disrupted lives. Here, the issue of rights becomes central. In the Czech case, politicians, worried about the impact of women's equality on the family, developed a capricious attitude toward rights. From the 1920s into the late 1930s, their concept of rights gradually became less absolute, and rights themselves were seen as less important than political, familial, or national needs. Once Czech democrats accepted rights as shifting, and citizenship as something that deferred to the nation rather than the law or the constitution, they began to find themselves making ideological common cause with their fascist or authoritarian neighbors. In the mid-1940s, individual rights would again be sidelined, this time in the name of social justice.

The legal issues that motivated Czech debates over women's citizenship were issues of Czechoslovak law, just as the Czech politicians who discussed them were working for the Czechoslovak Republic, not the Czech nation (although they may have well seen these two things as essentially identical). To help clarify this potentially confusing situation, I have used the adjective "Czech" to indicate that I am making claims that are only relevant for this particular group. I have used the term "Czechoslovak," when referring to institutions, laws, and policies that relate to the central government or to the country as a whole and not to any particular ethnic group.

Throughout the text, "Czech feminists," especially the women in charge of a group known as the Women's National Council, appears frequently. While this book is not intended to be an institutional history of the Czech feminist movement, its leaders, values, and goals provide the thread that holds the narrative together. I chose to feature these women for several reasons. First, because they proved to be so emblematic of the egalitarian democrats who hoped to transform society and politics in the Czech lands after 1918. Perhaps more than any other single group, Czech feminists had a positive vision of democracy and how they planned to achieve it. For them, democracy was not simply a government that substituted elected leaders for the Habsburg imperial system, nor was it purely a synonym for a Czech national state. It was a society with a strict code of egalitarian ethics. Their very explicit vision and their zeal made them stand out from many of their compatriots, who attached themselves to a concept ("democracy") without a firm content, which allowed them to accept a number of very different regimes that labeled themselves democratic. The Czech feminists provide us with a model of the possibility, and the limits, of progressive political action in interwar Central Europe. They were passionately committed to their ideals, but unable or unwilling to adapt those ideals to changing circumstances, which helped to lead to their ultimate end. Their story also serves to remind us that the lack of popular sympathy for feminism in Eastern Europe today is not something intrinsic to the region. In the Czech case at least, current attitudes toward feminism can only be explained as a legacy of Communism, which gutted the democratic Czech feminist movement and took its language, its organizational structure, and even its magazine for itself.[8] The decades of Communist rule effaced the memory of this earlier Czech feminism, just as they simplified the memory of the First Czechoslovak Republic, covering over its conflicts and contradictions and turning it into a mythical Czech golden age.[9]

# MASARYK, FEMINISM, AND DEMOCRACY
# IN THE CZECH LANDS

The attempt to strengthen and enhance a human being's energy and feeling of personal responsibility, to harmoniously cultivate all of his abilities, to place each individual in society on an equal plane—that is modern. . . . The attempt to destroy the privileges of some classes and individuals within those classes—that is modern. . . . It is from this standpoint that we can judge the old opinion of women: that a woman is for a man . . . this opinion is quite dubious, it is unseemly, it is immoral.

Tomáš Garrigue Masaryk, "Modern Opinions about Women"

IN THE CZECH LANDS, women got the vote after only a few years of work. Their rapid success was certainly not typical in Europe. Women's suffrage activism began in earnest in Great Britain in 1867, during the debate over the Second Reform Bill. John Stuart Mill, philosopher, feminist, and member of the British Parliament, stood up to demand votes for women on an equal basis with men. His proposal did not pass, but it did begin a period of intense, organized women's suffrage activity in Britain. For the next forty years, British suffragists worked tirelessly for their cause, but still did not gain the vote. In 1903, a group of women led by Emmeline Pankhurst and her daughter Christabel, decided to try a more radical approach. Their organization, the Woman's Social and Political Union (WSPU), adopted a strategy of sensational public protest. WSPU activists, dressed in white, green, and purple, sought to embody the group's slogan of "deeds, not words." They marched in the streets, organized demonstrations complete with banners and brass bands, attended political meetings and heckled party leaders, and even chained themselves to railings outside government buildings. After a few years and little progress, they turned to even more militant tactics. WSPU members broke windows, poured acid on golf courses, dropped ink into mailboxes, and cut telegraph and telephone lines in the name of women's right to vote. Their activities met with sustained resistance. Women selling the WSPU newspaper were heckled and pelted with rotten vegetables, and forced by the police to stand in the gutter to avoid arrest for obstruction of the pavement. On the infamous "Black Friday," November 18, 1910, WSPU marchers were beaten, kicked, and sexually assaulted by bystanders and police alike. Approximately one thousand women (and about forty men) were arrested for their participation in militant suffrage activities between 1905 and 1914. While in prison, some attempted hunger strikes and were brutally force-fed by tubes thrust down their noses. For the WSPU, fighting for suffrage really was war.[1]

The situation in the Czech lands makes an astounding contrast to the more well-known case of Great Britain. The first suffrage society in the Czech lands was founded in Prague in 1905, and after only seven years, its leaders had successfully convinced three Czech political parties to support their own form of spectacular public protest. They planned to take advantage of Bohemia's complicated electoral rules and run a female candidate in a replacement election for a provincial assembly seat. The nationalist writer Božena Vitková-Kunětická was selected as the candidate. Although she was the official nominee of three parties, her campaign was still controversial. Some local men were upset that their party leaders put up a woman as their candidate and placed their own male alternative on the ballot. Vitková-Kunětická and the suffragists who supported her faced their share of ridicule in the press, but in the end, she won the election.[2]

Czech men voted for a woman at the very time that Britain's militant suffragettes were being brutalized and imprisoned. Unlike the Brits who harassed suffragettes on the march, these Czechs did not see women's suffrage as a threat. Czech nationalists, who styled themselves as democrats fighting for their rightful freedoms, had been persuaded that women's equality was a part of their larger struggle against Habsburg imperial domination. This chapter examines this curious phenomenon by looking at the history of the Czech feminist movement and its relationship to Czech politics as a whole. It begins by considering the influence of the Czech philosopher and politician Tomáš Masaryk. Masaryk was certainly not the only influence on turn of the century Czech feminists, but his writing on democracy and humanity did provide an important foundation for much of their ideology. Taking their inspiration from Masaryk, Czech feminists began to see the issue of women's rights as an essential aspect of building an ideal democratic society. Creating democracy, they believed, was also a fundamental part of the Czech nationalist movement. It was the feminists' ability to convincingly link women's rights, democracy, and the good of the Czech nation together that led to their election victory in 1912. That victory would be deepened a few years later, when the Czechoslovak Republic was declared in 1918. Its new leaders, also heavily invested in the idea of creating a democratic society, would place women's equality prominently on their revolutionary agenda.

## Tomáš Garrigue Masaryk as Democrat and Feminist

One night in 1904, a controversial professor in Prague named Tomáš Garrigue Masaryk gave a stirring lecture on "modern opinions about women" at the Girl's Academy in the city of Brno. In this lecture, Masaryk made the astounding claim that women were just as intelligent and reasonable as men, arguing that the very real inequalities that existed between the sexes were a function of society rather than biology. He asserted that "women's nature" did not justify their subordination to men and set himself firmly against the notion that women's inferior place in society stemmed from their womanhood itself. In a Central Europe that had just the year before been taken with the vastly different conclusions about men's and women's natures presented in Otto Weininger's much talked about book *Sex and Character,* Masaryk's ideas were both fresh and startling. In contrast to Weininger's claim that sex determined the shape of an individual's character, Masaryk downplayed gender difference and emphasized the common humanity of both sexes. He declared that this human sameness gave society a moral imperative to treat men and women on equal terms. Denying women the rights due all human beings was, in Masaryk's estimation, a "fateful mistake" that had been wrongly "sanctified by religion," "implemented by the political system, the military and capitalism" and "defended by academia, especially medicine and psychology." Rectifying this "enormous mistake of the oppression of women" would be a complicated task. Many women's activists in Europe around the turn of the century concentrated on suffrage as the primary means for achieving women's equality, but Masaryk believed that any effort to end society's subjection of women had to look beyond the vote and consider how Europe's major social institutions helped to perpetuate this "error" of women's oppression. Solving the "woman question" required reorganizing society in a radical way, one that enabled women to become full members of the human community.[3]

When Masaryk gave his 1904 lecture in Brno, the society he criticized was not exceptionally democratic by any standard, let alone by his ideal definition. Ever since the crown of Bohemia had passed to the Habsburg family in 1526, the Czech lands had been part of their large empire, ruled ultimately from Vienna. At the beginning of the twentieth century, the Habsburg emperor's once absolute authority had been tempered by an elected Parliament (the Reichsrat), but it was chosen via limited suffrage and had restricted powers. Yet, alongside their long history as Habsburg subjects, early-twentieth-century Czechs were the products of a local liberal heritage stemming from events surrounding the aborted revolution of 1848 and carefully fostered by Czech nationalists ever since.[4] While the Czech liberals of 1848 were not democrats, they and their descendants helped to create a Czech political culture that venerated the liberal values of freedom, rights, and equality—concepts Czech nationalist politicians invoked as they struggled to gain local control from their Habsburg rulers.[5] Tomáš Masaryk built upon this tradition, but redirected the concerns of earlier Czech liberal nationalists, who were more interested in protecting local autonomy from the emperor's bureaucrats in Vienna and defending the rights and freedoms of Czech speakers against their German-speaking neighbors. As a politician and political thinker, Masaryk did not completely reject this focus, but he expanded it with a new way of thinking about democracy.

Masaryk's ideas about democracy had a profound impact on Czech political thought, and not just for feminists. To talk about what "democracy" meant to Masaryk is, however, a torturous enterprise. Though he wrote about the term constantly, he never formulated a precise definition, and "democracy" sometimes stands in for a whole host of ideas in his work. This mutability would allow Masaryk's ideas to be used by a wide array of later political groups for different purposes, making him the most widely used Czech political thinker in the decades after 1918. At the very least, most would agree that to Masaryk, "democracy" was much more than a political system based on free elections and universal suffrage. It described a society based on a respect for the humanity all people shared, and dedicated to preserving their rights and freedoms as individuals. A democratic society recognized the fundamental equality between people and refused to make distinctions among them or privilege one group over another. Masaryk did not believe that all people were equivalent in the sense of being equally talented or capable, but he did think that all people should be granted the freedom to better themselves according to their own abilities and merits and to live according to their own convictions.

Even before he began to think and write seriously about the political aspects of democracy, Masaryk vocally supported a democratization of society, which he defined as creating a community of equals to replace the master-servant relationships that characterized a monarchy.[6] What he advocated was, in effect, a different kind of civil society, one defined not by associational life but by a code of civil behavior. It was a way of living more than method of governing, where interpersonal relations mattered as much as holding regular elections. As he wrote in 1913, "universal suffrage does not guarantee democratic attitudes; a true democrat will not only be such in Parliament, but in the community, in a political party, in a circle of friends, in the family; he will feel and act democratically everywhere." This was democracy as a sort of civic morality, with respect for humanity as its foundation. It was, truly, "a new set of beliefs, a new angle of vision, a new method."[7]

Many Czech politicians used Masaryk's ideas about democracy to posit a special relationship between the Czech nation and democratic government. The nation was the category around which most Czechs at the turn of the century organized their politics. The tendency of most of these nationalist politicians was to essentialize the national group, imbuing it with certain "natural" qualities and characteristics. Masaryk tended to say that the Czech nation was not naturally democratic, but he argued that history had made the Czechs into a people particularly disposed towards democracy. He traced this orientation back to the experience of the Hussite Reformation, which, he claimed, acted as a crystallizing moment for the "character" of the Czech nation. As he remarked to writer Karel Čapek, "Look at us: For centuries we did not have our own dynasty, we did not have—but for minor exceptions—a nationally conscious aristocracy, we had no wealthy elites—in virtue of our history and nature we are destined for democracy."[8] Masaryk believed that the democratic heritage left by the Protestant reformer Jan Hus and his followers had been stifled by the intervening centuries of Austrian domination. Yet, at the same time, Habsburg rule had also made contemporary Czechs more receptive to democracy, by robbing them of a native nobility with pretensions toward governing the nation. Without a national aristocracy, the Czechs could more easily reorient themselves back toward the older democratic tradition of Hus. They only needed to work themselves free of this "old Austrian spirit" in order to put their history back on its democratic track.

While in some areas Masaryk's writing on democracy betrayed a real egalitarian spirit, his ideas were more contradictory than that. On the practical level of politics, for example, Masaryk stressed the skill of trained professionals over the equality of all citizens. While an individual's participation in politics (via voting and membership in a political party) was sacrosanct, as was one's right to express political views and critique government policies, Masaryk believed that the average person should have only a limited role in the actual process of governing. As he said many times, democracy was really a "discussion." In the political arena, this meant that voters and rulers talked to each other through the mechanism of elections and via the press but the groups remained, for the most part, separate. Democracy was "interaction between the governing and the governed, which allows for guidance from both sides with a constant revealing of interests and values." The will of the people should serve as the basis for policy, but the execution of that will was better left in the hands of more capable elites. As opposed to other forms of government, the ruling elites in a democratic system were supposed to have only the interests of the whole of society at heart. They did not rule out of self-interest, but merely "administer[ed] . . . the affairs of all in the best interests of all."[9] Sometimes the people did not really know what was in their best interest; in this case, the government would determine and carry out the proper policy for the good of the whole.

Masaryk was unwaveringly accepting of women's equality. For Masaryk, unlike so many liberal or even radical democrats before him, the concept of the "individual" was always gender-neutral.[10] His position on gender issues may have been due to the intellectual influence of his wife, the American-born Charlotte Garrigue.[11] During their courtship, they read John Stuart Mill together, and this helped to crystallize his/their opinions about the relationship between men and women. Like Mill, Masaryk refused to admit that women were naturally inferior to men. A crucial part of creating democracy involved making a world in which women and men could equally realize their abilities.[12] Women needed more than the vote—they needed to be self-sufficient, with equal access to educational opportunities and the job market. Masaryk thought that women should have the right to work outside the home and ridiculed arguments that claimed women were not physically or mentally fit for such employment, remarking that being an office clerk was probably much less stressful than running around after small children all day. He noted that not many people objected to peasants and working-class women in gainful employment, but when it came to middle-class women, opponents argued that they would compete with men who needed the jobs to provide for families. To this Masaryk pointed out that if both women and men were self-sufficient, men would not need to provide for the women in their lives and thus the problem of gendered competition for jobs would not be an issue.[13]

Although he was astoundingly radical in calling for women's equality in so many sectors of society, Masaryk was not radical on the subject of sex, even by contemporary European standards. While he did not believe a democracy should legislate its moral codes, he advocated a strict sexual morality for both men and women. Masaryk did not think of sex itself as immoral, stating, "celibacy is not higher and more pure than pure marriage," but he felt strongly that it should only take place between husband and wife. Unlike other moral traditionalists of his time, Masaryk insisted that both men and women should live up to the same strict sexual code and called for an end to the moral double-standard that had given men and women different sets of acceptable sexual behavior.

Masaryk was a strong believer in monogamous marriage; however, he had an unorthodox view of it.[14] For Masaryk, marriage was no place for domination or subjection, rather, the democratic ideals of equality and respect for others had to extend to the relationship between husband and wife. "Marriage," he explained, "is a fusion of two independent individuals, soul to soul," But, as he laconically added, "men today of course prefer a slave." For these men, Masaryk went on, "marriage means the end of spiritual aspiration and striving," yet, "to a strong, healthy individual it is the beginning of shared development, shared work . . . for eternity."[15] Though he sometimes exalted his ideal marriage bond to unwieldy heights, referring to it as the pinnacle of human existence and so on, Masaryk basically presented marriage as a working partnership, in which both spouses made equal contributions and where both had a say in making decisions.

Masaryk did not challenge the idea that domestic tasks were women's work. He did, however, call on society to recognize that such work was both difficult and worthy of praise. He thought it was disgraceful that men worked a mere eight-hour day and then happily spent their evenings relaxing at the neighborhood pub, while their wives put in eighteen-hour shifts at home for little reward and even less respect. As he wrote in 1929, "To have a child every year, to rear a half dozen children and take care of them day and night, to live half the day in the kitchen and carry out daily, as a rule modest, housekeeping, etc.—this is easier than a man's employment?"[16] This respect for housework was almost entirely unheard of in Czech circles at the turn of the century, when Masaryk first started publicly demanding that men value the tasks performed by their wives. Linda Vonková, a housewife from Nymburk, remembered how statements such as these surprised the local Realist Party club when Masaryk gave a lecture there in 1906. "We all listened to the words with wonder," she said, as Masaryk spoke with awe about his mother's ability to keep her household running on little money. "The men were surprised that such a learned man was speaking with respect about stupid women's work, and we women were proud that the leader of the Realists, Professor Masaryk, had such understanding for women's work." His comments made such an impact on her that she remembered them decades later and thought of that moment whenever she saw him as president.[17]

While he valued women's domestic work, Masaryk rejected the contention that wives should only be housewives. "Let the home be blessed and sacred," he said, "but for that it is above all necessary that women not be domestic slaves. We are removing women from public work in the name of the household, we are lowering their horizons, we are suppressing their energy, wasting their natural talents."[18] Society did not benefit from keeping women locked in their own homes. Masaryk saw wives as an untapped resource, capable of doing useful work in the world outside their households. While this usually seemed to refer to some sort of volunteering carried out in addition to their housework, he also recognized that not all women might want to be housewives and argued that those who wanted to work (or had to work) for pay should have that chance.[19] However, Masaryk never went so far as to see housework as an acceptable occupation for men. It was never precisely clear who he thought would take over the housework if a wife was working; presumably, domestic servants would take on that role.

Similarly, although he generally deplored the use of "nature" as an argument to justify women's subordinate place in society, Masaryk did believe that biology determined some parental responsibilities. He thought that women were uniquely suited to taking care of babies and that motherhood demanded greater sacrifices than fatherhood, stating: "I see the main and natural difference between men and women in that when a woman becomes a mother she must usually dedicate herself more exclusively and for a longer time to the functions and duties of maternity."[20] Still, Masaryk was more muted in his evaluation of maternity than most others of his era. While women needed to give up some of their other activities when they had children, this did not mean giving up all such activities and did not preclude their resuming other forms of work as their children matured. Giving birth was not the ultimate goal of women's existence or their primary contribution to their community. Neither was the family the sole province of women. Quite remarkably for the time, Masaryk suggested that husbands and fathers should also be considered vital to a healthy family life. What families were really missing, Masaryk claimed, was not omnipresent mothers, but good fathers. Men needed to involve themselves in raising their children and not just spend their leisure hours drinking beer and playing cards with other men in pubs.[21] Few others were willing to mesh gender roles in the family even to the rather limited extent that Masaryk advocated. Even well into the interwar period his opinions on this issue were far from accepted, but they were not forgotten. A mass-market Czech women's magazine generally devoted to fashion and movie stars celebrated Masaryk's eighty-first birthday by publishing an article that described him pushing his infant children in a baby carriage around the Prater during his early days in Vienna, making porridge for them, and playing with them in his study, writing about these acts as something bordering on a miraculous event.[22] If the idea of Masaryk feeding cereal to his children was seen as something so astonishing and wondrous, then his example of good fatherhood had clearly not been emulated by many other men, even several decades later. Yet women who read fashion magazines, as well as those who subscribed to more feminist periodicals, remembered and honored him for his deeds and words in behalf of a new kind of family life and continued to hope that his example would spread more widely into Czech society.

## The Czech Women's Movement Before 1918

The beginnings of what might be called a "women's movement" in the Czech lands can be traced back to the Czech National Awakening, a resurgence of interest in Czech language and culture.[23] Middle-class Czech women first began to organize in the wake of the failed national revolutions of 1848. They were led by female writers, such as Božena Němcová, Karolina Světlá, and Sofie Podlipská, whose work urged Czech women not only to support their nation, but to develop their own talents and capabilities. Ignorant women, they charged, were ill-equipped for the task most Czech nationalists assigned them: raising their children to be good Czechs.

To help the nation, women first had to help themselves. Accordingly, the first efforts of organized Czech women in their own behalf were in the field of education. The Czech Women's Industrial Association (Ženský Výrobní Spolek Český), founded in Prague by Světlá and Podlipská in the 1860s, took as one of its primary tasks improving educational opportunities for girls. It founded a secondary school, a school for poor girls, and a teacher's academy.[24] The association also sponsored lectures and created a journal devoted to women's issues. Other Czech women's associations proliferated in the 1870s and 1880s, most dedicated to education or charitable causes. These groups began to coalesce into a "movement" in the 1880s. The driving force behind their increased cooperation was a campaign to open institutions of higher education to women. At the time, the Habsburg Education Ministry denied women admission to state-run universities and gymnasia (preparatory high schools).[25] The campaign to make secondary education available to women was headed by Eliška Krásnohorská, a Czech writer best known outside her feminist activities for penning the librettos to several of Bedřich Smetana's operas. Krásnohorská began writing articles, organizing lectures, and starting petitions demanding that women be allowed to pursue university studies.[26] Her campaign was joined by other women's groups in the Czech lands and eventually received the political backing of a prominent Czech political party, the Young Czechs. Since a good high school education was required for university admission, Krásnohorská decided to start her own private gymnasium for women, the first such institution in the entire Austro-Hungarian Monarchy. Dubbed Minerva, the school opened in the fall of 1891, with the support of Prague's municipal administration but without recognition or financial assistance from the imperial Ministry of Education. Women were finally admitted to the universities in 1897, and then only to the Philosophical Faculties, but Minerva was a success from the start, and provided the basis for a new, elite class of educated Czech women.[27]

This campaign played an important role in establishing networks between Czech women and their organizations, but, perhaps more importantly, it also represented the beginning of cooperation between Czech women's groups and the Czech nationalist movement and its politicians.[28] The university protest was largely characterized by its organizers as a struggle of Czechs against Austrians rather than as a battle of women against the state, or women against men. Because the debate was cast in these terms, Young Czech delegates in the Reichsrat were willing to rally to Krásnohorská's cause and take up her demands in Vienna. While not all politically active Czech men looked favorably on Czech women's demands for educational rights, the fact that some did was crucial; Czech women's groups could now see Czech men and their political parties (which were at this time by law strictly male) as allies rather than adversaries.[29]

In the following years, a more self-consciously feminist group of women began to emerge in the Czech lands. Centered in Prague, it coalesced around the Czech Women's Club (Ženský Klub Český), founded in 1903. The club gathered together mainly educated and professional women, including some of the first Czech female doctors and academics, as well as teachers, writers, actresses, and others, to provide a meeting place for those concerned with the "woman question" and give them a place for debate and discussion. The club had a library of feminist literature, where members gathered to read works such as John Stuart Mill's *The Subjection of Women,* a text which had enormous influence among early Czech feminists. It had been translated into Czech by Charlotte Garrigue Masaryková, herself a member of the club. Aside from maintaining the library, the Club held frequent cultural events and organized several influential lecture series on women's history and the status of women in different areas of Czech/ Austrian society, which were attended by both women and men.[30] But the real legacy of the Czech Women's Club, which continued its existence until the 1940s, was its role in creating a community of dedicated women (and some men) who identified themselves as feminists and actively sought to change the subordinate position of women in society.[31] The Czech Women's Club did not represent all Czech women, and it was only one component of the multifaceted Czech women's movement, which was comprised of many ideologically different groups of publicly active women. But it was women from this group that would represent the Czechs (and later Czechoslovakia) in international women's organizations like the International Suffrage Alliance and it was this group that took the lead in creating and focusing a coalition of Czech (and later Czechoslovak) women to defend women's political and social interests. In this book, the term "Czech feminists" refers to the group of women involved with the Czech Women's Club and the later organizations founded by its members and/or their ideological supporters.

The feminists of the Czech Women's Club were profoundly influenced by Tomáš Masaryk, who began to write and speak on issues around the "woman question" in the 1890s, just as the first class of students, including his own daughter, Alice, was entering Minerva. He was lecturing at the Charles University when women first began to appear in its halls, initially as auditors and later as official students. Through his presence at Minerva, work at the university, and his many public lectures, Masaryk came into contact with most of this first generation of educated Czech women while they were still quite young. For many of these women, listening to Masaryk's lectures opened up their "eyes and their souls." Decades later, many of them remembered with perfect clarity attending his classes or talking with him at his home.[32] Those who were not in Prague devoured his frequently published essays. One provincial schoolteacher, Marie Vitková, remembered how a speech by Masaryk in her town changed her life: "His coming, his personal magic, which radiated from his bearing, from his gestures, from his manner of speaking, from his deep eyes, it all reinforced and emphasized in a wondrous manner all that had grown in our souls from his influence and deeds. We were his, we were his and we will remain his until our last breath: the generation of the 90s of the last century!" Vitková's experience was not unusual. Dr. Ludmila Nosilová-Zlesáková, an interwar feminist activist, remarked that when she was at the university just after the First World War, "*Humanitarian Ideals* [one of Masaryk's books] was our second Bible." Albina Honzáková, one of the first Czech women to earn a doctorate in history, a member of the Czech Women's Club, and a founder of the Czech Association of University Women, claimed that Masaryk was the only one who really understood the Club and aided its struggles. "For decades," she said, "exhausting our intellectual and physical strength, we used our energies in order to win new human worth for women and children. Who understood us? . . . Only Masaryk knew that we were people of equal value. From time to time his brilliance flamed through the dark of the age and then there he stood for us like a fiery column, spreading light far across half a century."[33]

Masaryk did more than reinforce the resolve of these young Czech women activists. His work gave them a vocabulary in which they could express their views about women's equality and tie those beliefs to a broader discourse about democracy. In accordance with Masaryk's insistence that a true democracy was based on a recognition of the essential equality of all individuals, Czech feminists could and did claim that their attempts to emancipate women were an essential part of the bigger project of realizing a democratic society in the Czech lands. This linking of feminism to the democratic project was a key feature of the ideology espoused by the Czech women's movement from the early twentieth century throughout the interwar period. These women saw the fundamental goal of their feminism as achieving "Masaryk's" democracy, which they defined as a society that realized the equality of all individuals in every area of life, from the political to the social, economic, and cultural.

But feminism for the Czechs was not only a democratic project, it was a national one as well. Czech feminists came of age and became politically active in the 1890s, when national fervor in the Czech lands was reaching new heights. Using their interpretation of Masaryk, they were able to link their national and their feminist aspirations in one united effort. Masaryk had claimed that Czechs were historically conditioned for democracy and had seen the creation of a democratic society as a continuation of an interrupted Czech national trajectory, which had started with Jan Hus and the Bohemian Brethren and been stunted by the intervening years of Habsburg rule. Czech feminists latched on to this idea, declaring that those who did not support women's rights were in effect betraying their national democratic heritage and standing in the way of the national imperative. Many of them went further than Masaryk did and portrayed Czechs as naturally or essentially democratic creatures, accusing those Czechs who went against democracy—or feminism—of being in conflict with Czech "national characteristics." According to Czech feminist leader Františka Plamínková, a "better human and national life" was one in which "the old Czech virtues of love and democracy" were manifest and "where hate [was] directed towards any oppression." Being Czech and being democratic, two components of a better and more humane life, became inextricably linked for Czech feminists, and both were part of what they were trying to achieve. Czech feminists felt as incapable of distinguishing between the part of them that was "Czech" and the part that was "feminist" as they did making a distinction between their support of women and their support of democracy. Therefore, Plamínková's essay did not stop with defining a better way of life, but continued, "we will work even more diligently, concentrating our private and political lives towards the success not only of our sex, but also of the national whole!"[34]

As a group, Czech feminists continually emphasized equality over difference in their rhetoric. While they did not deny that gender differences existed, they hoped to incorporate those differences within the context of an egalitarian society, one where being female did not preclude being a free person. They saw this project as something that transcended women's own needs and concerns; it was part of making a better world for everyone. Activists, asked in later years why they became feminists, repeatedly remarked on this. For them, feminism was simply "woman's path to humanity." It meant the "consciousness of the complete and unconditional human equality of men and women." For another woman it was "striving for a more just and better spiritual and societal order," a place where, in the words of another respondent, "women of all types . . . will be accorded the same human dignity as men in all areas of life and their acts will be evaluated according to their own abilities and merits." Or, as one woman pithily remarked, "Why did I become a feminist? I wanted to be a free human being."[35] These women saw themselves as working to fulfill the Masarykian mandate; their task was to ensure that women achieved their rightful place within his model.

This stress on equality and rights made Czech feminists somewhat of an anomaly in their part of the world, especially in the years after the First World War. Unlike their German and Austrian counterparts, Czech feminists never wavered from demanding strict legal equality for women and always justified their claims for women's rights on that basis of sameness.[36] They believed that women deserved the same legal rights as men because they shared a common humanity, not because of their special qualities or social significance as women. Because of their commitment to this ideal of gender equality, Czech feminists rarely utilized the maternalist rhetoric that was so common in women's movements throughout Europe during this period.[37] Although many thought highly of motherhood and sometimes spoke of it in exalted terms, leading Czech feminist organizations did not argue that women should receive rights or privileges because of their position as mothers or nurturers. For them, rights needed to be given on a basis of equality, rather than difference.

Armed with their conviction that women and men should be equals in society, some of the members of the Czech Women's Club began to venture into direct political agitation and to call for equal political rights for women. In 1905, some of them formed the Committee for Women's Voting Rights (Výbor pro Volební Právo Žen) to coordinate activities on behalf of women's suffrage. In the beginning, the committee had only twelve members, but they had the good fortune to be led by Františka Plamínková, a dedicated young schoolteacher who was already well known for her work with the Czech Women's Club. Plamínková became the driving force behind the Czech campaign for women's suffrage. Later in her life, she modestly said of herself, "I am simply an *active person*, a seeing person, a feeling person—the things were in the air. And because I am a thorough and responsible person, I could not rail on about them and then run away like many people, but I held on and tried to carry them through to the end."[38]

With the help of her friend and fellow teacher Marie Tůmová, Plamínková managed to take the cause of universal women's suffrage and make it a serious public issue in the Czech lands within the span of only a few years.[39] Albina Honzáková, also a participant in the committee's activities, recalled that during its first years, from 1905 to 1908, its members concentrated mainly on raising the consciousness of the Czech population about the need for women's suffrage. Their efforts coincided with a large-scale general campaign in the Czech lands for universal manhood suffrage in Reichsrat elections, a move supported by most Czech political parties. The committee participated in mass rallies held for this cause, using the opportunity to demand the vote for women as well as men. They organized numerous demonstrations and lectures of their own, both in Prague and in the countryside, wrote articles and brochures, and, perhaps most importantly, lobbied Czech politicians and political parties for their support.[40] While the committee's demands did not gain universal acceptance by any means, it did obtain the cooperation of some public figures and several political parties.[41]

The suffragists were particularly successful in establishing relationships with parties on the left of the Czech political spectrum. While they certainly had friends in the Progressive student movement, their biggest supporters were the various Czech socialist parties. The Czech Social Democratic Party (hereafter the Social Democratic Party) had formally supported women's rights since the 1880s.[42] Feminists also found a lasting ally in the National Socialist Party, a Czech radical nationalist party that also espoused a socialist program. This party was founded in 1898 and did not ever have an affiliation or ideological connection with the German Nazi Party. Programmatically opportunistic, the one constant feature of the National Socialist platform was its support of women's rights. Although this steadfastness may have been, as historian T. Mills Kelly claims, merely a pragmatic ploy for votes, it certainly helped the suffragists.[43]

This political support would prove crucial for the next phase of the committee's activism. In 1907, the Austrian government gave in to protests and agreed to universal manhood suffrage for Reichsrat elections. The new suffrage law, however, explicitly excluded women from the vote. Upset with this unfavorable decision, the committee decided it needed to push its stance a little more forcefully. The 1907 decision had dealt with elections on the imperial level; it had not touched laws regarding voting regulations for the Bohemian assembly. Plamínková realized that there was nothing in these older regulations that specifically prevented women from voting in Bohemian provincial elections. According to the laws, anyone who paid a certain amount of taxes or had an advanced degree could vote and the only formal qualification for being a candidate for election to the Bohemian assembly was to be an eligible voter. Plamínková decided that the committee should attempt to get a woman elected to the assembly as a form of protest. In 1908, the committee ran Marie Tůmová for election in the district of Vysoké Mýto, and also persuaded a few other parties (the Social Democrats and Progressives) to field female candidates. None of them were successful, but the committee continued to present Tůmová as a candidate in subsequent elections in hopes of eventual success.[44]

The women's suffrage movement was never able to push Tůmová to victory. However, they were successful in representing their fight as a battle of Czechs against the Austrian authorities in Vienna rather than as a women's war against a male-dominated government. This led to writer Božena Vitková-Kunětická's election to the provincial assembly in 1912. Vitková-Kunětická identified herself as a radical nationalist rather than a feminist, which undoubtedly helped to make her a more acceptable candidate to male voters. Her victory was short-lived, however. The Bohemian governor disputed Plamínková's interpretation of the election regulations and declared Vitková-Kunětická's election invalid, refusing to allow her to take her seat in the assembly. Still, the election had a positive outcome for both Czech feminists and nationalists. The public fracas between Austrian authorities and ardent nationalist Vitková-Kunětická gained the sympathies of many Czechs, who suddenly found themselves supporting a woman's election to public office as a means of opposing Habsburg central authority. In addition, the news of Vitková-Kunětická's victory spread all over Europe and was hailed by supporters of women's suffrage from around the continent. Vitková-Kunětická used her new notoriety to make nationalist statements decrying the Habsburg oppression of Czechs. Thus the incident allowed Czech feminists and nationalists to make a significant mark on the international scene and also increased their popularity at home.[45]

## 1918 and Beyond

At the turn of the century, even his admirers did not interpret Masaryk's espousal of democracy as a call for republican revolution. They looked to his democratic society more as a guide to personal behavior than as a formula for Czech party politics. Before the outbreak of war in 1914, most Czechs wanted no more than local autonomy from Vienna. Not even Masaryk, who was himself a delegate to the Austrian Reichsrat, seriously contemplated the end of the Habsburg Monarchy and the actual creation of a democratic Czech state. The unexpected events of the First World War changed that in a completely unpredictable way, abruptly pushing Tomáš Masaryk into a position of enormous political influence, moving him and his ideas out of the realm of philosophy, and giving him a very real impact on the shape of the new Czechoslovak Republic.[46] After hostilities began, the Habsburg state cracked down on nationalist politicians, forcing

Masaryk to flee abroad in order to escape imprisonment. After reaching a safe perch with the Western Allies, he quickly helped to organize an émigré Czech and Slovak independence movement that worked to gain Allied support for a new national state to be shared by these two closely related Slavic peoples. For Masaryk and his associates, however, this movement was about more than creating a national state; it was a chance to establish a foothold for democracy in Central Europe.[47]

On October 18, 1918, Masaryk and two fellow émigré leaders, the Czech Edvard Beneš and the Slovak Milan Štefánik, issued a statement describing their vision for a unified and independent Czechoslovakia. Known as the Washington Declaration, this document repudiated Habsburg attempts to reorganize and save the monarchy, proclaiming that Czechs and Slovaks could only be free if they had their own state. Alongside its assertion of Czechoslovak national self-determination, the Washington Declaration drew a picture of a new Czechoslovak state. Independent Czechoslovakia would be a republic governed by its people, a state that guaranteed and respected the personal rights and freedoms of all citizens, including non-Czechs and non-Slovaks. Since the Washington Declaration was written as political ammunition in the battle to convince the Western Allies to enable the peaceful creation of Czechoslovakia, it was not surprising that it included promises to respect the rights of the German, Hungarian, and Ruthenian populations that would find themselves turned into national minorities in a Czechoslovak Republic. But the Washington Declaration went further than that, proclaiming: gender, class, and religious affiliation would no longer have any bearing on how the state treated individuals; the nobility would be abolished and noble lands redistributed; church would be separated from state; and women would be "placed on a level with men, politically, socially and culturally."[48] It was not new for European democratic revolutionaries to attack the privileges of the nobility and the Church; they had been doing so ever since the French Revolution. The call for an end to class oppression was a new theme for a republican document, and undoubtedly an attempt to link Europe's older democratic tradition with the socialist fervor that had swept through the continent with the Russian Revolution, bringing class issues to the forefront of European politics. For Czechoslovakia's revolutionary leaders to so prominently mention women's equality in their declaration of national independence was also unusual, especially since there was no immediate political gain to be gotten by including it. These things signaled the beginning of a new era in European politics, where issues like class and gender, as well as nation and estate, would become impossible for any politician to ignore.

The Washington Declaration was successful in achieving its aims. The Western Allies accepted the petition and made an independent Czechoslovakia a condition of the peace agreement signed by the Habsburg emperor Karl IV on October 27. The following day, a coalition of leaders from the largest Czech political parties declared their independence and announced the formation of a provisional government. As they spoke, massive crowds swarmed the city, cheering the birth of Czechoslovakia. In their glee, the celebrants did not stop to think about the promises that had been made as conditions of their new independence, but simply rejoiced in the idea of freedom for themselves and their nation. But the Washington Declaration had committed the new state to protecting democracy, gender equality and respect for national minorities. The signatures of a few men given to a group of foreign powers took the place of a true national referendum. In October of 1918, this did not seem problematic, at least as far as Czechs were concerned. In their enthusiasm for their new state, Czechs gladly agreed to such conditions, praising the Czechoslovakia envisioned in the Washington Declaration and extolling Masaryk, its chief visionary, for his work.

In the arena of women's rights, this represented an extraordinary transformation. In the first few weeks after Czechoslovakia came into existence, the idea that democracy required women to receive the same rights as men suddenly became self-evident in the Czech lands.[49] Before the outbreak of the war, such an outcome seemed far from obvious. Members of the Committee for Women's Voting Rights reported that in 1914 women were often favorably disposed toward their activities, but men generally looked at them "with a smile" and did not take them very seriously, despite their successes. Understandably, some women activists worried that the backing they had received from Czech party leaders (all of whom had encouraged their parties to formally support women's suffrage by 1914) was a mere matter of convenience. Favoring votes for women was an easy way of annoying the Habsburg regime; few believed that the government in

Vienna would actually give women the vote. Feminists wondered if Czech politicians would still support women's suffrage if they actually had the power to grant it, and furiously lobbied those that remained in the country during the war to make sure this would be the case. Even as late as the spring of 1918, suffrage activist Plamínková reported that leading Czech politicians, including Agrarian Party leader Antonín Švehla, were hedging on their promises of support and arguing that Czechs were not ready to see women elected to public office.[50]

From October 28, 1918, onwards, however, the prospect of women as both voters and legislators was treated as a simple inevitability. According to F. V. Krejčí, a Social Democrat who became one of his party's representatives to the first Czechoslovak National Assembly, the experience of war and independence had caused even conservative Czechs to change their views about women and their place in political life.[51] The result was a mental turnaround so dramatic that "demands that would have been considered even by the liberal bourgeoisie to be too radical before the war, like, for example, universal suffrage in municipal elections or voting rights for women, did not encounter resistance from the Agrarian Party during the establishment of our Republic, and they [the Agrarians] were followed by the clerical [People's] party." Krejčí suspected that Czechs on the right may have suddenly accepted the idea of equal suffrage rights for workers and women in a studied attempt to forestall socialist uprisings like those that erupted in neighboring Austria, Hungary, and Germany right after the war. But he also recognized that even if it was motivated by tactical considerations rather than conviction, the Czech Right's voluntary acceptance of women's and worker's rights was really extraordinary.[52] In other parts of Central Europe, conservatives and socialists fought in the streets in an effort to maintain the old status quo. In Czechoslovakia, by contrast, all of the major prewar Czech and Slovak parties, socialist and bourgeois, entered into a single coalition and agreed to exchange monarchy for democracy. Together, they created a provisional National Assembly, allotting seats according to each party's showing in previous elections. Without comment or fuss, eight women were asked to be among its 256 representatives. These women were distributed across the political spectrum, with half belonging to various socialist parties and the rest split amongst the centrist Agrarian party, the right-leaning National Democrats (who gave a seat to

Božena Vitková-Kunětická), and the composite Slovak club. Less than a week after the new National Assembly opened its doors, all parties except for the Catholic-sponsored People's Party formally endorsed women's suffrage by cosigning a bill requesting that the committee charged with writing a Czechoslovak constitution work "with utmost speed" to come up with a document that would guarantee equal voting rights for both women and men.[53]

If any of Czechoslovakia's first legislators objected to women gaining the right to vote, they kept their opinions to themselves. Their first possibility to openly debate the matter came with a proposal for a new set of municipal voting regulations presented by the Constitutional Committee to the membership of the National Assembly in January of 1919.[54] The new law would grant all persons over age twenty-one equal voting rights in local elections, ending the complicated Habsburg-era curial voting system that had restricted suffrage at the local level to the propertied or professional classes and given the wealthiest voters a larger share of influence at the polls. It would also establish a proportional voting system to allow representation for minority populations. In the preamble to the bill, the Constitutional Committee presented its work as a response to the "wave of democracy" that had swept over the globe after the end of the war. It was this outpouring of enthusiasm for democracy, they said, that caused Czech parties to agree that "universal and equal voting for men and women is the only just basis for voting in municipal elections."[55] The other members of the Assembly concurred with this opinion. In two days of solid debate on the municipal voting law, not a single voice was heard opposing women's suffrage. In fact, every speaker embraced it wholeheartedly. As representative Bohuslav Franta from the National Democratic Party declared, "every friend of progress must welcome this with the greatest joy." Franta claimed that the reason women's suffrage had been controversial in the past was because the French revolutionaries of the eighteenth century had refused to accept women as political actors, setting the tone for an entire century of political struggle. The Czechs, Franta implied, would not make the same mistake. Where a century earlier the French had fought over the issue of women's suffrage, the "whole [Czech] nation recognize[d] the right of women not only to vote for municipal representatives but also to be elected themselves."[56]

Franta was joined in his enthusiasm by Antonín Němec, a Social Democrat. Němec declared that the municipal voting law was one of the foundation stones of the new republic and as such had to include the principle of women's equality. Because, he thundered, "it would not be a true democracy if women were not in public life, in political life, and placed on a completely equal social level with men!" As Němec spoke, shouts of "excellent!" rang out in the chamber as other deputies expressed their approval of his words.[57] This ebullient mood continued through the speech of Agrarian Party representative Cyril Horáček. Significantly, while Němec's Social Democrats had included women's suffrage in their party platform for years, the Agrarian Party leadership had been more wary of the issue.[58] But with the matter actually coming up for a vote, Horáček spoke glowingly of women's participation in politics. While commenting that there were "different opinions on women's roles in human society" and noting that "nature herself has on occasion certainly set them [women] different tasks than men," Horáček concluded that voting was not a gendered activity. "Justice demands that we give women the right to vote," he declared, once again to shouts of "excellent!" and "so it does!"[59]

By this time, everyone was clamoring to join the string of praise for women's suffrage. Two speakers from the People's Party, Bedřich Pospíšil and the priest Jan Šrámek, felt compelled to declare that they supported equal rights for women as well, even as others in the hall heckled them for refusing to allow women equality within the Church.[60] The one female delegate to participate in the debate, Social Democrat Božena Ecksteinová, praised her male colleagues for allowing women into Czechoslovak politics without a fight, noting that such "consideration and recognition of women's true needs was unusual in the world." However, Ecksteinová went on, the representatives needed to realize that suffrage was only the "framework" on which women's equality would be built. She exhorted her fellow legislators to "make women equal outside the walls of the Assembly house as well" and "call them into true collaboration on the local level," which she felt was the best arena for women's political involvement. Ecksteinová's demands for a more substantial equality were also loudly greeted with praise and her speech ended to enthusiastic applause.[61]

These kinds of sentiments about women's equality were not limited to the halls of the National Assembly. Everyone, it seemed, was praising women's new rights and pointing to them as proof positive that democracy had finally reached the Czech lands. An even more telling sign of the public mood, however, was that these words were matched by deeds. Responding to the "democratic spirit of the time," faculty and administrators voted to allow women into all of the university departments and academies that had still denied them access (including law, economics, and engineering), with the lone exception of theology. Women were also admitted into all secondary schools on an equal basis with male students.[62] In yet one more victory, the National Assembly agreed to abolish the Habsburg practice of firing female civil servants when they married, another prominent issue for middle-class, educated Czech feminists, many of whom were employed as teachers.[63]

For Czech feminists, it was an almost unbelievable, enchanted moment. In one stroke, they had been given national independence, a democratic government, and equal rights for men and women. Democracy brought them suffrage, equal access to educational opportunities, an end to discriminatory policies in the civil service, and the promise of a new era of equality. That these things all came together was significant for them; it made manifest the linkages between the Czech nation, democracy, and women's rights. The democratic Czechs had triumphed over aristocratic Austria; the oppression of the nation and its women was at an end. Plamínková saw matters in this light when she declared, "for women the proclamation of the nation's freedom was the proclamation of their human rights."[64] In this flush of victory, the air was heady and anything seemed possible. As Krista Nevšimalová exulted in the magazine *Ženský Obzor* (Women's Horizon), "Today the Czech woman is free. . . . All of a sudden, as if by magic, Czechoslovak women have been given all the rights and all of the concessions for which they had been fighting for years."[65]

## Constitutional Ambiguities

The crowning moment for Czech feminists came when the new Czechoslovak Constitution was finished in February of 1920. To their great joy, they found that it made women's equality into a constitutional right, giving legal heft to the promises of the Washington Declaration. Article 106 of the constitution decreed that "privileges of sex, birth, and occupation will not be recognized by the law."[66] When they included this article in the constitution, its writers effectively legitimized an egalitarian notion of citizenship, one in which the rights of state membership would be equally administered to citizens of both sexes. A citizen's gender, according to Article 106, would simply no longer have any bearing on the rights that person could claim. Women now had the perfect legal basis from which to challenge government-sponsored forms of gender discrimination and the means to force the state to actively create gender equality in its laws and institutions. Article 106, however, was complicated by other sections of the constitution which presented a different, and distinctly gendered, conception of rights.

The primary vehicle for this competing version of citizenship was contained in Article 126, which proclaimed that "marriage, motherhood, and the family are under the protection of the law." For most Czechs, "the family" was a distinctly gendered structure: a grouping of wife, husband, and children, where the husband had the role of provider and the wife that of homemaker and caregiver. Protecting this institution, then, would be taken by most to mean upholding the traditionally gendered roles and rights of individual family members. Article 126 thus gave legal weight to a very different set of ideals. Far from removing "the privileges of sex," it gave the lawmakers the duty to treat citizens, at least on occasion, as gendered beings, bestowing rights to men befitting their roles as husbands and breadwinners and to women in their roles as wives and mothers. Article 126 could easily be interpreted as giving constitutional sanction to laws that treated men and women differently, as long as the goal of those laws was to strengthen established gender roles within the family.

This did not necessarily have to be the case. Any disjuncture between Article 106 and 126 depended on how "the family" was defined. If the mandate to support the family was flexible enough to allow for multiple versions of familial relations, it would not come into conflict with Article 106.[67] However, since a traditionally gendered model of family relationships was dominant in the Czech lands, the combined effect of these two sections of the Czechoslovak Constitution was to create a legal tension around how women would be incorporated in the state. Taken together, these two articles both affirmed women as completely equal citizens "politically, socially, and culturally" and at the same time worked to perpetuate their status as the legal subjects of their husbands or fathers.

The reason for this ambiguity is that the writers of the constitution were divided about how the law should deal with gender, and especially about how it should treat the family. They could not satisfactorily answer the question of which was primary, a woman's status as a person or as a wife. The members of the Constitutional Committee had also written the municipal voting law that was greeted so warmly in the National Assembly. They were openly committed to the idea of a democratic, egalitarian, civil society as the proper form for a modern Czech nation and accepted Masaryk's notion that society could not be deemed democratic if it excluded women from the rights of citizenship. But equality seemed more difficult to justify when it involved changing the legal status of women within the family. While female suffrage fit unambiguously into the process of erasing the era of Austrian political domination and creating a modern democratic state, changing the structure of the family looked like a threat to the very core of the Czech nation. Seeing this dilemma, writers of the Czechoslovak Constitution waffled over how the law should treat "genderless" legal persons who also happened to be wives and mothers. This tension, naturally, rose to the surface in the debate the committee held over the draft of Article 106.

Several legislators objected to the article immediately, remarking that it would be wrong to legally bind the state to a policy of not recognizing gender privilege, because in some circumstances it should do just that. As National Democrat František Weyr, said, "privileges of sex do exist. I would not want Article 106 to change the civil code, which assigns a husband certain privileges . . . which we do not want to destroy."[68] While Weyr supported giving women equivalent rights as citizens outside of the family, he did not think the state should do anything that might change relationships within it. Similarly, Jiří Hötzel, one of the committee's nonpartisan "experts," remarked, "I cannot imagine marriage if the law was to legalize anarchy within it. . . . Where there is a society of two people, one of them must make the decisions." He believed that moving the authority of the state within the closed circle of the family was going further than democracy demanded, turning against established laws of society. Building on Hötzel's comments, People's Party representative Josef Dolanský noted, "we cannot suddenly eliminate privileges of sex. That would be against nature." These three committee members suggested the simple and expedient solution of eliminating the word "sex" from the text altogether and leaving only the categories of "birth" and "occupation" behind, because, as Dolanský remarked, "we cannot institute something which is against reality. 'Birth' [he was referring here to social categories determined by birth, such as nobility] is a creation of societal orders, but sex is given by nature."[69]

But other legislators, most prominently the Social Democrat Alfréd Meissner and National Socialist Theodor Bartošek, resisted this interpretation, arguing that the individualistic ideals of liberal democracy had to be awarded equally to both sexes, even if this meant eventually changing Czechoslovakia's civil codes. In their opinion, existing family law statutes were not based upon the natural differences between men and women anyway, but were the product of a concrete historical moment that was rapidly passing. Bartošek, joined by Václav Bouček from the Progressive Party, noted that Czech women were constantly taking on new roles in the working world and in political life. These social developments would soon make it impossible to justify the privileges given to husbands by the current civil code; Czechoslovakia needed a constitution that was prepared for such a future. As Bartošek remarked, "if we want to seriously consider things, there is not a doubt that it will be necessary to subject our family law, as it has been codified up to now, to revisions and I think that it will not be not possible to position women in civil law as they have been previously."[70] Bartošek's position, though, was essentially a pragmatic one. He believed that rights were dependent on a citizen's duties or functions in society, not on his or her general human worth. The reason that the state should no longer legally support the traditional model of the family was because that particular social structure had become outdated, not because it violated a woman's human freedom.

This argument about whether "privileges of sex" should or should not exist in the legal system was never completely resolved by its writers. They continued to argue over how to regulate the relationships between men and women, although the crucial sentence was finally allowed into the constitution by a vote of five to three.[71] Even some of those who voted to include "sex" in the text of Article 106 voiced doubts about doing so, but hoped that the wording was ambiguous enough to defuse any serious threat to the established gender order. The question of whether the state should regard the family as a collection of individual citizens or as a unit with its own internal hierarchies remained a matter of dispute. Interestingly and perhaps tellingly, however, these same men never challenged the basic importance of the family to the state, even as they disagreed on how the law should regard that family. The committee's debate over Article 126, which exalted the position of the family in Czechoslovak life, was brief and uneventful. The representatives on the Constitutional Committee agreed that it had merit as a "ceremonial declaration of the importance of the family as the foundation of society." This statement seemed incontestable, even though the committee's discussion of Article 106 implied that the representatives were not united in their definition of what constituted a "family." At this juncture, however, there was no debate over what variant of that term the state should endorse. Although a few stylistic changes were made, Article 126 was passed unanimously.[72]

DURING his very first official speech as president before the provisional National Assembly on December 22, 1918, Tomáš Masaryk looked around the hall and remarked, "I am happy to see women in this Assembly. I believe that women should dedicate themselves to public activities just like men."[73] Perhaps more than any other, he was responsible for putting them there. As one activist and writer, Věra Babáková, noted, the women's movement had had its share of unreliable friends, but Masaryk was different. "Never and nowhere else," she said, "has a man stood at the head of a state who so justly defended women when their human rights were concerned."[74] Considering the way his ideas allowed women to frame their own emancipation as a necessary component of Czech nationalism and of democracy, it is not surprising that Czech feminists retained their loyalty to Masaryk. His prestige and image as a sort of Czech philosopher-king gave their efforts the glow of legitimacy, and made it harder for other politicians to easily shunt them aside without at least considering their demands. It was via the medium of Masaryk that they had been able to move from the margins into the mainstream of the Czech political scene. Because of his staunch support, Czech feminists were not only able to have their concerns built in to the very fabric of the nascent state, but were able to link their agenda with the agenda of the country as a whole. As Masaryk claimed that gender equality was a constituent part of democracy, so they could claim that the fate of the nation rested on the extent to which their demands on the part of women's rights were realized.

Their efforts were extraordinarily successful and made Czechoslovakia a rather unique place in Europe. It was not just that the independent Czechoslovakia granted women suffrage, or even that it included a promise of gender equality in its constitution. When it gave women the vote, the Czechoslovak state was not acting in a very radical fashion for the times: the new regimes in Germany, Austria, Hungary, and Poland also included women in the electorate just after the First World War, as did Britain, the United States, and others.[75] Even Czechoslovakia's constitutional guarantee of women's equality was not unique, but was echoed in the constitution of Weimar Germany. Similarly, using the rhetoric of women's emancipation as a marker of their nation's "modern" and "progressive" traits was not particularly Czech, but could be found elsewhere on the continent and even echoed the rhetoric of a number of non-Western nationalisms, particularly from Turkey and India.[76] What made what happened in Czechoslovakia in 1918 rather unusual was the way in which suffrage seemed to have become genuinely popular, its beginnings tied to the establishment of an even more popular regime, for Czechs at least. Czechs in 1918 wanted their republic, and if women's rights were part of creating that republic, they wanted them as well. In contrast, women's suffrage in Germany was identified with a Weimar Republic that few liked or wanted to defend. Things were similar in Austria, where popular imagination connected women's voting rights with the socialist victory of 1918, while in Hungary an expanded suffrage became the tool of Christian nationalists hoping to use women's votes to sustain a conservative regime.[77]

Czechs were willing to cheer for women and praise them as equals because they had accepted the idea that democracy was the best form of government for their nation and were told that democracy required a polity of equal citizens. But the impetus for this idea didn't come from below. Instead, it was the belief of educated politicians and university graduates, men and women who been inspired by the speeches of Tomáš Masaryk, now their President-Liberator. In 1918, few thought to question it. But few had also really begun to ponder the possible ramifications of such a radical rhetoric of equality. When forced to consider the outer limits of "the privileges of sex," even a number of men on the Constitutional Committee began to balk at the prospect of gender disappearing from the law. They wanted women to vote—they had themselves written the first law that would allow them to do so—but to deny the rights a husband had over his wife? This was an entirely different question, and one for which they, and most other Czechs, did not have ready answers.

# 2

## THE FIGHT OVER THE
## CZECHOSLOVAK CIVIL CODE

Today's granting of equal rights acknowledges women, but it does not
understand them. . . . We must be concerned with keeping equality with
men, but not forget to value a woman's domestic activities and maternal
profession, where she cannot be replaced by anyone or anything.

Unsigned article, "Ženské hnutí," *Naše Doba*, 1924

AFTER THE FOUNDING of the Czechoslovak Republic in 1918, the legal
equality of women was taken as a given in the Czech lands. The provisional
National Assembly made women's rights a priority; admitted women as
members, granted suffrage to men and women on an equal basis, and ended
discriminatory policies toward women in the educational system and the
civil service. Rather remarkably, the Assembly's decisions concerning
women's rights met with little debate. Acceptance of women's suffrage
was more widespread in the Czech lands than in the world's most established democracies, including republican France, where women would not
get the vote until 1944, Great Britain, where women under thirty could
not vote until 1928, or in the United States, where anti-suffrage sentiment
was much more vocal after 1918.[1] In contrast, Czech women were openly
welcomed into politics. Even the region's more socially conservative political parties, the Agrarian Party and the People's Party, quickly embraced

women's suffrage and urged women to take their place on the public stage. By 1919, even a magazine for conservative Catholic women in the province of Moravia told its readers that the old adage "women should not be concerned with politics, only with the home" no longer applied in the Czech lands.[2]

While the Czech public may have agreed that women deserved something called "equality," there was a wide variety of ideas about what this might mean in practice. The author writing in the Catholic magazine quoted above would have probably answered that question by replying that some felt gender could not be exterior to citizenship, but needed to inform and shape it. Women, she would have said, should have equality, but only within the context of their specifically gendered place in society. Women's responsibilities and rights should stem from womanhood itself and be based on their distinct social roles as wives and mothers. Czech feminists, on the other hand, did not believe that rights could be determined by gender and protested that for women to truly be placed on a level with men, the law had to treat them equally in all areas, even within the family. Their demands touched a nerve in Czech society. In the political environment of the Czech lands after 1918, it was not problematic for feminists to demand voting rights for women. It was, however, troubling for them to assert that the law needed to treat women as people, rather than as women. And it was even more controversial for them to declare that women should have equal rights even within the family. For many people, the idea of political equality was just, but the idea of spousal equality was threatening, representing a wanton attack on the family itself.

These differences over how Czechoslovak democracy should bring equality to its men and women came to a head around Czechoslovakia's civil law code. These laws regulated many kinds of interpersonal relationships, including contracts, inheritances, marriages, and family life. At the time Czechoslovakia was founded, the Czech lands still used the Austrian Civil Code of 1811. Its laws concerning marriage and the family were similar to those in other European civil law codes, such as the Napoleonic Code. It reflected what feminist scholars have called a "liberal" or bourgeois notion of gender relations, where citizen-husbands were the rulers of their households.[3] The Austrian Civil Code presupposed a world split into gendered domains, where the husband was the family's public representative and provider, while his wife stayed at home minding the house and children. Like elsewhere in Europe, men in the Czech lands had the power to legally represent their wives and children, administer their property, and make decisions about their future. In legal terms, a wife was on a level with her own children; even as their mother she had no rights toward them. A father could even leave custody of his children to a guardian other than their mother in event of his death, leaving her with no legal connection to her own offspring.

In other parts of Europe, feminists had begun to challenge a wife's legal subordination to her husband during the nineteenth century, with mixed results. British women fought and won the right to own their own property, to obtain legal separations from abusive husbands, and to keep custody of their children after such separations. They were, however, not able to convince many legislators to support a true equalization of power within marriage. Closer to the Czech lands, German women had tried to influence the creation of a new unified German civil code in 1900, but had little success in reducing a husband's patriarchal authority.[4] Czech feminists before 1918 had not prioritized civil law in their campaigns, preferring instead to give their energy to suffrage and nationalist causes. They began to look more intensely at the issue after the creation of Czechoslovakia, as new Czechoslovak legislators considered devising their own civil code. Lawmakers agreed that something needed to be done with the old Austro-Hungarian laws they had inherited and began the process of revising them. Their project served to bring uncertainties about women's legal place in the republic into focus, forcing politicians and the public to articulate how they felt about the concept of women's rights and the reach of the democratic system they had created.

## Democracy and Divorce

As predicted during the debate over Article 106, the civil code quickly came under the scrutiny of the National Assembly. The Assembly's main concern, however, was not explicitly linked to women's rights, but was instead focused on changing the relationship between the state and organized religion. The Habsburg government had deferred to religious law in matters relating to marriage, ceding authority over registering births and marriages to the various faiths it recognized within its borders. All citizens were registered by religion at birth and, regardless of their degree of religiosity in later life, had to follow that faith's rules for marriage and divorce. In the Czech lands, over 80 percent of the inhabitants were registered as Catholics, which meant that they were legally unable to marry outside the Church or get a divorce. Aside from the rare annulment, Catholic residents of the Habsburg Monarchy married for life. This policy of forcing even nominal Catholics to abide by Church marriage laws had been unpopular throughout the monarchy, but it took on additional significance in the Czech lands, where nationalists often associated the Catholic Church with Austria's Habsburg family. In 1918, many Czechs linked removing the Church's legal privileges with their plan to rid the new Czechoslovak state of the Habsburg legacy and create a "modern" democratic state in its place. Alois Hajn, a prominent member of the National Democratic Party and government minister, wrote that the Church's power over marriage was "absolutely unacceptable for a modern state, it does not satisfy us as citizens, or as progressive, modern people who look at religion and marriage quite differently than they did in the Middle Ages."[5] Taking authority over marriage from the Church was a very visible (and popular) aspect of the de-Austrianizing process that consumed the provisional National Assembly in the early weeks of the Czechoslovak Republic.

Czech politicians from parties across the political spectrum initially proposed a sweeping array of changes, including mandatory civil marriage. They also attacked old prohibitions on interfaith marriages and marriages of former clergy and proposed legalizing divorce for all married couples, regardless of their faith. The symbolic importance of these issues to the creation of the new state was reflected in the speed with which politicians worked to realize them. Within two months after the declaration of the republic, the first proposals for a new marriage law were being debated in the legal committee of the National Assembly, before borders had been stabilized or the problem of getting food to the hungry masses in the cities had been solved.

The Catholic Church and its political allies, the Czech People's Party and Slovak People's Party, strongly objected to these proposed reforms and vigorously defended their hold over marriage and divorce. Especially in the countryside, parish priests worked to mobilize the faithful against the perceived danger of civil marriage, warning that the state was trying to "make a mess out of marriage."[6] The Catholic press targeted women in this effort, and argued that divorce would allow husbands to abandon their hardworking, devoted older wives in favor of younger and prettier brides. They also defended the religious content of marriage, calling a civil ceremony a sacrilege. Church leaders denied that having marriage under the control of organized religion went against the ethos of the new Czechoslovakia, claiming that the values of the Church had a place in Czechoslovak society, and that marriage was only meaningful as a moral and religious pact. If it was sanctioned by the state rather than God, marriage would become just a legal category, devoid of its special social significance.

Despite these vigorous objections, the Church could not effectively counter the idea that separating religion from state policy was necessary for a modern democracy, even if it meant legally permitting divorce for Catholics. Even the women's section of the rural and heavily Catholic Agrarian Party came out strongly in favor of the proposed new marriage laws, calling them both a moral demand and a social necessity. They rebuked local priests for trying to unfairly use their influence among rural women and charged that the Church had forgotten the line between religion and politics.[7] However, the Czech and Slovak People's Parties, the political arms of the Catholic Church, had enough strength in the National Assembly to force a compromise in at least one respect. The final bill, hammered out after six months of negotiations, legalized civil marriage, but did not make it mandatory. Religious ceremonies would still be legally valid. But divorce would be legal for all, available virtually on demand to any couple who mutually agreed to dissolve their marriage.[8]

When the formal debate on the new marriage law began in the Assembly on May 20, 1919, there was little doubt it would be passed. The Catholic Church simply did not have enough votes to defeat it. But despite the lack of drama, the parliamentary debates over divorce illustrate the conflict that surrounded marriage as a social institution at the start of the Czechoslovak

Republic. Should marriage be dissolvable or inviolable, under the control of the state and society or of the Church and God? Jan Rýpar, a representative for the Czech People's Party, claimed in his speech to the plenum of the Assembly, "it is not allowable to touch this moral foundation on which humanity, the family and the state rests. And this foundation is being undermined in the way in which this bill would legalize the violation of marriages conducted according to religious law, the way in which firm religious beliefs are being subverted."[9] In his choice of rhetoric, Rýpar showed the influence of the language of democracy on Czech politics, even for its Catholic practitioners. He argued that Catholics should have the freedom to conduct marriages as they wished, even if this took authority away from the state. With his use of this vocabulary, Rýpar tried to change the terms of the debate, making it into an issue of religious freedom rather than Church privilege.

His efforts were not enough to sway the other side. For the government and its supporters, marriage was a social institution that demanded state regulation. The Minister of Justice, Social Democrat František Soukup, explained, "we all realize perfectly that marriage is a social institution par excellence, that the state has an enormous interest in the forms by which marriage law is regulated; it is self-evident that the state is bound to solve this matter of civil law by means of its own legislation and in this manner also legally declare the absolute equality of all state citizens."[10] Because it separated religious practice from legal practice, the proposed law was characterized as a victory of reason and democracy over the forces of faith and superstition. As another representative, the Czech (National) Socialist Theodor Bartošek, declared rather bluntly, "The union of a democratic state which recognizes only the rule of the people with the absolute monarchy of the Pope is a legal and political monstrosity and would be a diseased phenomenon and a curb on all cultural and political progress in our republic."[11]

The issue of legal divorce was framed in the debate as part of the larger project of creating democracy. As the newspaper *Národní Politika* (National Politics) noted, removing barriers to divorce was a logical step in the creation of a truly modern country because it "answers modern culture, freedom and justice."[12] Divorce brought democracy's sense of legal justice to marital relationships, allowing those who had broken their marriage vows to be punished for their crimes. Divorce was also characterized as being humane, in that it could end the suffering of those whose marriages had disintegrated through no fault of their own. Such people had previously been trapped in their unhappiness forever; now divorce would enable them to construct new lives and, even more importantly, new functional families. In Theodor Bartošek's dramatic words, "Daily experience teaches us that marriage sometimes founders, it breaks down, that sacred bond of the spirit dies, the spouses are at odds with each other . . . what sense does it have to hold on to that dead form, what justice can sentence a person to lifelong suffering for a single fateful mistake?"[13]

Proponents of the new divorce law were not, they claimed, out to undermine the traditional family or in favor of wantonly destroying salvageable marriages. All speakers emphasized the importance of stable families to the state, especially in rearing children to be responsible citizens of the republic. But, they said, sometimes divorce was the only fair and moral choice. As Representative Václav Bouček asserted, "marriage is in its whole nature an indissoluble bond which should not be allowed to be touched with a capricious or frivolous hand." However, he continued, "divorce is in certain cases absolutely necessary."[14] An unhappy marriage could not succeed in its duties to society, especially where children were concerned. The only way to save the children created by such marriages, the only means by which they could be made into good citizens who would found strong families of their own, was to get them away from the pernicious influence of the dysfunctional family from which they had sprung. As Josef Černý of the Agrarian Party asked, "What kind of effect does the unhappiness of the parents have on the children? Dear Sirs, certainly a pernicious and even immoral one. How can the children of such a marriage become useful members of human society?"[15]

The only dissenting voices to these attitudes about divorce were from the People's Parties. Despite occasional taunts from the gallery or even from other representatives on the floor, they staunchly defended their position that making divorce legal would cheapen marriage and threaten the stability of the family, potentially causing great harm to the nation. They first cited religious grounds for their rejection of divorce, noting that "what God has joined, man should not break apart."[16] They also enumerated many social reasons for their stance, especially the problems that would be faced by the children of divorced parents. These "half-orphans" would probably live with their mothers in reduced financial circumstances, and the combination of poverty and lack of a father could only have disastrous effects. Additionally, as Catholic delegate Karel Novotný claimed, the possibility of divorce would undoubtedly increase use of contraception among married couples who would put off having children in case the marriage broke up. This, he said, could be catastrophic for a small nation whose numbers had already been reduced by the First World War. In order to compete with other, larger nations, Czechoslovakia simply could not allow divorce.[17] These arguments did not find many sympathetic ears in the Assembly chamber, but some of them would resurface in later years, as divorced women found themselves in precarious financial straits. These unhappy ex-wives would become a powerful political voice in later discussions about revising Czechoslovak marriage law.

At this juncture, however, it was most striking that delegates from all sides of the debate agreed that the family was the foundation of society and that its primary function was to rear children for the future of the nation. The family was supposed to be the source of culture, decency, and most importantly, morality. The argument was over who should be able to determine the content of those chosen codes of behavior that the family would then promulgate. The Catholic representatives argued that the family was essentially part of the private and religious sphere and that it was God's teachings that should dictate how the family should function. But the majority of the National Assembly members wanted to harness the family to support their secular democracy. The importance of being able to control how the family transmitted the messages of society was clearly stated by one of the last speakers in the debate, the Social Democratic representative Ludvík Aust. He acknowledged women as ones who had the primary role in child-rearing and the greatest influence on future generations. He declared: "the whole debate has not come to anything but and is nothing different than a fight about women, about her being, which has its own destiny and so much power and strength that it can change even the foundation of the social order." The church, he claimed, wanted to keep women enslaved to their husbands and to traditional values and mores. He painted organized religion as a sinister controlling force that was battling the democratic state for the souls of Czech women, and through them, the Czech family.[18]

Ostensibly, democracy would bring women freedom, but Aust's portrayal of women as objects to be fought over gave a more ominous tinge to his words. Both groups wanted to "win" the women, to use them and their position as mothers to influence the values of future generations. In this contest, conducted in the aftermath of a successful and nonviolent revolution and in an unelected Assembly dominated by liberal "progressives," socialists, and die-hard nationalists, the supporters of the state won easily. But what would they do with their victory? Would wives be freed from slavery to their husbands, as Aust implied? Or would they simply enter a different kind of servitude? While they had easily asserted their overt control over marriage, Czech politicians now faced a much greater—and more contentious—task: redesigning the family to fit the new country they were creating.

Only one representative gave a substantive speech about what a reform of the family should entail. Czech (National) Socialist (later Communist) and feminist activist Luisa Landová-Štychová chastised her colleagues for not considering anything beyond the pending marriage bill. She argued for sex education rather than moralizing as the way to combat prostitution and debauchery, releasing women and children from the control of their husbands and fathers (including equal pay for equal work so that women could be financially independent of their husbands), and encouraging women to develop their natural abilities away from their roles as wives and mothers. To this end, she demanded that priests, political poets, writers, and artists stop telling women that love for their husband was the only meaning in their life.[19] Landová-Štychová's radical stance on family policy did not garner much support. One deputy, National Democrat Josef Matoušek, claimed to agree with her, but did so in a backhanded way in which he also denied the emotional, physical, and intellectual equality of men and women. His statements reiterated the belief that men and women already held the roles in the family to which they were most naturally suited and implied that few, even in this radical, revolutionary parliament, really wanted to equalize the balance of power in the family.[20] Landová-Štychová's demands for substantive change were largely ignored, and the debate remained preoccupied with disputes between the godly and the godless. In the end, the divorce law passed easily and was widely hailed as a symbol of social and moral progress, especially for its rejection of religious dogma in favor of a more modern sensibility.[21]

## A New Czechoslovak Civil Code

The drive to revise family law in the new Czechoslovakia did not end with the passage of the marriage law of 1919. Lawmakers agreed that the entire civil code of 1811 would need to be rewritten to meet the needs of the new republic. Since this was considered a complicated and technical job, it was taken over by a special commission established in 1920 by the Ministries of Justice and Unification. The commission's mandate was multipronged. First and foremost, it was to create one unified civil code for the Czech lands and Slovakia. Before 1918, though they had both been part of the Habsburg Monarchy, these regions had been governed by different legal systems. The Czech lands, in the monarchy's Austrian half, had been administered under the Austrian civil code of 1811. Slovakia had been part of the Kingdom of Hungary, which had its own civil laws, dating largely from 1894. The new Czechoslovak version was to be based on the Austrian law, but there were numerous small differences between the two systems that needed to be negotiated. The commission's second priority, closely related to the first, was to provide a complete and authoritative translation of the original German codes into Czech and Slovak, which had never been done during the era of Habsburg rule. Its third and last task was to make changes to the existing laws as needed, including, for example, integrating the new divorce legislation into family law statutes. However, a radical revision of the civil code was never part of the commission's mandate.[22]

The revisory commission was soon divided into four topical subcommissions, each staffed by experts in its area. The subcommission concerned with family and marriage law, headed by the legal scholar Bruno Kafka, was composed of a mixture of law professors, practicing lawyers, judges, and notaries, along with representatives from the Ministries of Justice and Unification. A later request made by the Women's Center of Czechoslovak National Democracy to include female representatives on the subcommission was summarily rejected by Kafka. The subcommission discussed the stylization of individual paragraphs of the code in a series of fifty meetings carried out over the course of over two and a half years, from the end of 1920 until June of 1923.[23] In early 1924, the initial drafts of the individual subcommissions were published and presented to the legal community for comment. The Ministry of Justice then established a single "super-revisory" commission to collect feedback, combine the work of the four subcommissions into one document, make such revisions as seemed necessary, and create a final version.

In the area of family law, three years of work had done little to change the old code. The subcommission's draft continued to label the husband the legal "head of the household" and empowered him to direct his home as he saw fit. The husband remained the family's sole legal representative, with full power over the property and persons of his wife and children. He alone had the right, for example, to determine the family's place of residence and set its standard of living. In return for these rights, he was required to provide for his wife.[24] Wives were legally obligated to obey their husbands' wishes in domestic matters. They also had a legal obligation to see to household chores and even to assist in their husbands' professional activities, by working on the family farm or in the family business without pay. The fact that wives owed their husbands such service made it hard for them to be economically self-sufficient if their husbands did not want them to be. As Marie Mikulová, one of the first Czech female lawyers, commented in her analysis of Czech family law, while a husband's formal agreement was not explicitly required for his wife to work, "an independent profession or public activity conducted against her husband's will could cause difficulties for the wife, if she was not able to balance them with her legal wifely duties." As Mikulová noted, a woman who did not give up her job at her husband's request could be sued for divorce for not fulfilling her responsibilities. As the guilty party in the divorce suit, she would be denied alimony, no matter what her salary. If she did as her husband asked and left her profession, she placed herself at his economic mercy, since he was not required to share any information about his assets and earnings with her.[25]

When it was first published in 1924, the revisory commission's initial proposal for a new Czechoslovak civil code was greeted by intense dissatisfaction from all along the political spectrum, primarily in regard to family and marriage law. However, different groups violently disagreed over what it should have done. Catholics thought too many changes had been made to the 1811 code. They protested against the incorporation of civil marriage and divorce, decrying the commission's proposal as antifamily and a threat to the Czech nation. In marked contrast, others argued that the revisory commission had failed to modernize Austria's century-old family law, thus saddling Czechoslovakia with a civil code that was out of date and out of sync with the new state's democratic basis. Within each of these two main camps of opinion, there were numerous subgroups and ideas about what should or should not be included in Czechoslovak family and marriage law. The problem of women's equality was a common thread between many of them, as people struggled to fit democratic legal principles into the context of the intimate relationships between husbands and wives.

## The Response of the Women's Movement

The debate that emerged over the new civil code was heated, producing a flood of articles, speeches, and protest meetings. There was much more at stake in these discussions than the format of Czechoslovak family law. The contest over the legal representation of family life provided a political context in which concerns and anxieties about the relationships between men and women could be articulated. The civil code became one battleground through which different groups tried to gain state sanction for their own vision of gender relations and family life. As such, although the civil code was an issue that concerned all Czechs, it was women's organizations that were the most vocal, taking the lead in setting the outlines of the debate.

From the perspective of the Czech feminist movement, the revisory commission's initial proposal was laughably inadequate. The feminist response to the commission's proposal was led by a new organization, the Women's National Council (WNC, or Ženská Národní Rada), which emerged in 1923. It was founded by Františka Plamínková, the former leader of the women's suffrage campaign. After Czech women got the right to vote, Plamínková had gone into politics as a member of the National Socialist Party. She served on the Prague City Council for several years before being elected to the Czechoslovak Senate in 1925, a post she would hold until 1939. Like others from the prewar Czech women's movement, she had assumed that after gaining suffrage women would no longer need to organize politically in gendered organizations. But although she herself found a place in party politics, Plamínková soon realized that the established parties were not very responsive to women's concerns over issues like the civil code. She decided to create a new association that would act as a center for women's political action. The resulting Women's National Council was an umbrella organization for existing Czechoslovak women's groups, similar in design to other nationally based European women's federations like the Federation of German Women's Associations or the League of Austrian Women's Associations.[26] Under the leadership of the well-connected and charismatic Plamínková, the Women's National Council quickly became the most influential lobbying group for women in Czechoslovakia. It also became the voice of Czechoslovak women internationally, via its membership in a number of prominent international feminist organizations, including the International Council of Women and the Alliance for Women's Suffrage and Citizenship Rights.[27]

From its beginnings, the WNC declared itself dedicated to achieving cooperation between all Czechoslovak women, regardless of nationality, creed, or political affiliation. However, although the WNC federation did eventually incorporate the largest Slovak feminist network (Živena), and even included token German and Jewish groups, the organization was really quite Czech in its orientation. The women who dominated WNC's central office were generally Czech themselves, and they tended to speak of "Czechoslovak" women as if they were all of the same national/cultural heritage, effectively erasing any women who identified themselves primarily as Germans, Slovaks, and so on. WNC leaders also insisted on using only the "Czechoslovak" language in meetings and correspondence, a practice that, because of the volatile history of German-Czech language disputes in the Czech lands, drove away German-identified women's groups.[28] In addition, the WNC leadership was fiercely anticlerical, and rarely attempted to work with Catholic women's groups.

The organization was much better at bringing together women who supported different Czech political parties. WNC leaders usually labeled themselves feminist, but aside from that their political affiliations varied. While most supported one of the three Czech socialist parties—the Social Democrats, the National Socialists, or more rarely, the Communists—the executive board often included women who favored the more conservative National Democrats and rural women involved with the Agrarian Party. Similarly, WNC campaigns would often reach out to both socialist and Agrarian women leaders. The WNC's core constituency, however, was educated, middle-class Czech women. Many of the groups federated under the WNC were professional in nature, including unions of female teachers, civil servants, and social workers. Middle-class feminist organizations like the Czech Women's Club and groups devoted to causes such as women's education and women in the arts also joined. Czech housewives' associations had already formed their own federation (Ústředí Československých Hospodyň) and declined to enter the WNC, but there was communication and cooperation between the two organizations.[29]

At time of its founding, one of the WNC's biggest priorities was to elicit a feminist revision of family and marriage law.[30] Initially, the WNC members involved in this project assumed that the Czechoslovak Constitution's own admonition to abolish the "privileges of sex" made such changes all but inevitable. When the actual recommendations of the government's subcommission on family law became known, the WNC was shocked. Angry that a group of "legal experts" could so boldly ignore the constitution, WNC leaders went on the offensive. The legal basis for their attacks was Article 106, which, they contended, mandated erasing all legal privileges that existed between citizens, even if they were members of the same family.

The Women's National Council based its arguments for changing the civil code on constitutional issues, but Czech feminists also believed that it was socially important for the state to recognize women's civil equality.

They accepted the prevalent view that the institution of the family was the foundation of society and the state. But, they quickly pointed out, both state and society were now supposed to be governed by democratic principles. For the sake of maintaining democracy, marriage had to be transformed from a dictatorship into a partnership, where spouses shared decision-making authority. Czech families could only produce future generations of good democrats if equality was the defining characteristic of domestic life as well as public life.[31] With this kind of argument, the WNC proposed a new set of family values for a democratic age, where family members were, first and foremost, equal citizens.

As part of its work, the WNC's legal section developed its own radically egalitarian set of revisions to Czechoslovak family and marriage law. This plan for a new civil code began by treating all adult family members as legal persons, each endowed with the same fundamental rights and privileges. Husbands and wives became "spouses," and their legal duties to each other and their children were mutual, and not gender specific. Even a couple's married name, said the WNC, should be the result of a joint decision. The WNC was particularly adamant that spouses not be legally shoehorned into a gendered division of labor. They demanded an equal right to work for both spouses, unfettered by gendered responsibilities for housework. But the WNC realized that housework would have to be done, potentially limiting the economic equality of the spouse who performed it. Therefore, the WNC's model civil code granted any spouse who devoted his or her time to unpaid work for the household the legal right to half of his or her partner's salary. In interwar Czechoslovakia, this would realistically only benefit women, but the WNC was quite careful to leave the possibility open that men might also receive a wage for housework in this fashion. Moreover, WNC members suggested that in a divorce, all property gained in marriage should be divided equally and the spouse with the lower income be granted a right to alimony from the other, whatever that spouse's sex might be.[32]

The WNC's legal section sent its proposals for a new civil code to the super-revisory commission as well as to other members of the government, hoping to influence later stages of the civil code revision process. In addition, the WNC heavily lobbied the Ministry of Justice to place newly minted female lawyers on the commission. These demands were rebuffed. The Ministry claimed that, while the commission welcomed the comments of interest groups on specific issues, it was an objective, academic body and could not show preference for one specific group over another. While it advocated egalitarian laws, the WNC still claimed to represent women, which made it a group that spoke for special interests. However, the Ministry did seem to find some meat in the WNC's arguments. It wrote that it would "think seriously about meeting the WNC's demands, or at least about arranging the possibility for it [the WNC] to express its opinions about the new revision of family law before the text of the entire new civil code is ready."[33] And in fact the WNC did wrangle an opportunity to negotiate, sending its president, Františka Plamínková, and the lawyers Milada Králová-Horáková, Marie Svozilová, and Hana Vichová to an official symposium on family law sponsored by the ministry in 1929.[34]

The WNC certainly did not represent the attitudes of all Czechs or even all Czech women on the subject of family law. Its views tended to be shared mainly by those members of the intelligentsia (including many members of the state bureaucracy) who supported President Masaryk and his ideas over any particular political party. Many of the WNC's specific proposals for new family and marriage laws were also favored by the political parties of the Left and their supporters, meaning primarily the Czech National Socialist Party, the Social Democrats, and the Communists, each of which at least formally advocated women's equality in their platforms.

In the 1920s, especially, some of the WNC's ideas about the civil code also found broad-based support among more socially conservative segments of the population, represented politically by the Agrarian, Free Trade, and National Democratic parties. But although many members of these groups, especially their female constituents, approved of some of the WNC's proposals, they did so from a completely different ideological perspective. They agreed that husbands should give up some of the legal powers they still enjoyed over their wives, but rejected the WNC's belief that men and women should be able to choose the roles they played within their families. For these groups, the definition of the family itself hinged on its strictly demarcated gender roles. After the revisory commission's preliminary proposal was published in 1924, women from these three parties met with representatives from the People's Party to hammer out their own specific set of suggestions on the subject of family law, which they published in 1927. Somewhat like the WNC, the Women's Coalition (as they called themselves) asserted that the family of the future could not be strong if its women were weak, and demanded that the legal rights a husband had over his wife's person be removed. The Coalition wanted husbands and wives to share legal authority over children and property, but it also wanted to emphasize the distinct roles men and women played in family life. Unlike the WNC, the Coalition's proposal did not affirm the right of a wife to pursue her own career outside the home. Rather, it attempted to make a wife's domestic role equal in status and power with her husband's by seeing it as the functional equivalent of a career outside the home, complete with salary, benefits, and guarantees of job security. The Coalition borrowed the feminist usage of the gender-neutral term "spouse" to suggest that any spouse who took on housework as a full-time job receive a legal right to a portion of the other's wages. However, it is clear from the text of its proposal that the Coalition believed that women were naturally suited to domestic work and should concentrate on that after marriage. The traditional division of labor in the family was the correct one, it simply needed to occur in an atmosphere where wives were no longer financially or legally dominated by their husbands. By giving wives a legal voice in the household and payment for their work, the Czechoslovak state could fulfill its promises of equality for women while maintaining their important social differences from men.[35]

It was not surprising that many women in Czechoslovakia were wary of embracing the "opportunity" to reject the traditional role of wife and mother. For many, the risks associated with such a choice did not seem worth the greater personal freedom it might have to offer. The WNC's strongest supporters were members of the new class of educated professional women, who had a vital interest in being able be a wife without being a homemaker. Yet even though this group was growing rapidly, its numbers were small compared to the masses of women who considered, or wanted to consider, being a wife and mother as their primary career.[36] Being a full-time housewife was generally the ideal toward which middle-class Czech women were directed by their parents, spouses, and society, and it was also a dream to which many poorer working women aspired. Throughout the interwar period, most of those wives who did work held menial or low-level clerical jobs strictly out of necessity. Such women could not afford household help and were therefore responsible for all of their family's domestic needs in addition to their waged work. After spending years suffering under this double burden, it is no wonder that many such women looked approvingly upon laws which would help them in their quest to be financially and legally independent while being "just" home-makers.

Women who were full-time housewives had rarely been trained for any other sort of work and did not generally find the limited employment options open to them appealing. Their priority in thinking about family and marriage law was to protect their career choice to the greatest extent possible. Therefore, they often also disapproved of the divorce law of 1919, because it took away one of the greatest advantages to the job of home-maker: its security. A woman who believed her marriage contract had bought her employment and sustenance for life now discovered that she could be summarily fired. For the housewife with no other profession, divorce was a calamity that threatened her very existence. Harsh stories about the plight of ex-wives and their children thrust into poverty after the flight of the male breadwinner struck at the heart of how many women had always imagined their lives. By 1924, there were sixty thousand divorced women in Czechoslovakia, and a steady four thousand or more were being added every year. According to statistics from 1928–1932, only one-third to one-fourth of newly divorced women had had an occupation other than housewife during their marriage.[37] Such women found themselves thrust on a depressed economy and meager job market with no skills or job preparation and often with the burden of children to look after. A divorced woman had a right to alimony and child support, but only if she was not the guilty party in the divorce suit, and there was no good mechanism for forcing former husbands to pay if they fell behind. Divorced wives thus often found themselves dependent upon their parents or state aid for survival.

Groups like the WNC and the Women's Coalition did not object to the legalization of divorce. Both recognized that divorce could be devastating for women, but they also believed, along with the Czechoslovak National

Assembly, that divorce was a necessary freedom that democracy could not do without. However, there were many other women who were more frightened than exhilarated by the possibility of such freedom, which threatened to destroy the lives they had built as wives and mothers. These women, primarily conservative and middle class, but not exclusively so, were so alarmed by the havoc they saw divorce creating among women like themselves that they banded together to demand that the government make divorce illegal again. The existing Austrian civil code helped to disadvantage women who came to the divorce court by making it possible for husbands to divorce wives who refused to follow their orders and leaving such women without a right to alimony for being "at fault" in the case. Yet most women who wanted to see the divorce laws repealed did not find the civil code's distribution of powers between the sexes problematic. Their goal was to protect tradition, even traditions that disempowered them. While this drive to defend the old code was present among women and men of all religions, it was especially strong amongst Catholics. The Federation of Catholic Women and Girls, one of the largest women's associations in Czechoslovakia, became a leading force in the drive to repeal the divorce law of 1919 and to prevent any changes in the rest of the civil code that might threaten the security of a woman's position as wife and mother.[38]

The anti-divorce groups designed their public campaigns around a very conservative interpretation of Article 126 of the constitution, which promised that marriage and the family would be under the protection of the law. Unlike the WNC, these groups believed this could only mean protecting the family in its traditional form, with strongly differentiated roles for husbands and wives. Catholic women, positioned to the right of the Women's Coalition, wanted to be treated as wives rather than individuals, believing that gender roles within families were sanctioned by human biology. In their view, the essential differences between the sexes not only justified the gendered division of labor, but also mandated the husband's authority within his family. The Federation of Catholic Women and Girls and its allies wanted to restore a civil code that would protect the position of the husband as head of the household, forcing men to remain responsible for making the family's financial and legal decisions so that their wives could focus on their domestic tasks. Like their more feminist compatriots,

Catholic women demanded that domestic work be recognized as essential and important, but doing it was never a choice for women. The Catholic women's movement was not supposed to help women achieve greater mobility outside the family, but to increase their power within its confines; to make wives the rulers of their hearths, while removing them from most responsibilities outside the door of the home. As an article in the Federation's journal, *Křest'anská Žena* (Christian Woman), declared, "The husband is the head of the family, but the wife is its soul. In domestic quiet, she has her own empire."[39] Another author noted, "a woman does not have a right to her body, she is inseparably tied to the company of the family and the nation, she does not answer only to herself, but above all to God."[40] Catholic women activists therefore advocated returning all married women to the family. They claimed that married women had to be homemakers in order for a family to function properly and for its children to be educated as good, contributing members of society. Breaking the barriers between husband and wife as the WNC proposed was, for them, a serious threat to healthy family life.

## The Super-revisory Commission

The super-revisory commission began its work in February of 1926. It listened to the cacophony of voices raised in response to the first phase of revisions to the code and deliberated upon them until November 4, 1931; their results were published at the end of that year. However, the commission's six years of work did not reward the public with many substantive changes. While it had continued to modernize and simplify the language, most of the old law remained behind the new words. In the area of family law, the commission did not tamper with the unequal distribution of powers between spouses and still awarded husbands legal authority over their wives, their children, and all the family's property.[41] In its accompanying statement, the commission claimed that it was "necessary for the husband to represent his family." The commission implied that groups who demanded otherwise (it mentioned the Women's National Council by name) were not thinking realistically. "It is easy," the commission wrote in its report, "to say that husband and wife should have the same position in the family, that is, the same duties and the same rights."[42] But the result would be chaos. Couples, constantly arguing over petty matters, would be forever turning to the courts to arbitrate disagreements over where they would live or how to allocate household earnings. Seeing this "anarchy" as the consequence of spousal equality, the commission concluded that leaving decision-making power with the husband was the only rational solution. The men on the super-revisory commission found it impossible to believe that two sovereign persons could live together peaceably and work out mutually acceptable solutions to everyday problems. A harmonious family life simply could not exist if one person did not have the authority to quell all opposition, the subjection of one spouse the necessary sacrifice for domestic tranquility.

However, while the commission was not inclined to implement changes in family law simply to bring it in line with the constitution's mandate of legal gender equality, it did prove itself committed to asserting bureaucratic authority over organized religion. The most substantial change enacted by the super-revisory commission was to write mandatory civil marriages into the civil code. The commission claimed that it was only interested in streamlining administrative procedures, saying that any modern nation should have just one authority responsible for registering marriages. It denied that this decision was an attack on the Catholic Church.[43] The Church, of course, did not see it this way and many Catholics were deeply upset by this newest draft of a Czechoslovak civil code.

With its lack of respect for the demands of both the feminist viewpoint and the religious right, the commission managed to alienate just about everyone who had an interest in seeing the civil code revised. Angry protests rolled in from all quarters, though those outside the Catholic camp applauded the move to make civil marriage mandatory.[44] Even the man nominally in charge of the project, Minister of Justice Alfréd Meissner, came out strongly against the commission's work. Meissner, a prominent member of the Social Democratic Party and a longtime associate of Plamínková's, criticized the commission for not taking more seriously the need to equalize the status of husbands and wives. In a speech given to the Syndicate of Czechoslovak Reporters in Plzeň he remarked, "the super-revisory commission's proposal does not completely satisfy this demand [of equality] and it will be necessary to revise many of its statutes. For example, the mere sentence that the 'husband is the head of the household' is in many cases a mere fiction."[45] He went on to say that in a world where more and more women were taking on nontraditional roles and supporting their families, it would be necessary to reject the old legal traditions still present in the commission's work. But although Meissner himself criticized the new proposal, it remained unclear what effect this might have on the newly proposed version of the civil code itself. Meissner might be Minister of Justice, but he did not have the personal authority to set policy in this matter. He was simply one member of a fractious multiparty coalition government that was strongly divided on these issues. Now that it had been completed, the super-revisory commission's proposal left his jurisdiction. It was sent to the various government ministries for comment, and the delicate process of negotiating its recommendations began.

While this official process was carried out in an atmosphere of silence and secrecy, the public reaction was loud and vociferous. The lines between the different interest groups became more clearly drawn and each became more preoccupied with addressing its specific concerns than engaging the others. One the one side, Catholic groups were incensed by the renewed prospect of mandatory civil marriage, as well as the further integration of the 1919 divorce law into the civil code. While they admitted being motivated by religious conviction, they labeled the commission's new draft a blatant attack on the family, not the Church. Catholic leaders loudly declared that a strong nation needed strong families and a strong family could not exist in a land where divorce was legal. Their standpoint was convincingly articulated by the Archbishop Karel Kašpar in a speech given at a mass protest meeting called by the Federation of Catholic Women and Girls in Prague on March 15, 1932. While Kašpar caused controversy among non-Catholics by proclaiming that even "barbarous" nations recognized that marriage was a matter of the sacred and not the profane and calling civil marriage "nothing but concubinage," he also made a concerted attempt to rally the entire nation to the cause by emphasizing the importance of an unbreakable marriage bond for Czechoslovak society as a whole. He even quoted Masaryk on the virtues of monogamy in an effort to prove this point. Far from wanting to undermine the state, he declared, Catholics were the ones who loved it the best, more than those who would undermine its stability to satisfy their own selfish desire for divorce. "In the interest of the state," said Kašpar, "we appeal to everyone who holds our state dear . . . to demand that this law be changed, not out of love for Catholics, but for those miserable, abandoned, forsaken wives . . . for the love of the children to whom they gave life . . . for love of the nation and the state, which only then will be strong, only then will be moral . . . for the love of our republic."[46]

Catholic women's groups also stressed the centrality of the family to the state and the destructive force divorce exerted on it. As characterized by the Federation of Catholic Women and Girls, divorce was "a work of modern progress and at the same time the biggest evil and unhappiness of every state. It disrupts its foundations, destroys peace in families, rips the bonds of marriage, and does not even stop in front of the fearful little faces of the children and moves like an avalanche, dragging with it everything that stands in its path."[47] These women saw marriage as a serious commitment that demanded sacrifices from both husbands and wives. It was not the "mere communal co-existence of two people of different sexes for the purpose of tasting life's pleasures"[48] but a societal mechanism for raising children to be good and moral citizens. Getting married was a social duty and it was both irresponsible and selfish to leave a marriage for personal reasons. The children were what mattered and they had a right to a stable family life that exceeded their parents' individual rights to self-determination. The attitude that children's rights exceeded those of their parents was not limited to Catholics by any means. As an article in the generally anticlerical newspaper *Národní Politika* (National Politics) put it, "Where is true democracy for the children? We are revising the civil code—family law; where should it place its emphasis? The law should strengthen the family, limit divorces, force parents to honorably care for the children they bring into the world. . . . Do we want to protect the tradition of the family or live like animals in herds?"[49]

This was an argument that groups like the Women's National Council could not accept. For the WNC, a functional family depended upon being led by two equal individuals. While feminists could agree that children had a right to a stable family environment, they did not believe that this could be prioritized above the rights of both parents to exert their freedoms as independent citizens of a democratic state. This second revision of the civil code from 1931, which blatantly disregarded those rights for wives in its proposal for the new family law, surprised and disgusted the WNC and left many of its members bitterly disillusioned. They could not believe that the commission could support laws which were so obviously in conflict with the constitutional guarantee of gender equality and with the ideals of democracy. Additionally, they felt betrayed by the Ministry of Justice, which had not fulfilled any of its written and oral promises to take their demands into consideration or to give them the opportunity to express their views before the commission.[50] The whole affair caused them to wonder how committed their government actually was to democracy. As an article in the WNC's journal, *Ženská Rada* (Women's Council), asked, "Do the leaders of the republic really want a true democracy? Do they want it from internal conviction that it is the correct path for our nation? If they want it, they cannot want, they are not allowed to want a family law which would come outside the democratic spirit of equality between spouses and between parents."[51]

The WNC leapt into action. In addition to calling their own protest meetings and making their dissatisfaction with the new proposal known, they also began work on a new set of detailed suggestions for changes to Czechoslovak family law. The legal committee of the WNC, headed by the young lawyer Milada Králová-Horáková, held a set of twenty-four meetings throughout 1932–1934 in which they went over every line of the latest proposal for the civil code and worked out their own alternative.[52] This was not an easy task. Even in this relatively small forum, disputes broke out over whether women might actually benefit more by more restrictive laws, especially in the case of divorce. In the end, a poll of the WNC's federated organizations ratified the leadership's more gender-neutral approach, but only after a group called For Women's Rights, dedicated to helping divorced women, left the WNC federation in a huff.[53] After the legal committee had completed its own proposals in October of 1934, it met with the women's sections of various political parties to formulate a common set of basic demands in an effort to create a united front from which to petition the Czechoslovak government for more change.[54] In November, the WNC sent a letter to the new Minister of Justice, Ivan Dérer, a Social Democrat who had been sympathetic to the WNC in the past. They demanded the opportunity to present their suggestions to the ministry and hold personal negotiations with its representatives. They argued that such a request was only just, since no women had been allowed to participate in the super-revisory commission's work and the result was a document "in absolute conflict with Article 106 of the constitution, even though select university professors wrote it. Is that not," the WNC scathingly commented, "enough proof of the mind of Czech men as far as women are concerned?" If law professors, "whose first and fundamental duty is to be imbued with the spirit of the constitution," could not be trusted to remember its words without women in the room, then the WNC could only conclude that the male ministry officials who would be taking up the commission's suggestions would benefit by hearing what they had to say.[55]

Dérer agreed, and directed ministry officials involved with the project to meet with WNC representatives to go over their suggestions. In September 1935, Milada Králová-Horáková met three times with senior justice officer Dr. Srb to debate the fine points of the super-revisory commission's proposal. As they both noted separately later, they agreed on many issues, including parental rights and bettering the legal position of illegitimate children. Srb, however, disagreed with the WNC's stance on the legal relationship between spouses, particularly regarding property rights during marriage and divorce. Srb remarked that the WNC's proposal on this issue could "meet with very serious resistance," but the WNC refused to change its position and requested that Srb send its suggestions to the other members of the interministerial group working on the civil code. Srb refused, explaining that the ministry would only forward the parts of the WNC's proposal it recognized as important. He claimed that no other organization was given the opportunity to negotiate personally with the ministry like the WNC, implying that they should be happy they had gotten as far as they had. Králová-Horáková retorted that since the government was not allowing any women to participate directly in the proceedings relating to the civil code, this was not exactly a concession.[56]

This incident with the Ministry of Justice illustrated both the strength and weakness of the WNC. It was generally successful in using its clout and influence (or the influence of its president, Plamínková) to get a hearing from government officials. However, it remained completely at the mercy of those officials and had no means by which to force actual policy changes. Though there were a few female representatives in the National Assembly, they were basically powerless to help in any significant way. Political power in Czechoslovakia was heavily concentrated in the leadership of whatever parties were members of the governing coalition, and women had yet to make their way into those higher circles, much less obtain a ministerial portfolio. Instead, the WNC had to rely on what they hoped were the democratic principles of others and this often proved to be a futile exercise.

## A Body without a Heart

The government debated the super-revisory commission's proposal in closed sessions until the summer of 1935. That fall, the Ministry of Justice recalled the commission to make some amendments based on the outcome of these sessions. By this time quite a few of its original members had died. They were replaced, however, with other older, male legal scholars: no representatives from other sources were admitted. The commission finished its work in November 1936, but the government did not release the results to the public until a final version was presented to both houses of the National Assembly for preliminary debate in April 1937.[57] The occasion was heralded as a significant moment for the Czechoslovak legal system and for Czechoslovak national unity, since the proposal was the first to join the Czech lands and Slovakia in one system of civil law. As Representative Ladislav Rašín stated in his speech in the National Assembly, the new civil code was a "historical act because it is the first extensive codification [of Czechoslovak law], a codex which should lay the foundation for a new Czechoslovak legal order, for a new legal basis for everyday life and everyday relations between citizens."[58] In the opinion of Rašín and others, completing the civil code project marked a final break with the heritage of the Habsburg Monarchy and sealed the status of Czechoslovakia as a united, democratic republic. For the Czechoslovak government to resist the pull of authoritarian ideas in the sphere of civil law, despite the growing European political crisis and threats of war, was tangible proof that Czechoslovakia was truly a democratic state. However, the proposal presented to the National Assembly in 1937 was not quite complete. The sections on family law were left out. Statutes dealing with property in marriage were included in the sections dealing with property and inheritance, but the bulk of regulations covering marriage and the family were missing.

Speakers in the National Assembly, where the new code was first debated, loudly proclaimed their horror at this omission. Oldřich Suchý from the Agrarian Party dramatically declared that a civil code that did not include marriage and the family within its scope was "like a body without a head, and I think even like a body without a heart." Suchý claimed that the reason the family law sections were not present in the government's proposal was because of partisan disagreements within the governing coalition about how to deal with civil marriage and divorce. However, in a sharp contrast to 1919, when only Catholic representatives dared criticize legalizing civil marriage and divorce, in 1937 the Agrarian Suchý expressed doubts. While he did acknowledge that "obligatory civil marriage is the logical conclusion of logical legal thought," he also claimed that it "does not answer well enough the conditions we have been living under for some years, and particularly not the state we are currently living in."[59] He did not propose abolishing divorce, but he did suggest that it had not strengthened marriage as its supporters had claimed it would in 1919. While not explicitly renouncing the bold statements of twenty years earlier, Suchý talked about how faith and religion were moving back into the center of people's lives and how the law had to respect this.

In his speech to the Senate a few days later, Minister of Justice Ivan Dérer admitted that civil marriage and divorce were the primary issues behind the government's failure to include family law with the rest of its proposal for the new civil code. Dérer refused to name any party as specifically at fault, but simply pointed to general differences of opinion that had, up to that point, eluded a solution. He claimed that having such political differences was "not a sin" and declared that family law was "in its nature political and has always and everywhere been considered as such." A compromise solution, he said, is just as political as an extreme one and there can never be a purely legal approach to such matters. He noted that the government was still working on the problem and that it would continue to negotiate until it could reach a solution. However, Dérer did not seem optimistic that the situation would be resolved any time soon and urged the Senate not to hold up the completed portions of the civil code in vain attempts to reach an agreement on the family law problem. While he did not actually say that the situation was hopeless, he certainly implied that the government doubted that its internal difficulties on the subject could ever be resolved.[60]

After a few days of such preliminary speech making, in which the most prevalent comment concerned the sad lack of the regulations concerning family law, the government's curtailed proposal for the new civil code passed into special committees of the Assembly and Senate for more detailed negotiations and debate. The government apparently continued to debate about the proper form of the family and marriage law components, but its negotiations were carried out in secret and no draft proposal of these sections was ever released to the public, nor did the individual parties give out any details.

A few months later, in December of 1937, Františka Plamínková used the opportunity of a Senate debate over the 1938 budget to publicly rebuke the government, including her own National Socialist Party, for its failures with the civil code. Plamínková argued that a truly democratic state could not choose when it would allow equality between its citizens and when it would not, regardless of the circumstances or difficulties involved. For Plamínková, any law that did not meet basic standards of justice and equality was unacceptable, and she criticized the government for being unwilling to hold to those standards. Plamínková scathingly took Justice Minister Dérer to task for hiding behind the "high academic qualification of the specialists who prepared this proposal." This, she felt, was poor justification for a set of laws that did "not respect the democratic spirit of the constitution in fundamental matters of policy." It was this "spirit of democracy," that needed to inform the law, Plamínková charged, not "legal scholarship" more preoccupied with clinging to old ways than executing its constitutional duties. According to Plamínková, the issue was not one of *women's* rights, but of the rights of all citizens within a democratic society more generally. The problem with the civil code was that it regarded women only as wives, mothers, and daughters and not as citizens. The Czechs, said Plamínková, liked to think of themselves as an island of democracy, swimming alone in the middle of a Central Europe rapidly being engulfed by various forms of authoritarianism. But if there was no democracy in the family, if children were not raised in a democratic atmosphere, then how long could the Czechs hope to keep fascism from obtaining a foothold in their republic?[61]

The government did not see the problem with the same urgency as Plamínková did. The matter of a new family law remained mired in the mud of coalition politics, never to see a satisfactory solution. The rest of the government's proposal for a new civil code remained with the committees that had been assigned to debate it until the outbreak of war in 1939 halted all such projects. The Czechoslovak government would only return to the task in 1945. It was only after another war had yet again revolutionized the political scene that Czechoslovakia would finally get a new civil code.


IN 1918, CZECHS found themselves becoming a nation that supported women's rights. In their drive to replace the imperial subject with the democratic citizen, they brought women into politics, seeing universal suffrage as part of the process of making democracy. But the story of these debates over the civil code shows that Czechs were more ambivalent about the idea of equality than many of them might have wanted to admit. Throughout the decades-long arguments over family and marriage law, few denied that women were citizens, entitled to some form of legal equality. But while Czechs generally continued to support the idea of women's rights in the abstract, they began to think about how they might qualify those rights. When men were first recognized as citizens by the liberal state, they received not only the right to represent themselves as individuals politically, but also the right to exercise their will in their own homes. Equal under state law, men could make their own laws in private. When women gained citizenship, this division between public and private spheres was called into question.

When the Women's National Council made the potential consequences of Article 106 of the constitution clear, many Czechs reacted negatively. The WNC's proposals for a new civil code, which included the possibility of wives who supported their husbands economically, removed the responsibility of housework from women and even threw the idea of a wife taking her husband's name into doubt, were much more frightening than the idea of women voting, or even being elected to public office. While even a radically changed civil code would not in fact mandate any change in the way ordinary Czechs lived their lives, it seemed, perhaps, to make the possibility of such change more real.

In many ways, the widespread resistance to changing the civil code in Czechoslovakia is a familiar story. Feminists across Europe had been generally unsuccessful in getting their governments to agree to civil laws that truly treated husbands and wives as equal persons, each endowed with their own individual right to autonomy and freedom.[62] What was new, however, was the context in which this battle was played out. Czechoslovakia was a new republic, popular with its Czech citizens. Czechs had a declaration of independence that promised to make women equal and a constitution that seemingly prohibited men from having legal privileges over women. For anyone who might have forgotten this, the WNC's activities served as a reminder. It is perhaps a testament to the strength of their constitutional argument that few chose to debate the WNC on its own terms. Members of the Czechoslovak government often accepted the validity of the WNC's position, but seemed incapable of actually acting on their convictions. Justice Ministers Meissner and Dérer supported the WNC in principle, but failed to insert a single meaningful change for women into the existing civil code, or even into the draft for the revised version. In their defense, they could only claim that their hands were tied by the requirements of partisan politics. The non-partisan super-revisory commission defended its choice to leave a husband's powers in his household essentially intact by ignoring the issue of constitutionality. Instead, they claimed that they made the only practical choice, speaking in the name of a sort of extra-legal reason. The loudest voices against an egalitarian civil code also put the issue of the constitution aside and spoke with a different kind of vocabulary. Instead of talking about the kinds of laws a democracy could allow, they argued for the stability of the family and its importance to the nation and the state. The best civil code was one that insulated the family and protected it from change. This was also a powerful argument, and one that seemed to gain in force during the tense 1930s, as economic and political crises swirled through Central Europe. But the opposition of these two kinds of arguments could create a troubling dichotomy, setting the cause of democracy against the idea of the family and implying that one existed to the detriment of the other. Feminists claimed that democracy needed to rely on the rule of constitutions and laws and to respect values like equality, even within the family. Their opponents tried to set the family outside of politics, subject to natural laws instead of constitutions and bound to the Czech nation more than any system of government. As the feminists argued their case, however, it began to look more and more as if democracy itself was the issue threatening the family.

# 3

## ONE FAMILY, ONE NATION

### *The Problem of Married Women's Citizenship*

The family is the basis of human society. Its perfection and sanctity
is a condition of the physical and mental health of individuals, of nations,
of humanity. If an individual, a social class, a nation loses its respect for
the sanctity of family life, it is condemned to extinction.

Jan Zachoval, *Rodinná výchova*, 1923

PAEANS TO THE VIRTUES of family life such as the one above were constant features of political discourse in the Czechoslovak Republic. These
flowery explosions of prose might seem insignificant, merely banal sentiment. But, in the Czech case at least, they graphically illustrate the difficulties feminists faced in achieving civil rights for women. The ideal family
required a wife/mother who was willing to sacrifice herself for the good
of the other family members. For Zachoval, the primary characteristic of
a wife was her selflessness: she was a "helpmate, an advisor and support
for her husband."[1] Ideally, she had no personal desires except to serve her
family, depending upon that service to find fulfillment in life. Others described her as being the family's heart—the living instrument that made it
live too. Without her, the whole institution might crumble, and with it,
the nation itself.

For most Czechs, therefore, equality for women was acceptable only
to the extent that it did not disrupt their vital role in the family. Within

those bounds, it was not only tolerable, but even desirable. This was the peculiarly Czech twist to what were otherwise relatively common European beliefs about the family as an ideal institution. Even Zachoval conceded, "attempts to make husbands and wives morally, educationally, legally and socially equal are a sign of all eras that strive for the moral progress of humanity."[2] But, even for Czechs, relationships between wives and husbands were generally considered to be outside the purview of the egalitarian impulses of the democratic system. When Czech feminists struggled to get their lawmakers to adopt a more expansive vision of equality, one without marital restrictions, they met with little success. Even after the establishment of the republic, most Czechs continued to believe that when a bride said her wedding vows she was signaling her willingness to live under her husband's authority and to have her relationship to the law shaped by her relationship to him. For the most part, laws that would have changed the rights husbands could claim over their wives either simply failed to materialize or did not win enough political support to be enacted. Wives continued to be deprived of their status as legal individuals more systematically than any other group in Czechoslovakia, despite the constitution's decree not to recognize the "privileges of sex."

Perhaps the most glaring example of this failure to reconcile beliefs about the family with a concern for equality was the case of citizenship law. The ability to choose one's state allegiance is one of modern society's most basic privileges, straddling the divide between political and civil rights. Where you claim citizenship determines not only where you vote, but whether you are able to vote at all. It indicates where you can live, which legal system will regulate your life and business, what kind of social assistance may be available to you, and what you owe your government in return (in the form of taxes, military or jury service, and so on). In the interwar Czechoslovak Republic, the right to determine one's own citizenship status was taken away from women when they married; a wife's citizenship was determined solely by her husband's state of allegiance. As long as she chose a partner who was also a Czechoslovak citizen, the fact that her husband had the power to determine her country was invisible. But if she married a foreign man, or if her Czechoslovak husband decided to emigrate and be naturalized elsewhere, then his power over her became devastatingly clear. Such a woman found herself renounced by her own country, stripped of her citizenship, and thrown out of the polity. Once the deed was done, a wife had no legal power to reverse the process.

Legally, this practice was justified by the so-called "doctrine of family unity." As its name implies, this stream of legal thought began from the premise that a family's internal harmony depended on all of its members being citizens of the same state. Since the husband was the "head of the household," it was his task to determine his family's country. The practitioners of this doctrine claimed that the goal of protecting the family was well worth the loss of a wife's personal freedom.

In 1918, the citizenship regulations of most of the world's nations, including Czechoslovakia, followed the doctrine of family unity.[3] This began to change in the 1920s when several nations, including the United States and the Soviet Union, changed their laws to allow women more autonomy over their state allegiance. While such moves were applauded by feminists around the world, they also had unforeseen effects; because countries used different criteria in assigning married women citizenship, conflicts could occur. Wives who fell between the cracks of different national legal systems might find themselves literally without a country—unclaimed by their husband's nation and denied by their own. And as those who became stateless would discover, in a world where access to even the most basic human rights came only through state-based citizenship, those who could not claim membership in any polity literally had no rights at all.[4]

## Married Women, Citizenship Law, and Nationalism

The matter of making women equal persons in citizenship law might seem separate from nationalist concerns, but in the Czech lands citizenship laws were always entangled with nationalist politics. When the Czechoslovak state was established in 1918, Czechs and Slovaks hoped to cement their majority status by limiting the number of citizens from other nationalities. Like the other Habsburg successor states, Czechoslovakia was ostensibly based on the principle of national self-determination. However, the country was home to many people who did not identify themselves as either Czech or Slovak. Czech leaders were particularly concerned about the large German population in the Czech lands, but international pressure prevented them from using national criteria to decide on who would be recognized as a Czechoslovak citizen. The 1920 Czechoslovak law settling the question of who was to be a citizen was, in large part, dictated by the Treaties of Versailles, St. Germain, and Trianon, which forbade the expulsion of residents based on their nationality.[5]

According to this 1920 statute, the right to claim Czechoslovak citizenship was primarily based on an individual's official residence status (*domovské právo/Heimatsrecht*) in 1910. Persons (and their children) who possessed the legal right of residence in the Czech lands or in Slovakia in that year became Czechoslovak citizens, regardless of the language they spoke or the national group they identified with. Former citizens of the Habsburg lands who had been formally granted residency in Czechoslovak territories after 1910 could also claim citizenship, but they were required to formally apply for the privilege. The offer of Czechoslovak citizenship could be refused, but only to those who were not "Czechoslovak by language and race." According to the postwar peace settlement, residents of Czechoslovak territory who did not consider themselves of Czech or Slovak nationality were allowed to "opt out" of Czechoslovak citizenship and claim membership in whichever country of the former Habsburg lands fit their national allegiance. Similarly, Czechs and Slovaks who had been living in other parts of the monarchy were allowed to opt for Czechoslovak citizenship.[6]

This decision to use the year 1910 as a baseline was actually a measure aimed at excluding as many non-Czechs and Slovaks from the polity as possible. In the Czech lands at least, an official right of residence could only be obtained after the applicant had already lived in the locality of his application for at least ten years. Therefore, only those who actually had lived on Czechoslovak territory since 1900 would have the documentation necessary to automatically be recognized as Czechoslovak citizens. While those of Czech and Slovak nationality could always exercise their right to opt for citizenship in the country aligned with their nationality, those of other ethnic backgrounds would have to resort to the petition process. Basing the criteria for citizenship largely on residence rights was especially problematic when dealing with territory outside of the Czech lands. Regulations regarding residence were looser in the Hungarian half of the Monarchy, where formal proof of residence rights was rarely needed or given. This meant that thousands of inhabitants in this part of Czechoslovakia, mostly poor Ruthenian and Hungarian speakers, had no papers enabling them to prove that they had been legal residents in 1910. This bureaucratic oversight cost them their right to citizenship.

The text of the 1920 law spoke of generic "persons," implying that both men and women (or Czechs, Slovaks, or Germans) over eighteen would be treated in the same manner. This was true, but only if they were not married. Wives were a special category. Under both Czech and Slovak civil law, a woman lost her right to control her own residence status when she married; her husband determined that for her. So, if citizenship was allotted according to residence rights, wives and children followed their husbands or fathers. The right to opt for citizenship according to national identification was explicitly denied to married women and children under eighteen. For example, a Czech-identified woman married to a German-identified man could be forced to formally renounce Czechoslovak allegiance if her husband opted for Austrian citizenship after 1918, even if they had always lived in Bohemia and regardless of her wishes in the matter. Even if her husband later died, she would legally remain an Austrian.

When the citizenship law of 1920 was released, there was very little comment on its decision to stand by the doctrine of family unity, even though this was not mandated under the peace treaties. The 1920 law was controversial, but mainly for its decision to give Czechoslovak citizenship to German-speaking citizens living in the Czech lands.[7] Czech women did not protest that the law denied women legal autonomy. There were a number of reasons for this. First of all, in 1920 the organized Czech women's movement was in disarray and would not recover its momentum until after the founding of the Women's National Council in 1923. When this legislation was passed, most former women activists were trying to make their way in the political parties of their choice and no party saw fit to delay the law over this issue. But perhaps more importantly, in 1920, a wife's ability to choose her own country seemed but a part of the much larger issue of achieving equal civil rights for wives and husbands within marriage. Thus, feminists' concerns with the citizenship law were largely subsumed into their greater campaign to revise the civil code along egalitarian lines. For women like National Assembly representative Luisa Landová-Štychová, achieving gender parity within citizenship law was simply part and parcel of this larger project. If the family law statutes were changed so that wives were recognized as legal persons, then things like citizenship law would have to fall into agreement.[8]

Moreover, the inequities in the citizenship law affected only a small number of Czech women, those who had married foreigners or whose husbands had abandoned the state. From its inception, the Czech women's movement had seen itself as part of the Czech nationalist milieu. Its leaders defended their egalitarian beliefs about gender by linking them to ideas about the Czech national character and democratic destiny. Such women may have preferred to not spend their energies defending women who had married non-Czechs.

Gradually, however, the inequities of Czechoslovak citizenship law became more apparent. In 1922, the United States passed the Cable Act, which made U.S. immigration and naturalization regulations more gender-neutral. Under its provisions, American women who married foreigners were allowed to keep their U.S. citizenship. Although the Cable Act represented an advance for American women, and perhaps also for the greater cause of gender equality, it had disastrous consequences for women from other countries whose husbands became Americans. Previously, the wives and children of men who were naturalized as United States citizens had automatically received American citizenship. The Cable Act changed this policy, requiring the wives of new U.S. citizens to apply separately for naturalization. They were allowed to follow a slightly abbreviated procedure —the residence requirement for applying was shortened from five years to one for such women—but were not exempt from quota restrictions on immigration, which were quite strict. Thus, there was no guarantee that a wife who was not already living in the United States would even be able to enter the country to join her husband.[9]

The Cable Act had a tremendous impact on Czechoslovak women. Unaffected by the American legislation, Czechoslovak law still mandated that a woman whose husband was naturalized elsewhere immediately lost her Czechoslovak citizenship. After the passage of the Cable Act, a Czech woman whose husband acquired American citizenship became stateless. If, as commonly happened, her husband had gone to the United States alone, intending to find work and send for her later, she abruptly found herself in the uncomfortable position of being an alien in her own country. She lost her political rights, but this was often the least of her worries. As the contemporary American legal scholar Waldo Emerson Waltz remarked, "There is a romantic ring to the phrase a 'man without a country,' but there is stark realism in the situation of a 'woman without a country.'"[10] In particular, the economic consequences of losing citizenship could be devastating. In the Czechoslovak Republic, noncitizens were forbidden from practicing certain professions, such as law and medicine, and were ineligible for employment in the civil service. This ban included most work in education, since public school teachers in Czechoslovakia were state employees. It also affected legions of postal clerks, railway employees, workers in the state tobacco factories (almost all women) and so on. Additionally, foreign nationals in Czechoslovakia were not eligible to receive social services, such as welfare assistance or medical care, and neither were their children.[11]

Leaving the country also became a complicated task for the wife made stateless by the Cable Act. Since it no longer recognized her as its citizen, the Czechoslovak government would not give her a passport. It was possible for her to apply for an immigrant visa from the United States Consulate, which would get her to America without a passport, but quota restrictions made obtaining these visas difficult, even for the wives of American citizens and their families. Although most women eventually received visas, it could take years of waiting and paperwork, and the separation and stress could have serious ramifications on their marriages. A wife might finally get her visa to discover that her husband no longer wanted her to join him. Throughout the whole ordeal, she could not turn to a single government-sponsored office or agency for legal or financial assistance. Czechoslovakia no longer recognized her as worthy of aid, and the United States felt no obligation toward her. When she did manage to get a visa, she had to fulfill a one-year residence requirement before applying for citizenship. While she fulfilled the residence requirement, the woman remained officially stateless. Although, as a legal immigrant she could not be deported from the United States during this time, as a woman without a country (and hence without a passport), she could not leave it either. This sometimes forced such women into difficult situations, requiring them to choose between seeing a dying parent for the last time or staying with their husbands and rectifying their statelessness.[12]

A similar set of circumstances was faced by female Czechoslovak citizens who married refugees. The Russian Revolution of 1917 had sent many people of Russian and Ukrainian nationality fleeing to Czechoslovakia. These refugees were permitted to stay in the Czechoslovak Republic, but they were not citizens. Many of them had the so-called "Nansen passports" issued by the League of Nations, but these documents did little but recognize their refugee status. The Czechoslovak government viewed these people as temporary residents, hoping that they would eventually go back to Russia to oppose the Soviet regime. In fact, most of them had no intention of returning to what was now the Soviet Union, and in any case a Soviet decree of 1921 officially expatriated anyone who had fled the country after 1917 and had not returned. Seen as Russians by the Czechs, and traitors by the Soviets, these people were locked in their stateless condition.[13] A number of Czech women married such refugees, and afterwards found themselves also without a country. After 1933, this experience was repeated by women who married Germans fleeing from Hitler's regime into Czechoslovakia. While refugees might be naturalized in Czechoslovakia, this process required at least a ten-year residence. During this lengthy waiting period, both the refugee and his formerly Czechoslovak wife would face the social and economic difficulties of statelessness.

Faced with these hardships and confronted by a government that took little notice of their plight, women who had been forcibly deprived of their Czechoslovak citizenship began to appeal to groups like the Women's National Council for aid. An attachment to a report prepared by the WNC on the issue of citizenship law in 1930 contains many harrowing stories about the dangers women might face as a consequence of losing their Czechoslovak citizenship. A recurrent problem in these tales was the economic hardship of being declared an alien. A typical example was given by one woman had been a home economics teacher for twenty-two years, but was forced to give up her job after marrying a Russian refugee, since the Education Ministry would only employ citizens. She and her newborn became financially destitute, but as noncitizens they were ineligible for public aid. Many women found their existence similarly threatened because they were deprived of the social services they had enjoyed while citizens. One such woman had lost her Czechoslovak citizenship by marrying a Yugoslav and moving with him to his country. Her marriage was unhappy, her husband infected her with venereal disease and then abandoned her. Alone in a foreign land, she fled Yugoslavia and went home to Bohemia, but once there was refused treatment for her disease at the state hospital because she was not a citizen. Although she would have liked to reclaim her Czechoslovak allegiance, she could not legally do so because her husband was still living and her citizenship was irrevocably tied to his. Czechoslovak law contained no procedure for the repatriation of women who had once been its citizens. They could apply for naturalization like any other immigrant, but only if they were no longer married to their foreign husbands. Many found their way home blocked by this restriction, even though they no longer wanted to be in the marriage that had removed them from their country. One woman, for example, had married an Austrian citizen and wanted to divorce him and return to Czechoslovakia. But divorce was not legal in Austria, and Czech authorities refused to perform this act, since neither she nor her husband were Czechoslovak citizens. She remained trapped in a loveless marriage in a foreign land, legally a citizen of a country she did not recognize as her own.[14]

The WNC sympathized with these women, but the problem of statelessness resulted primarily from the new disparities between Czechoslovak laws and the laws of other nations. The dimensions of the problem were international in scope and had wide-reaching ramifications for women all over the globe. Since this was the case, solving the problem of married women's nationality demanded action that transcended domestic politics.

## Married Women's Citizenship in International Perspective

International feminist organizations first took up the problem of married women's citizenship around the turn of the century, but their interest intensified in the years after the First World War. Groups like the International Council of Women, the Women's International League for Peace and Freedom, and the International Alliance for Women's Suffrage placed the issue prominently on their agendas. The Alliance, which soon renamed itself the International Alliance for Women's Suffrage and Equal Citizenship, formed a special committee on the subject, which included representatives from each of the other two organizations and delegations from twenty-five countries. After its founding in 1923, the WNC was a member of both the Alliance and the International Council of Women and worked with them on their campaigns.[15] The goal of these international feminist groups was to end statelessness on their terms, by severing all legal links between citizenship and marriage. Their efforts to accomplish this task focused on international solutions to the problem. In contrast to suffrage, which had to be won on a country-by-country basis, groups like the Alliance envisioned achieving citizenship reforms in one global swoop, via an international treaty that would require its signatories to give women complete control over their own citizenship, regardless of their marital status.[16]

The Alliance prepared a model of such a treaty at its congress in Rome in 1923.[17] To turn this model into reality, the Alliance approached the newly formed League of Nations about sponsoring an international symposium on the matter.[18] To their joy, in 1925 the League began to organize a conference to address the issue of stateless wives, among other legal matters. However, the League's position was not what the international feminist community had hoped. The committee of experts assigned by the League to survey the problem in advance of the conference pronounced the model treaty the Alliance had composed "very desirable" in the abstract, but concluded that it was not a practical or realistic option for the time. Following the Alliance's proposal would simply require too many countries to change their laws, something most nations were loath to do, especially at the behest of the international community. Indeed, a number of nations, including Austria, Belgium, Denmark, France, Norway, Romania, and Sweden, had liberalized their citizenship laws to allow some women to retain their citizenship after marriage to a foreigner, but in 1926, only six countries—Argentina, Cuba, Paraguay, Uruguay, the United States, and the Soviet Union—adhered to policies that met the Alliance's requirement of complete gender equality.[19]

The author of the committee's report, the Polish jurist Szymon Rundstein, did not believe that the conference would be able to agree on anything other than a bare-bones solution to the problem of statelessness. Although most states recognized that this growing global problem stemmed from their own citizenship laws, they were not willing to do much to solve the problem. Protecting their national sovereignty was the priority, not helping the stateless or giving women greater legal equality. Therefore, Rundstein suggested that the League sponsor a limited convention that would require its signatories to allow women who married foreign nationals to keep their original citizenship only in cases where the woman would otherwise be rendered stateless. If a woman somehow became stateless anyway, her husband's nation would be asked to give her a special passport even if she was not admitted to the full rights of citizenship there. In all other instances, states that signed the convention would be permitted to do as they pleased.[20] Rundstein's solution was an expedient one. It addressed the vexing problem of statelessness, but tried hard not to tread into ideological waters. However, by advocating only such change as was absolutely necessary, Rundstein effectively privileged the doctrine of family unity over a policy of legal equality between men and women.

The Alliance, along with other international feminist organizations, was deeply disappointed by the committee's report. Despite this setback, they continued to hope that the League of Nations would be the venue for an international accord on a woman's right to determine her own citizenship. To this end, they campaigned to have female representatives placed on the League's committee of experts, a project which was not successful.[21] After the League of Nations Conference for the Codification of International Law had been officially scheduled to take place at The Hague in 1930, the Alliance worked hard to get its representatives and ideas admitted to the bargaining table, and encouraged its national chapters to get women appointed as part of their country's official delegation. This proved to be a very difficult proposition. Even in the United States, where the issue of citizenship rights had not only been a major concern for the domestic feminist movement but one of its biggest postwar successes, feminists faced enormous resistance to placing their own representatives on the American delegation to The Hague. In the end, one woman, Ruth Shipley, was appointed as a delegate for the United States, but she was not a member of any of the major U.S. feminist organizations and did not claim to represent them.[22] On this point, the Czech Women's National Council proved somewhat more successful than the Americans. The question of women's citizenship was not a prominent issue in Czechoslovakia, and the WNC's own efforts on this problem throughout the 1920s had mostly been limited to its work with the Alliance and its Committee on the Nationality of Married Women. However, through their strong personal connection to Czechoslovak foreign minister Edvard Beneš, they were able to have WNC leader and respected lawyer Milada Králová-Horáková placed on the delegation that traveled to The Hague. Králová-Horáková was not an official delegate; she had the designation of "expert," which meant she could attend conference sessions and give input, but did not actually get to cast a vote. To have her on the delegation at all, however, was quite a coup for the WNC, since few women were present in any official capacity at The Hague and fewer still were connected to the international feminist community.[23]

The WNC had reason to be optimistic on the eve of the conference. The two voting delegates from Czechoslovakia, Minister Božin and Dr. Joachim, were favorable to the WNC's position on married women's citizenship. Even more significant was the Czechoslovak government's response to the preparatory questionnaire sent out to conference participants. Though only asked for information about current Czechoslovak citizenship laws, the respondents, presumably bureaucrats in the Foreign Ministry, went further than the questions demanded on the subject of a wife's state allegiance. First, they admitted that current policies often resulted in statelessness, which they recognized as a serious problem. Therefore, they wrote, Czechoslovakia would welcome an international agreement on this issue. They suggested that the simplest solution to the tragedy of statelessness would be for a woman who would otherwise become stateless to retain citizenship in her original country. In terms of policy, this would mean little real change: only women who did not receive citizenship from their foreign husband's state would be allowed to retain their rights as Czechoslovaks. However, the response continued, the simplest solution might not be the best answer to the problem. In a vein far more promising to the

WNC, the authors wondered whether "in certain circumstances and provided suitable guarantees were stipulated and definite formalities and time-limits described, a woman, should not, on marrying, be allowed the option of retaining her nationality."[24] Although the language was qualified and tentative, this passage certainly suggested that the Czechoslovak government was considering allowing women to retain control over their citizenship and definitely implied that Czechoslovakia would be willing to sign an international agreement that advocated such a policy.

The conference itself opened on March 15, 1930, and lasted for a month. Although they were not allowed their own representation at the conference, and although most sessions were closed to the public, women's rights advocates from all over the globe flocked to The Hague to observe and hopefully influence the proceedings. They recognized that any agreement would have the potential to direct the future development of citizenship laws in countries around the world. A coalition of women's groups, including the Alliance and the International Council of Women, sponsored a joint conference and demonstration from March 12 to March 16 as a sort of shadow meeting to the League of Nation's conference. The event included private meetings, where members presented reports about their work, as well as public demonstrations designed for the consumption of the delegates. The women's groups held a reception and party on the evening of March 14 for all of the participants in the League conference, the WNC proudly noting that the Czech delegate Dr. Joachim enthusiastically attended. At the reception, the delegates were treated to a pageant of young girls carrying flags, with those representing nations whose laws adhered to the Alliance's principles dressed in white, and those representing nations whose laws did not dressed in black. The evening also included speeches from female lawyers, politicians, and academics from a range of countries. To Milada Králová-Horáková, the spectacle of such a large gathering of accomplished, educated women eloquently underlined the injustice in laws which refused to recognize them legally as adults.[25]

However, the Alliance was not as successful as it had hoped in making an impact on the program of the conference itself. On March 13 it issued a joint resolution with the International Council of Women publicizing proposals for an international agreement on married women's citizenship and demanding that "a woman should herself have the same right to choose [citizenship] as a man." Alliance leaders were allowed to make a formal presentation of their suggestions to the Bureau of the Conference on March 15, but their request to speak before the entire assembly of delegates was denied, and they were subsequently forbidden from even entering the Peace Palace, where the conference was taking place. In protest, they demonstrated outside its gates. But throughout the remainder of the deliberations, feminist organizations had to struggle to make their voices heard, and their dreams of actively participating in the work of the conference were spoiled. Without the goodwill of the conference organizers, there was little they could do to improve their position and gain access to the delegates. In this sense, the conference was a rude awakening for feminist organizations, forcing them to see that any influence they might have on the international scene was dependent on the approval of the men who controlled the League and its institutions. Just as the WNC had discovered that sweeping statements of egalitarian principle had only a limited political effect, the Alliance found that the sympathy of some League officials did not necessarily translate into concrete advantages.[26]

Most of the work of the conference was not carried out in its general assembly, but in specialized committees devoted to one of the three topics being considered: nationality, territorial waters, and the liability of states toward foreign residents and their property. The Nationality Committee, headed by the Greek lawyer N. Politis, met from March 17 to April 8 in closed sessions, working out a draft convention on citizenship law, which it then presented to the full assembly for debate. The issue of married women was only one part of its agenda, and was only considered for three days toward the end of its deliberations, despite the efforts of some delegates to give it more consideration. The presidium of the Nationality Committee refused to allow observers from women's organizations to be present at the negotiations, although in the end, a small deputation representing a number of feminist groups was allowed to briefly address the plenum of the committee at a special evening meeting. The meeting was strictly regulated, with the women allowed only three speakers, each of whom had thirty minutes to make their case. No formal discussion between the delegates and the feminist representatives was allowed. In fact, there was no discussion following the women's presentation at all, and the very next morning the committee voted on the points of its draft convention dealing with the issue of marriage and citizenship. Králová-Horáková, who participated in the work of the Nationality Committee, speculated that the decision to allow the women to speak was mere pretense on the part of the committee's leaders. In her opinion, allowing the meeting to be held only outside the committee's regular working hours was the committee presidium's way of emphasizing its control over the proceedings and demonstrating its magnanimity in permitting the women to be heard at all, since no other "special interest" groups were given a hearing.[27]

Although the women's groups who had gathered at The Hague were not given much opportunity to participate in the conference, the committee's own debates on married women's citizenship were dominated by women. Králová-Horáková recalled that, for this issue, the women who were on the committee in an official capacity—mostly "experts" and not actual voting delegates—took over the discussion. These female experts, however, did not always have views acceptable to the feminists standing outside the gates of the Peace Palace. The Dutch expert, for example, eloquently defended the importance of using citizenship laws to maintain family unity. Others, including Králová-Horáková, were constrained by their positions as official representatives of their countries, whose priorities may not have matched their personal views. Each country's goal was to reach an agreement as much in accord with its existing policy as possible; this seemed to be the case with Czechoslovakia as well, despite its answers on the preparatory questionnaire.[28]

The Nationality Convention that came out of these meetings was designed to create as little change as possible. It acknowledged that marriage was often a factor in determining women's citizenship status and did not condemn this in principle. In most cases, it merely required its signatory nations to adjust their rules if statelessness was the result. The one exception was in cases where a husband decided to change his allegiance after marriage. In this circumstance, the convention required that a wife be allowed to retain her original citizenship. While the convention itself was a very moderate document, it also contained a written recommendation that was much more radical. The framers of the treaty recommended that participatory nations "introduce into their law the principle of the equality of the sexes in matters of nationality." The recommendation further advised countries to make any changes to a wife's citizenship dependent on her consent. But these were merely nonbinding suggestions, not mandated by the convention itself.[29]

Once formulated by the Nationality Committee, the Nationality Convention was hotly debated by the general assembly of the conference. In the end, it was signed by all of the participating nations except the United States, although some of the signatories exempted themselves from specific articles that conflicted with their existing policies. The United States did not sign the convention because it diverged too much from its citizenship laws after the Cable Act. The American delegates were also reacting to opinion from home, where U.S. women's groups opposed the conference proposals. They were angry that the convention did not grant women and men the same rights to determine their citizenship and demanded that the United States not support such a flawed document. The American decision not to sign was taken as a tremendous victory by these American feminists, proof that their government supported their drive for equal citizenship rights.[30]

For women who came from nations where citizenship laws were not quite as liberal as in the United States, however, the Hague Convention of 1930 seemed like progress. This was the position of the WNC. The Hague Convention, which was signed by the Czechoslovak delegation without reservations, would end the problem of Czechoslovak women left without a country and give wives more of a measure of control over their own citizenship than they had ever had. Perhaps more importantly, the recommendations contained in the convention, while not binding, gave the WNC reason to hope that their government would consider a more radical change of its citizenship laws than the convention demanded. As Králová-Horáková remarked, the results of the Conference "did not bring a true victory, but they clearly showed the path that future laws must take in states where the question of married women's nationality rights has not yet been solved in accordance with women's real contemporary position."[31] The WNC's task now was to make sure that their country followed that path.

## Czechoslovak Citizenship Law after the Hague Convention

Although the Hague Convention on Nationality did not totally repudiate the principle of gender equality in citizenship law, it was not the international treaty that most feminist organizations had wanted. While there was still feminist agitation for a new international agreement on women's citizenship, particularly in the Americas, more attention now turned to the individual signatories of the convention, who were faced with the task of deciding whether or not to actually revise their laws to meet the convention's guidelines. It was at this point that the WNC began to actively campaign for a change in citizenship laws at home. Although the WNC had its problems with the Hague Convention, it also realized that was a useful tactical lever with the Czechoslovak government. While it was true that the convention would not be valid until at least ten nations had ratified it, Czechoslovakia had signed it. The WNC hoped to use this fact to force its state to change its citizenship laws, at the very least to comply with the Hague guidelines, but preferably more radically. The WNC believed that the tone of the conference had made it clear that the international tendency in legal thinking was toward gender equality in citizenship policy, a trend that was emphasized and endorsed by the Nationality Committee in its recommendations. The WNC was optimistic that Czech lawmakers, always concerned with being perceived as "modern" and "progressive," would not want to obviously place themselves with the "backward" nations of the world by denying the conference's marked approval of an egalitarian means of determining citizenship.

Initially at least, it seemed that the League of Nations conference might have had the desired effect on Czechoslovak citizenship law. While the conference did nothing to awaken public interest in the issue—it was hardly reported in the Czech press—it managed to spark some legislators to action. One, the prominent Social Democrat Lev Winter, drew up his own draft of a new law to overhaul existing legislation on citizenship. The text of the Winter Bill, as it became known, stressed the need to modernize existing laws and bring order to the confused jumble of decrees still in use, which often came from the previous century. The Winter Bill's authors claimed it was time to root out the Habsburg legacy from citizenship law and replace it with democratic values. Instead of attempting to restrict their citizenries, states needed to allow people—except for those who posed a security risk—the freedom to choose their country of allegiance. The Social Democrats who wrote the bill were explicitly thinking about the problems of working-class immigrants and refugees, hoping to make it easier for them to claim the benefits and protection of the state (and perhaps also enable them to vote for the Social Democratic Party).[32]

The tone of the Winter Bill, and especially its comments on respecting the rights of individuals to choose their citizenship, suggested that it might also look favorably on feminist demands for women's citizenship rights. However, although it was a step in their preferred direction, the bill was not everything the WNC could have wished. The Winter Bill ideologically aligned itself with the doctrine of family unity, assuming that wives should share their husbands' country of citizenship. Winter had declared the democratization of citizenship law to be his ultimate goal, but he did not believe that limiting women's personal autonomy in favor of protecting their ties to the family ran afoul of his purpose. In the text of his bill, the family stood outside the democratic realm, a simple social good that did not need to defend itself from charges of "backwardness." Although Winter did not see the need to categorically step away from the legal doctrine of family unity, he had been influenced by the language of equality, freedom, and choice used by Czech feminists. While the bill proposed laws that would, by default, treat married women more as family members than individuals, it nonetheless provided an option for women to retain control over their citizenship status. Any woman who wanted to keep her own citizenship after marrying a foreign national could do so by petitioning the appropriate office within six months after her marriage. But, although it allowed wives greater freedom in determining their own citizenship, the Winter Bill kept a child's citizenship status under its father's control. Only illegitimate children followed their mother, since their paternity was uncertain.[33]

While the Winter Bill would have made it possible for women to exercise many (though not all) of the same citizenship rights as men, it still made a very visible legal distinction between the sexes. Women who wanted to keep control over their own citizenship were deviations from the general rule, much as the civil code allowed married women to control their own property only via special petition. This distinction worried the women of the Women's National Council and caused them to look suspiciously upon the Winter Bill, despite the legal gains it represented for women. When Františka Plamínková read it for the first time, she immediately wrote to Milada Králová-Horáková, saying that she was "afraid that this bill will be a cruelly heavy beam lying in front of our feet." Plamínková was upset because the bill so self-consciously represented itself as a compromise on the issue of married women, even labeling itself as such several times in the text. She would have preferred a much more complete renovation of the old law. But she also wondered to what extend the bill represented a compromise at all. She noted indignantly that while Winter had explicitly mentioned the League of Nations conference as a major influence behind the proposed law and claimed that his bill met Czechoslovakia's obligations to the international community on the citizenship issue, he had completely neglected to take into account the Nationality Committee's recommendations to promote equality whenever possible when creating new citizenship legislation, and had instead merely tweaked existing Czechoslovak regulations to make them fit the convention.[34]

Mainly, however, Plamínková was afraid that the Winter Bill could put the WNC in a compromising position. As she wrote to Králová-Horáková, "The main thing is—and this we, feminists, must fundamentally decide: if we are satisfied with the practical results this law will bring (if the Winter Bill becomes a law) or if we want the principle of equality."[35] It was true that the proposal represented a sincere advance over the existing law, and in many ways, it made sense for the WNC to support the measure. As written, the bill granted many of the feminists' demands, making it generally possible for married women to keep their own citizenship independently from their husbands. But it did so by burdening them with time limits and special applications, forcing them to go initiate special proceedings in order to have that independence that the WNC felt should be their right. The bill was based on the premise that wives and children should follow the male head of the household in citizenship and construed this as the "normal" situation. Although it did not force this "normality" on women, it implied that anyone who wished to deviate from the standard regulations was acting outside of usual social norms. Aside from these troubling questions of principle, there were other problems with the bill, especially in its treatment of parents' rights over their children. In Winter's proposal, mothers still had no say in determining the citizenship of their legitimate children. This remained a huge area of the law in which women would not even have functional equality with their husbands, a circumstance which had the potential to cause tremendous harm, especially if a mixed-nationality couple became divorced.

But, at this stage, the choice between supporting Winter's Bill and a principled opposition to it did not have to be so starkly made. In the Czechoslovak parliamentary system, only bills backed by the government had a chance of being enacted into law. Lev Winter was a member of the National Assembly, but he did not hold a ministerial portfolio. Therefore, his bill had little chance of making it to the floor of the Assembly, and it did not. The significance of the Winter Bill lay in its potential to focus political attention on the issue of citizenship law and influence the shape of further attempts at writing new legislation. Winter's proposals were debated in the Legal-Constitutional Committee of the Assembly and considered by the Ministries of Justice, Foreign Affairs, and Unification, just as the government decided to draft its own new citizenship law. But the fall of the ruling party coalition after the 1932 elections, as well as the death of Lev Winter, turned the government's initiative into an extended project that lasted for several years.[36]

Knowing that a new law would eventually be forthcoming, the Women's National Council began to devote more time to the issue. Its legal committee, chaired by Milada Králová-Horáková, began to study the citizenship question intensively in 1935. Their goal was to come up with a consensus among the WNC's federated organizations, so that they could lobby the government in their name. Those involved in the discussion quickly agreed to advocate a law that did not allow marriage to have any bearing on the citizenship of Czechoslovak nationals. While it was easy to advocate equality for adults, children posed a bigger problem. This aspect of the law was of special concern for Králová-Horáková, who was employed by the Social Welfare Office of the city of Prague, where she had become an advocate for the legal rights of mothers and children, especially illegitimate children. Children's citizenship was especially problematic in Czechoslovakia because its legal tradition held to principle of *jus sanguinis*, in which citizenship was passed through blood—i.e., the child of two Czechoslovak parents was a Czechoslovak citizen. As long as wives had automatically taken on their husband's citizenship, the children had simply followed suit. But if it became possible for children to be born of only one Czechoslovak parent, some other criteria would have to be used to determine a child's country of citizenship. The Winter Bill's solution was simply to give fathers the right to determine the citizenship of their legitimate children, regardless of the citizenship of the mother. This was in keeping with the tenets of existing Czechoslovak family law, which held that fathers had the sole rights over their children's futures. In its fight over the revisions of the family law codes, the WNC had already taken a strong stand in favor of giving mothers and fathers equal legal powers over their children. This issue became even more contested with regard to citizenship law. How would parents be able decide where their children would be citizens? Would this tension over the children's country of allegiance strike a mortal blow to family unity? Even within the WNC, some members thought that it would be best to continue to have children follow their fathers in citizenship. But the legal committee tried to come up with a proposal that would not rely on singling out either fathers or mothers for special rights. The eventual solution was to partially depart from the doctrine of *jus sanguinis* in cases where the parents were citizens of different countries. In the WNC's model law, children born of one Czechoslovak parent on Czechoslovak territory would take the citizenship of the land on which they were born, while children born of one Czechoslovak parent outside of the republic (presumably in the country of the other parent) would receive dual citizenship.[37]

The WNC's legal committee finished its work early in 1936. Around this time, the Ministry of Unification completed its first draft of a comprehensive new citizenship law, which would knit the legal systems of the Czech lands and Slovakia together. Hoping to persuade the law's writers of their position on married women's citizenship, the WNC prepared an extensive memorandum detailing their requirements for such a law and sent it to the ministry in April. Interestingly, the ideological and legal support the WNC marshaled in this memorandum departed significantly from its usual strategies. Here, it did not stress the constitutional validity of its claims, although it could have, since the existing practice of allowing husbands to determine the citizenship of their wives certainly counted as a "privilege of sex." Instead, the WNC emphasized the international aspects of the citizenship question, declaring that Czechoslovakia was frustrating the global attempt to end statelessness by refusing to modify its citizenship laws, and charging that the state was making a mockery of its signature on the Hague Convention. The WNC tried to paint the Czechoslovak state as a prime violator of international legal trends, noting how recent League of Nations resolutions had supported the feminist line in citizenship law. It also stressed that its suggestions did not simply represent its own opinion, but were the product of a large, international movement of women. The tone challenged the Czechoslovak government to overcome its legal backwardness and finally join the progressive elements of the international community on this issue.[38]

This mode of argument seemed to have much more effect in government circles than the constitutional arguments the WNC favored in dealing with domestic issues. The Ministry of Unification not only listened to the WNC's concerns but also agreed to negotiations. Eventually, the ministry accepted many of their demands. The government's preliminary citizenship bill, which was released for debate in 1937, no longer automatically tied women's citizenship to their husbands. In fact, the government's decision to grant this demand seemed to be quite uncontroversial, occasioning little discussion or protest among government ministers or the public. This was striking, considering that in the simultaneous debate over the civil law code, Catholics and conservatives argued vehemently in favor of sustaining the legal authority of husbands. On the citizenship issue, however, the nationalist feelings of those groups proved stronger than their social conservatism. Allowing Czechoslovak women to keep their own citizenship after marrying a foreign national was, after all, not taking power from Czechoslovak men, but from foreigners. In 1937, when the position of the Czech nation looked increasingly precarious both at home and abroad, it perhaps seemed advisable to keep as many reliable people in the national community as possible. In this kind of political climate, the

WNC's argument that a woman had an "emotional and moral relationship" to her country that existed outside of her relationship to her husband found sympathetic ears, even amongst those who otherwise did not favor granting wives more legal autonomy.[39]

This broad-based acceptance of a Czechoslovak woman's right to choose to keep her native citizenship was linked to a new fear of the former practice of unconditionally giving citizenship to the foreign wives of Czechoslovak men. The WNC had initially objected to this practice because it deprived women of autonomy in making decisions about their own political allegiance. They were joined by Czech conservatives who considered it a defense risk to award citizenship to people who might have no real feeling for the country. The government's proposed new law would stop bestowing citizenship automatically on these alien wives; only those who otherwise had become stateless would receive a Czechoslovak passport, and then only after making an official application to their local authorities. Even so, this was too much for some. One author, writing in the Agrarian Party journal *Brázda* (The Furrow), noted that the love of a person did not necessarily translate into the love of a country and urged stricter regulations to keep potentially traitorous elements from claiming membership in the state.[40] Undoubtedly linked to Czech fears about the increasingly vocal German minority in Czechoslovakia's borderlands, this argument about the specter of potential fifth columns of foreign wives within Czechoslovakia had a widespread popular purchase among Czechs. It would even be used by the WNC, whose members were definitely not above nationalism. Though they never stated it so baldly, the Czechs were mostly worried about expanding the Sudeten German population with a crop of Reich-born wives. The combined pressure from feminists and more conservative nationalists eventually worked to get a qualification inserted into the bill which reserved the right to refuse citizenship to any wife of a Czechoslovak citizen if she did not appear likely to be loyal to Czechoslovakia. The government's final bill also contained the stipulation that persons applying for naturalization be proficient in the "Czechoslovak" language, a measure obviously designed to keep German-speaking minority populations from increasing.

This nationalist argument did help the feminist cause, and the WNC was willing to use it in their struggles with the government over the citizenship bill. However, the idea that nationality could run deeper than romantic love worked better as a rationale for excluding foreign wives than in persuading lawmakers to fully realize women's legal autonomy. The government's proposal answered most of the WNC's demands, but it also did not abandon the doctrine of family unity. Its proposal still treated married women differently from all other adults, making it clear that marriage represented a significant change in a woman's legal status, while it did not for her husband. Like the Winter Bill, the new proposal characterized a wife's desire to control her own citizenship as exceptional rather than normal, requiring her to file special petitions within very definite time limits if she wanted to deviate from her husband's citizenship status. While the proposed law would have allowed Czechoslovak women who married foreign nationals to keep their native citizenship, its restrictions on that right cast doubt on her loyalty. Women who married across national lines and allowed foreign men access to their bodies and wombs betrayed the state in a way that men did not. They had to prove their allegiance to their state, to beg in writing for their rights or lose them.[41]

Worse, however, was the new proposal's treatment of children's citizenship. The WNC's suggestions in this area were completely ignored, in the practical as well as the principled sense. The new law would make a child's citizenship entirely dependent upon its father. Only in cases where the father did not legally recognize the child would the mother be able to pass her citizenship on to her children. On this issue, the WNC found no outside support. Women who married foreign men, it seemed, could not be trusted to raise children who would be loyal to the Czechoslovak state. The WNC had suggested dual citizenship for some children, at least until they reached legal age, but many Czechs thought that the idea of dual citizenship was both dangerous and impossible. How could one truly have allegiance to two countries? Fighting with this conviction proved a losing battle for the feminists. The final version of the bill, which was printed and released to the National Assembly in March of 1938, did not change its original position on children.

Some possibility for change still lingered, however. The new citizenship law was debated in the Legal-Constitutional Committee of the National Assembly in May 1938. The "rapporteur" (*zpravodaj*) for the bill, the Social Democrat Ivan Markovic, gave the bill a high recommendation, noting that it answered the "years-long attempts of women's circles, which were manifested at the Hague Conference and in international negotiations and were interpreted even in our Republic." Nevertheless, Markovic recommended that the National Assembly address a few of its omissions before voting it into law. One of these was the issue of children's citizenship, which Markovic felt should be legally the right of both parents to decide. However, while this indicated that the bill might yet be amended to suit feminist demands, the outcome of that debate remained undecided.[42] This report in the Legal-Constitutional Committee took place only a few months before the Munich Conference put an end to the First Czechoslovak Republic. The Czechoslovak legislature always suspended work over the summer months, and the committee did no further work on the citizenship law before its recess. After the summer holidays, lawmakers and politicians were far too concerned with the crisis situation in the Sudetenland to worry about other matters. The government's citizenship bill never left the committee and Czechoslovak citizenship laws stayed in their existing form until after the Second World War.

## The Problem of Citizenship in the Czechoslovak Republic

The question of married women and citizenship law proved to be a problematic area in the history of interwar Czechoslovakia. On one level, it provides a particularly damning example of the Czechoslovak state's refusal to recognize its own avowed principle of equal rights for women. Here, as elsewhere, women's personal rights were very explicitly subordinated to the assumed needs of the family. Family harmony seemed to dictate that all family members be of the same nationality, and the ability of wives to control their own citizenship was sacrificed to this cause. Even in its attempts to "modernize" citizenship laws, Czechoslovak lawmakers endorsed this ideal of family unity over the democratic principle of equal rights. Although their proposed laws would have made it legally possible for a married woman to retain control over her citizenship, this was treated as a deviation from the norm, a sop to women who refused to follow the accepted pattern of renouncing civil rights with their marriage vows. In these proposals, the ability for a married women to choose her own citizenship was given the form of a dispensation, or a privilege, rather than a right.

Czechoslovak's failure to change its citizenship laws during the decades between the wars is especially striking when considered in its international context. In their attitudes toward women's suffrage and general acceptance of the concept of women's equality, Czechs generally showed themselves to be more supportive of women's rights than other Europeans. In its approach to citizenship law, however, Czechoslovakia remained on the conservative end of international legal opinion. Holding fast to the doctrine of family unity, the Czechoslovak government publicly set itself against Western democracies as the United States, Britain, and France all liberalized citizenship laws for married women. Although these states did not all implement truly egalitarian policies, they showed a willingness to change and a marked tendency to support women's right to determine their own citizenship. Czechoslovakia may have been heading towards such changes themselves by the end of the 1930s, but the fact remains that Czech(oslovak) politicians were never able to agree on a way to revise their citizenship laws, despite their signature on the Hague Convention. That agreement would have represented only a limited divergence from existing Czechoslovak citizenship regulations, but lawmakers still proved unwilling to commit to making this step. By 1938, Czechoslovakia had one of the most restrictive citizenship laws for women in the world. It was one of only fifteen countries to unconditionally deprive a woman of citizenship if she married a foreigner, and one of only nine to do so if her husband acquired another nationality during marriage.[43]

While the Czechoslovak government eventually prepared and gained support for a law that would have allowed married women to exert much greater control over their citizenship status, it did not do so as a way of legislating a woman's personal autonomy. This law served multiple agendas: it gave Czech feminists most of the things they asked for, though not in the way they desired; it upheld the doctrine of family unity unless a woman specifically asserted her right to deviate from it. It also satisfied the wishes of Czech nationalists, who decided that automatically granting foreign women who married Czechoslovaks the rights of citizens could be a dangerous policy. This strange confluence of competing influences shows us the complicated interplay of imperatives motivating Czech politics. Realizing women's rights to legal equality was something to be taken seriously. It was required by the democratic ideology that stood behind the Czechoslovak Republic, represented by its constitution, and it was necessary for maintaining Czechoslovakia's "progressive" face on the international stage. Equally important was the imperative to protect and support the family. And next to these stood the idea of the Czech (or "Czechoslovak") nation as a priority in defining national and international interests. In the government's 1937 draft for a new citizenship law, it seemed possible to balance each of these priorities, the needs of democracy and women's rights, the family, and the nation, and to create some sort of workable compromise between them. But this was an uneasy balance. Even within the law itself, the tensions were apparent. Women who married foreign citizens could assert their rights to Czechoslovak citizenship, but their fitness for such a privilege was still called into question. In order to keep their Czechoslovak passports they had to affirm their continued loyalty to the state, to prove that they were true to their nation, and they were barred from passing their rights on to their children.

In broad terms, this question of married women's citizenship shows that it was possible for the needs of the nation and the requirements of democracy to diverge. A crucial part of the enthusiasm Czechs had for democracy was their conviction that it suited and strengthened the Czech nation. In this case, both of these priorities found a small patch of common ground. The principle of legal equality required that the foreign wives of Czechoslovak citizens go through the same requirements for naturalization as other applicants. So did the nationalist desire to limit the number of non-Czech speakers who entered the polity. However, the idea that protecting the nation required excluding the untrustworthy pointed to the potential for rupture between the two. Democracy served a purpose if it was good for the nation, but what if protecting the rights and freedoms of all citizens began to look like a threat to the national interest? The link between democracy and Czech nationalism was not as organic as Czech feminists might have liked to believe. In a Europe rapidly turning toward authoritarianism, democracy began to be more of a liability to national survival than it had appeared in 1918.

# 4

## WOMEN IN THE CIVIL SERVICE

> It is true that the bill [to fire married women from their jobs in the civil service] is reactionary. Today it is a step back to return a woman to her family and direct her toward its care against her will. But wouldn't it be a good thing if we women took more such reactionary steps?
>
> Unidentified working woman, quoted in Beneš,
> "Nesnáze celibátu a nesnáze necelibátu," *Přítomnost* 1, no. 36 (1924): 576

THE ULTIMATELY IRRESOLVABLE conflicts over how to revise Czechoslovak citizenship laws and the civil code showed that for many Czechs "equality" was a rather problematic concept when applied to women. Although they were formally recognized as citizens like any other, women could never simply partake of equality like other individuals in a democracy; they were always women first. As feminists discovered when they attacked inequalities in civil law, democratic ideology was not very effective in helping women to escape the remaining legal limitations of womanhood. Women might have an equal say in the voting booth, but inside their homes they remained subject to their husband's authority.

This ideological dispute about the limits of equality for women reached far beyond the walls of the home itself, and spilled into debates over the rights of citizenship more broadly. During the interwar years, Czechs pushed the definition of citizenship beyond the rights of political participation, residence, or legal personhood. They argued over the extent to which their republic should also guarantee social or economic rights to its citizens, wondering whether the state should acknowledge a "right" to subsistence or a "right" to work. But if work was a right, could it be claimed by all citizens equally? Or was it something that more correctly belonged to those who sustained families, presumably men? Breadwinning was already legally defined as a masculine task in Czechoslovak family law. It was a husband's status as a provider that justified his authority as the "head of the household." It was also socially marked as a "naturally" male responsibility, linked to a man's biological traits. Women did not short-change their femininity by being supported by their spouses. A man who couldn't provide for his family, however, was a failure both as a man and as a husband.

While the ideal of the single-breadwinner family influenced beliefs about gender and work in Czechoslovakia, its power as a model for defining citizenship was complicated by the fact that the domestic reality of most Czechs differed from it significantly. Even before 1918, relatively few families had actually conformed to this picture. Most rural and working-class women, both married and single, had worked for wages, and young middle-class women had also been sometimes forced to take jobs to help their families or support themselves. The economic crisis that followed the First World War, a catastrophe that destroyed the economic security of many middle-income families, made work a necessity for most women at some point. By the 1920s, gainful employment had become a fact of life for millions of Czechoslovak women. In 1921, almost one-quarter of all Czechoslovak women had jobs, a number that remained fairly constant for the whole of the interwar period.[1]

Most Czechs accepted paid female labor as a necessity, a belief that was reflected in laws that opened women's access to better education, allowing them to aspire to more kinds of professional work. But, even though women were seen as viable workers, the way their "right to work" was conceived was still inherently different from men's. For a man, the right to work was basic and inviolate, like the freedom of speech or the right to vote; it was something the state was bound to protect. A woman's right to employment, however, was usually seen as contingent on her financial need. She was accepted as a worker only insofar as she had no other means of supporting herself or her family. Women who worked for reasons other than need were reviled for going against their true feminine nature. They were made into villains, accused of taking jobs from men, the ones who had the "real" right to them. These accusations often had serious consequences, including pay cuts and layoffs targeted specifically at working wives.

These measures were vigorously protested by many female workers and by men who agreed that all citizens should have equal access to the labor market. They were led in their dissent by the feminists of the Women's National Council, who took a commanding role in organizing campaigns to protest the discriminatory measures that often threatened women's employment. The WNC argued that all citizens should be allowed the freedom to sell their labor and be justly compensated for it, regardless of gender or marital status. The role of the state, it said, was to advocate equality and fairness in the workplace. Women might choose to be homemakers, but this had to be their choice. The state could not force them to bow out of the labor market when they married.

This chapter outlines the feminist struggle to assert and protect women's equal right to work during the interwar period. It does so by looking at one specific area of employment: the civil service. The civil service is not just a convenient example for illustrating this battle to define work as either a right of citizenship or the social right of male breadwinners; it is a crucial point for assessing the way the state itself regarded women as workers and how it conceived of their citizenship. Only in the case of the civil service was the state itself the employer. Regulations governing salaries, hiring policies, and so forth were written by the government and voted on in the National Assembly— they were laws like any other, technically bound by the same constitutional standards. Civil service policies, therefore, were not like the practices of private companies. They represented the attempt of Czech lawmakers to practically implement their beliefs about work, compensation, and women's rights.

The Czech public saw the civil service as distinct from other types of work, as an unusually secure form of employment that functioned partly as state-sponsored social assistance for the middle class. Because of its special status, the civil service became the focus of a heated national debate about working women and the rights they deserved, a debate which the news media fanned into a frenzied series of attacks against married female civil servants, despite the fact that these women represented only a tiny percentage of all female workers.[2] During the Depression, these so-called "double earners" in the civil service were constantly vilified by the press for supposedly abetting the unemployment crisis by taking jobs from unemployed young men. The government allowed itself to be swayed by this public outrage, making employment conditions for such women far less favorable than those of their male colleagues. The changing nature of the Czechoslovak government's policies toward working women illustrates how political concerns began to lead Czech lawmakers away from the legal guidelines of their constitution. When government ministers placed restrictions on female civil servants, they clouded the state's duty to protect individual rights, giving legitimacy to the idea that limiting the freedoms of certain groups of people was acceptable political behavior.

## The Celibát in the 1920s

Like the civil code, the practice and policy of gender discrimination in the Czechoslovak civil service was a legacy left from the days of the Habsburg Monarchy. Women had started to enter government employment in Austria during the last decades of the nineteenth century. These first female civil servants were usually single women from impoverished middle-class backgrounds who found work as teachers or, if less educated, as clerks, primarily in the postal service. The Austrian state agreed to hire these women, but did not treat them in the same fashion as their male colleagues, often paying them less than men in similar positions and requiring that they abstain from marriage and family life. If they married, female government employees were summarily fired from their jobs, without the benefit of severance pay or pension.[3] Fighting this policy of enforced celibacy for female teachers and other government workers, known in Czech as the *celibát,* was one of the highest priorities of the pre-1918 Czech women's movement. Many of those involved in the women's movement during this period were themselves teachers who deeply resented being forced by the state to make a choice between marriage and work. As they had done with the suffrage issue, Czech feminists sought to portray the celibát as an instrument of Austrian oppression directed at Czech women. Using this tactic, they managed to gain the support of most major Czech parties for their campaign.

After the establishment of the Czechoslovak Republic, some of the female representatives to the provisional National Assembly quickly introduced legislation to abolish the celibát. Their law, which passed on July 24, 1919, represented a great victory for working women in Czechoslovakia. It not only permitted teachers who married to keep their jobs, but also gave severance benefits to those women who chose to leave work after marriage, provided for paid maternity leave, and enabled the children of deceased female teachers to receive their mother's pension.[4] Although it seemed to end discriminatory policies against women in the civil service, the law had its limits. It dealt only with teachers and did not extend its benefits to other female government employees. Thus, although it was indeed a feminist victory, this law did not represent a complete condemnation of the government's practice of firing female employees who married.

The public reaction to the 1919 law was very positive. The measure was widely hailed in the press as a progressive advance over the dictatorial policies of the former Austrian regime. However, those who welcomed the destruction of the celibát often still did not approve of working wives. Even some women activists, who praised the idea of equal rights for women in abstract form, worried about the effects such rights might have on marriage and family life. They pleaded with women not to use their new legal freedoms in ways that would undermine the traditional family and women's place within it. For example, the journalist Marie Loucká-Čepová wrote in the magazine for female Agrarian Party members that it was entirely appropriate for the state to award women the same legal rights as men; this was required in a democracy. But if democracy demanded that women have rights, it did not require that they take advantage of them. Loucká-Čepová urged her female compatriots to refuse some of their new freedoms, such as the right to work after marriage, calling on them to concentrate on being good wives and mothers instead. In her opinion, women could not work for wages and still adequately fulfill these roles.[5]

The writer Marie Tippmanová also doubted that lifting work restrictions really benefited women. In an article in *Nová Síla* (New Strength), the women's journal of the National Democratic Party, she worried that married women who accepted paid employment were in reality signing up for two jobs. While their husbands worked only one eight-hour day, working wives were consigned to two consecutive shifts, one in the office and one at home. Tippmanová worried that these exhausted women would have no time for their own self-improvement, unlike their husbands, who would have plenty of free time to read and inform themselves about the world. In a society that saw worth in intellectual attainment but not in domestic labor, working wives would continue to be less valued than their husbands, despite their double labors. Tippmanová did not believe that wives could ever refuse their household work, and so she came to the conclusion that married women might find themselves better off by avoiding paid employment if possible, in order to spend the extra time educating themselves instead.[6] She, like Loucká-Čepová, believed it was important for women to formally have the legal right to pursue employment whenever they wished, but also saw married women as having a primary duty to their family, a duty that nature itself called them to fulfill.

Whether or not she chose to take it, a woman's right to employment was not as secure as these writers blithely assumed. Lifting the *celibát* for teachers did not appear to stop other women from being indiscriminately laid off from their government jobs. National Assembly representatives Luisa Landová-Štychová, Anna Malá, and Anna Sychravová presented an interpellation to Prime Minister Jan Černý in October 1920, in which they charged that female workers in government offices were being systematically fired for no reason other than their sex. They claimed that several ministries had explicitly directed their staff to fire female office workers and replace them with men. The women urged the government to remember that such practices were in direct conflict with Article 106 of the constitution, writing that "every direct or indirect attempt to exclude female workers [from government offices] devalues the single principle of equality upon which the republic's constitution is based."[7] They asked the government to investigate the situation and demanded that the discriminatory practices be reversed and the women who had been fired allowed back to work. However, their demands did little. Responding to their charges a few months later, Černý wrote that the government had investigated and found that no *official* policy of replacing female clerks with men existed in any of its ministries. All offices, he claimed, looked only to their needs and the qualifications of the individuals applying for the job in making employment decisions.[8]

Despite Černý's assurances, the incidents involving women being summarily fired or restricted in their work continued to mount. In April of 1922, the Czech newspaper of record, *Lidové Noviny* (The People's News) reported that the Ministry of Justice had decided it was no longer going to accept women in its service. In response to this news, National Democratic Assembly representative Anna Vettrová-Bečvářová met with the Justice Minister, Josef Dolanský, to ask for an explanation. He told her that the policy was not "personally" directed at women, but that there were simply not enough jobs to meet the needs of all applicants. Therefore, he had decided that any available positions should go to legionnaires rather than to women. Vettrová-Bečvářová accepted this reasoning as just, since the beneficiaries were war veterans.[9] However, other women were enraged at this exchange. Božena Novotná, a leader in the women's section of the Agrarian Party, angrily demanded that workers be judged by their qualifications alone. She further remarked, "a Minister of Justice in a democratic republic should just not speak that way and it is a great, a great shame that he did so. It is a shame on him and a shame on the entire republic."[10]

Minister Dolanský and other government officials seemed to believe that their actions were justified, though they might be unconstitutional. Similar incidents continued throughout the next few years, and the issue erupted in the summer of 1924, when it was rumored that the government was planning to reinstate the *celibát*, a mere five years after it had been revoked. Worried, the newly constituted Women's National Council sent delegates twice a week during July and August to meet with members from each of the parties involved in the governing coalition and officials from every ministry. Each of the WNC's many delegations was told that the rumors were not true and that the government was not planning such a step.[11] However, it came out a few months later that an interministerial commission had indeed drafted a proposal to lay off the married female employees in the civil service. Although the proposal was not implemented, its existence indicated that the government had never really accepted the idea that married women had a right to keep their jobs, despite its formal protestations to the contrary.

The government's contradictory position, which led its ministers to declare women's equality in the workplace even as they tried to fire them, was voiced by the writer Jiří Beneš in the weekly journal *Přítomnost* (The Present). Beneš admitted that a policy of mandatory celibacy for female employees conflicted with Article 106 of the Czechoslovak Constitution and that such regulations were reactionary rather than progressive. Women had a right to work that the *celibát* ignored. However, the antidemocratic and backward-looking nature of the *celibát* was not enough to make him condemn the practice. For Beneš, the crucial issue was not equality or the lack of it, but the massive unemployment problem among the economically strapped intelligentsia. The *celibát*, in his view, was the most effective way of providing desperate men with good government jobs. Even Františka Plamínková, he said, should agree that it was more just to fire a married woman who had a husband to take care of her than a man who had a family to support.[12] That solving the unemployment problem would require firing someone was self-evident to Beneš. He, like many other Czechs during this period, believed that the number of jobs in the country was finite and that it was simply not possible to find work for everyone who wanted it. Strategies for ending unemployment, therefore, did not concentrate on creating more positions, but on devising ways to move some people out of the workforce in order to more equitably redistribute their jobs. Married women were the logical targets in such a scenario.

One problem that defenders of women's right to work faced was the lack of a general set of regulations concerning the civil service. Because there was no formal code of conduct for the government as employer, women with grievances had no basis from which to protest the discriminatory policies of individual offices within the state apparatus. This situation was remedied in 1926, with the publication of several laws designed to standardize salaries, benefits, practices, and codes of conduct in the civil service. In general, these laws represented a victory for working women, a fact due in large measure to the lobbying efforts of the WNC.[13] The laws that dealt with higher-level bureaucrats, policy makers, judges, university professors, and teachers carefully avoided making distinctions between men and women in almost all areas, including pay grades and hiring policies.[14] Officially, only the abilities and qualifications of an applicant mattered in hiring decisions, with salaries assigned according to a single scale keyed to an employee's seniority and educational level. In addition to the base salary, most employees received a monthly "active-duty supplement" called the *činovné*, which adjusted their base pay to compensate for the rigors of their particular position. In addition, employees with children were eligible for an additional supplement called the *výchovné*. This supplement, however, was earmarked for fathers, since only they were legally considered heads of their household. Married women with children were never eligible to receive the *výchovné*. Single mothers could be granted this payment, but this required a yearly petition to the Ministry of Finance, an involved process that was, in practice, seldom successful.[15] Although the 1926 civil service laws refused to consider mothers as providers for their families in the same fashion as men, they did make some provisions for them. Where previously pregnancy had been grounds for dismissal, now women were granted a generous three-month maternity leave, during which they would receive 80 percent of their base salary. Thus, despite the injustice of the *výchovné*, these laws were generally seen by female government employees as a positive step, since they did not include any hint of a *celibát* and did not officially permit gender discrimination in hiring policies or in most forms of compensation. Indeed, according to the Imperial Union of Czechoslovak Women Teachers, these laws "resolved the legal situation of married female civil servants" and ended the ambiguity over their position in the government work force.[16]

However, the above-mentioned laws did not cover all government employees, only higher-level bureaucrats and teachers. The regulations concerning lower-level office staff were presented separately, in Law 113/1926, which was not as favorable for women.[17] Although the second section of the law proudly proclaimed that its regulations would apply to employees without regard to their sex, it restricted female employees' right to receive *výchovné* payments. But much more seriously, it stated that a female job applicant who was married or had children could only be hired in exceptional circumstances and only with the approval of a central office.[18] Though the law did not list marriage as admissible grounds for dismissing women who had already been hired, it required employees who married to inform their superiors of that fact within fifteen days of the wedding, an ominous-sounding regulation for women frightened of the *celibát*.

This law provoked outrage from working women and their supporters. Plamínková, in her role as senator, presented a interpellation to the government in response to its discriminatory passages, charging that the state was attempting to use the law to reinstate the *celibát* and claiming that its tactics were unconstitutional since they gave men preferential treatment.[19] The government's reply, which took over a year and a half to arrive, partially vindicated working women, but also showed how the state's views on women's equality were severely limited by its prejudices about women's abilities and the proper place of married women in society. The response, written by Jan Šrámek, a deputy from the prime minister's office, denied Plamínková's charges. It claimed that the creation of Law 113/1926 effectively repealed all older legislation that had permitted the practice of the *celibát*. While the new law had not stated this in so many words, the fact that it contained the same provisions for maternity leave as the laws covering teachers and other bureaucrats meant that there could be no official barrier to married women working in the lower levels of the civil service. However, he went on, while marriage itself could not be used as a reason for dismissing an employee, anything that affected the ability of an employee to perform their job could indeed be grounds for dismissal. This meant that while there was no officially sanctioned *celibát*, in practice, a supervisor could easily fire a recently married woman simply by claiming that her work had suffered in quality since her wedding.[20]

Šrámek denied that the parts of the law directed at women went against the constitution. Article 106 did not, in his view, mean that all regulations that applied to men should be mechanically applied to women. Laws could establish different provisions for men and women if those provisions were in response to actual differences (physical or otherwise) between the sexes. Indeed, he said, this was why allowing women maternity leave was not in violation of the constitution, although this was a marked advantage for women that men did not share. It is unclear how Šrámek believed this could justify excluding women from the right to *výchovné* payments, since both sexes were capable of being parents, but his pronouncements opened up a troubling area for female government employees. Many people in interwar Czechoslovakia believed that women were less physically and mentally capable than men, that they could not work as well independently, and that they lacked similar powers of reason and concentration. Šrámek's statement made it clear that the government would not contest such beliefs and that the state found it perfectly acceptable to limit some jobs to male candidates on the grounds that only men could perform the position's functions adequately. Similarly, it was possible to condone firing married women on the grounds that, as wives, they were no longer capable of performing as they had before their marriage.[21] This kind of reasoning was later expanded by various ministerial officials to justify excluding women from upper-level positions based on their presumed physical or mental weaknesses.[22]

## Controversy over the Christmas Bonus

The year 1930 marked a turning point in women's struggles to achieve parity with men in the civil service. It was then that the impact of the worldwide Depression began to make itself felt in Czechoslovakia. While the effects of the financial crisis were not initially as dramatic in the Czech lands as in the United States, the fallout from this global economic catastrophe reverberated through the region, increasing unemployment and intensifying a general sense of unease and uncertainty. Public attacks on working women grew in force and virulence in response. Increasingly, they focused on married women employed by the state. There were a number of reasons for this. First of all, the economic crisis had struck hard at the educated classes and the masses of unemployed degree-holders captured the imagination of the largely middle-class media. The specter of the unemployed intelligentsia was haunting to those who had never contemplated poverty. Previously in the Czech lands, a secondary education had been seen as the ticket to lifelong employment, very often in the civil service. Economic hard times changed that rosy picture. The government jobs that had once seemed certain for gymnasium graduates became subject to even stiffer competition. Many people had to wait for years before finding employment, while those who were hired found their pay reduced. Although the salaries and benefits attached to government jobs fell along with their numbers, they still remained an idealized form of work for the educated classes, with more status and security than higher-paying private-sector jobs. In this tight labor market for the civil service, unsuccessful job seekers grew to resent the women who had positions, seeing them as interlopers in what had once been an exclusive and elite male club. Even as the number of jobs decreased, women were becoming more visible within the ranks of the job-seeking intelligentsia as more and more of them took advantage of the new educational opportunities that had been awarded to them. Indeed, because the economic future looked so uncertain, large numbers of middle-class parents decided that an education was a better investment for their daughters than the traditional dowry, because it enabled them to support themselves or contribute to their family's earnings whatever the inflation rate. Unemployed men, and often their wives, looked upon these newly educated women with loathing and fear.

Attacks on female civil servants had unofficially influenced hiring and salary decisions for years, but in 1930 they had an impact on official policy toward government workers for the first time. In June of that year, the government submitted a bill to the National Assembly as part of a drive to reduce its employment expenditures. The target of the bill was the annual Christmas bonus traditionally given to all state employees in the upper pay grades. This bonus was not merely a frill; also known as the "13th paycheck" (*13. služné*), it was often equal to an entire month's base salary. The bonus was not linked to job performance, rather, it was given annually to all employees whose positions entered them in the bonus category. As such, those who received it counted it as part of their normal yearly earnings.[23] The government's plan to lower the annual Christmas bonus was, therefore, viewed by its employees as an attack on their pay, even though their official salaries were not touched.

The bill proposed standardizing the bonus at 70 percent of a qualified employee's monthly salary, and also bumped whole categories of workers out of the bonus category. Most prominent among these were married employees whose spouses also worked for the state. Also included were those who had not worked for at least ten months out of the year, effectively excluding all women who taken their recently won maternity leave from the bonus pool. Hourly workers would also no longer be eligible for the bonus, a move that mainly affected already badly paid language and home economics teachers, another group that was largely female.[24] Though the proposed legislation carefully avoided mentioning "women" by name, these exclusions were quite obviously directed specifically at female employees and "double earner" couples.

Subsequent events proved that working wives were at the heart of the matter. When the Christmas bonus bill was presented to the Assembly, it was greeted with vociferous protest from civil servants and their professional organizations, who were angered at the prospect of losing such a large part of their yearly earnings in the middle of a financial crisis. These protests, which were led by extensive efforts on the part of the Women's National Council, succeeded in pushing the bill back to the Cabinet for reworking. Just before the legislature left for its summer break in late June, the government proposed a compromise. Instead of taking the bonus away from both spouses in a marriage of two civil servants, it would allow the husband to receive his.[25] This new development shocked and disappointed the women who had initiated the fight against the bill, but it pacified the rest of the protesters, who considered it fair.

As the legislature went into its summer hiatus, female civil servants, led by Plamínková and the Women's National Council, went into action to try and persuade the government to come up with a more equitable solution. The WNC exhorted its member organizations to send appeals and memoranda to the various ministries and organized deputations to present their demands in person. Plamínková herself met personally with most of the government ministers, as well as with the members of the National Assembly's social-political committee.[26] The WNC's position was that the Christmas bonus was compensation for work done, not some form of government-sponsored social assistance. When it denied married women their proper benefits, the government cheapened their labor and made it seem inherently less valuable than other people's work.[27] And in any case, the WNC charged, it was foolish to think that it was socially just to deny benefits to married couples who both worked, regardless of their salary level, when a single high-ranking official who might make more than two office clerks combined would still be receiving his bonus.

The government did not share this standpoint. Some parliamentary representatives and even a few Cabinet members, such as Postal Minister Emil Franke, privately agreed with the WNC's stance.[28] Their support, however, was not enough to engineer a change acceptable to a majority in the governing coalition. As Social Democrat Lev Winter told WNC functionary Irene Malinská, most of the government was looking at the matter from a "social perspective."[29] In their view, a paycheck from the government was not simply compensation for services, it was also a way of giving financial aid to middle-class households—almost more like charity than work. But the goal was not merely to assist the intelligentsia; it was also to help traditional single-breadwinner families to stay afloat. Therefore, if the government needed to trim its budget, this had to be done in such a way that the least damage fell on those kinds of families. In the prevailing government opinion, primarily formulated and defended by Finance Minister Karel Engliš, gender helped determine who would get access to the government's limited funds. According to Engliš, the government had a social duty to use its money to insulate married men from the effects of the economic crisis. Even under WNC pressure, Engliš refused to bend from his plan to dock the pay of double-worker families to support single-earner ones. But although he firmly believed that there could be only one bonus given per family, he was willing to concede that, if both spouses did work, the husband did not have an intrinsically greater right to the extra money. In the final compromise reached with the WNC in the fall of 1930, it was decided that in two-employee families, the spouse with the larger salary would receive the bonus, maximizing the amount each family was entitled to receive and removing the explicitly gendered aspect of the deductions. The government also granted the WNC's requests to exclude maternity leave from the mandatory ten-month work period to be eligible for the bonus.[30]

For the feminists in the WNC, this was an empty victory. Although the compromise eliminated any explicit references to women, the implicitly gendered content remained. Single-breadwinner households, almost all headed by men, would emerge unscathed, while double-earner households would be punished for going against the normative ideal of the Czech family. By denying the feminists' argument that compensation should be given in accordance with work accomplished, the government set a dangerous precedent, making salaries dependent on nebulous "social factors" that supported a very specific version of gender relations. As Plamínková remarked in a speech to the Senate, "The spouse with the lower salary is cut out! That might mean that it wouldn't be the wife. But, let's not play games, that is dishonorable for a parliament. It will almost always be the wife."[31] It was common knowledge that women almost always made less money than their husbands and everyone knew that the financial burdens of the new policy would be borne almost entirely by working wives. This sent a chilling message to women in the civil service. Throughout the 1920s, women had frequently been paid less than their male colleagues for equivalent work, but such practices had not been officially sanctioned. Now, however, the government quite openly stated that the civil service was, at least in part, a means of maintaining the middle-class, male-headed family, a project quite at odds with these women's sense of their rights as citizens.

## The Media Campaign against the Double Earners

In the fall of 1930, shortly after the fracas over the Christmas bonus bill wound down, Finance Minister Karel Engliš placed an article in the influential daily *Lidové Noviny,* in which he suggested that one way to deal with the unemployment problem would be to ban all married women whose husbands earned a living wage from the labor market.[32] Although the opinions he expressed about working women were not new, Engliš's article was the first major public statement of this kind by a sitting government minister. Though the Engliš plan was not actually put into effect, it reinforced the belief that excluding married women from the civil service was the key to solving the economic crisis, or at very least the problem of the unemployed intelligentsia. After its publication, working wives found that few people, other than feminist groups like the Women's National Council, were willing to defend them. Over the next few years, their position in the public eye steadily worsened, as even many single working women excoriated them for remaining on the job. The number of written attacks against them published in local and national newspapers and journals in the years after Engliš's article are too many to count. Double earners even found their way into novels and short stories, and were the subject of at least one stage play.[33] However, while numerous, these attacks and the responses written to them all relied on a similar set of arguments, making it possible to see from a few examples how the groups for and against the right of wives to work in the civil service formulated their positions.

The scope of the debate was neatly laid out in a series of letters to the editor published in the journal *Přítomnost*. The letters were occasioned by a small article in the October 5, 1932, issue entitled "Second Jobs." In it, the author (known only as "V.G.") claimed that "secondary" jobholders, such as married women, were abetting the unemployment crisis. V.G. specifically mentioned the working wives of "highly paid" state employees as a "glaring example" of this phenomenon. According to V.G., all such "secondary" workers should turn their jobs over to the unemployed immediately. If they did not want to do so, the government should force them out of their positions.[34] This letter betrayed a number of common assumptions about work and who was justified in having it. For V.G., the right of individuals to have jobs and thereby acquire their own wealth was subordinate a family's right to basic sustenance. The state could most easily protect this entitlement by employing husbands. Therefore, the civil service had a public duty to hire husbands above all others, even at the expense of a few current employees. By this logic, married women were the people least entitled to government jobs, since their husbands ostensibly earned enough to supply their basic needs.

V.G.'s attack on working wives provoked a letter from Mila Grimmichová, a feminist who worked with the WNC. Her letter was obviously not inspired just by V.G.'s diatribe, but also by the appearance of many such articles in the popular press. Grimmichová's first point was that the civil service should not be considered social assistance for the elite, but a job like any other. Grimmichová went on to ridicule the way in which married women in the civil service were singled out for retribution. She sarcastically wrote that if jobs were to be taken away from married female civil servants, the same logic would demand taking diplomas away from married female doctors, ordering female shop owners to cease business if they married, and even forbidding peasant women from working on their farms. But, Grimmichová added, if second jobs really posed such a threat to society, then there was no excuse for only targeting women. The male factory or estate owner who had made enough from his enterprise to be able to live comfortably should also be forced give up his job for the benefit of the less fortunate. Though this might seem absurd, said Grimmichová, "it is no more absurd than the continual references to married female state employees. If only these women could finally be allowed the peace and quiet they need to do their work!"[35]

Grimmichová's letter provoked a wave of responses. The tenor of many of these retorts was captured by Josef Kremer, an engineer, who accused working wives of leading decadent lives with their "extra" income, ignoring that these women actually worked for their salaries, portraying them as selfish and profligate spenders who cared only about their own material gain.[36] Kremer was joined in his opinions by an unmarried woman who worked in the private sector, Helena Neswedová. Neswedová affirmed the right of qualified women to work for the state, but felt that this right only extended to single women or wives who needed the work to survive. She also believed that a government job was inherently distinct from work in the private sector and should be regulated differently. Privately employed individuals, like the doctors or shopkeepers Grimmichová mentioned, operated in an uncertain environment, dependent on outside forces like customers and competition for their earnings. Civil servants, however, were removed from vagaries of the market, could only be fired with difficulty, and had excellent pension benefits that guaranteed them an income for life. In Neswedová's reasoning, this luxury of a stable income, which had become a precious commodity during Czechoslovakia's years of economic uncertainty, needed to be reserved for heads of households, who had the legal and social responsibility of providing for others.

If a husband's duty was to provide, a wife's was to devote herself to domestic cares, and Neswedová argued that all married women who could afford it should leave paid employment. "Indeed," Neswedová remarked, "I know from the large number of marriages that surround me that the household of a working wife is not a household at all and if there are children, they are the most miserable creatures, left for the whole day in the hands of an irresponsible servant."[37] With this comment, Neswedová took the discussion to a new plane. Rather than arguing that wives should not have jobs during times of economic crisis, she claimed they should simply not hold jobs outside the home at all. Their proper workplace was their household, their proper tasks being a homemaker and mother. For Neswedová, a working wife was automatically a failure. Absent from her home, she virtually guaranteed the unhappiness of her husband and children.

The following week's issue of *Přítomnost* included a host of other letters elaborating on these points, talking about why the civil service was different from the private sector and labeling married women who chose to work as selfish and irresponsible. One, a male civil servant who signed his letter only "A.B.," belittled married women who worked for only being concerned with "personal gain," and suggested that firing them was "more just and more reasonable than lowering the pay of male bureaucrats," who presumably were more interested in helping others than bettering their own personal situation.[38] Letters like A.B.'s showed a distinctly gendered view of sacrifice and duty, declaring that it was in the nature of wives to live only for others and sublimate their own desires for the welfare of their husbands and children. A woman's insistence in staying on the job after marriage could therefore only indicate some sort of moral deficiency, a betrayal of her womanly nature, or even a crime against nature itself. Another letter writer, a male teacher, called two salaries for one couple "an abuse and horrible social evil" and accused married women who worked of taking food out of the mouths of the starving young intelligentsia.[39] Often in graphic and emotional terms, letter writers decried the hoarding of wealth that two working spouses seemed to represent and pleaded for some sort of justice that would give jobs to those who truly needed them. They insisted that that wealth should be distributed throughout society according to need. But despite this corporatist thread running through the letters, the letter-writers tended to express it with a democratic vocabulary based on rights and duties. As one of the writers, A. K. Emanov, put it, "democracy demands that each have the ability to live."[40] But Emanov really meant that each family should have the ability to live, not each individual. The fact that protecting families might entail taking individual rights from some groups of people (like married women) did not seem to trouble him.

After two weeks of printing letters that attacked working wives, *Přítomnost* began running some responses that tried to defend them. The first, written by a "Dr. H," concluded, "any lawyer, used to thinking without passion" would have to side with the sentiments originally expressed by Grimmichová. The right to work must be sacred for all, not merely for some. To start limiting the freedoms of certain individuals and not others, no matter what the cause, was to "go back to Austria" when an arbitrary monarchy ruled instead of a democratic state. If we allow ourselves to fire married women simply because of who they are, Dr. H wrote, then "we can stop believing in our freedom-loving constitution as far as ideas are concerned." Dr. H. warned against abandoning the constitution in search of solutions to short-term economic goals and appealed to the public's sense of democratic responsibility to get them to agree that whatever benefits might be gained from excluding married women from government employment were not worth the potential dangers posed by such attacks on civil liberties.[41]

A similar argument came from Irene Malinská, WNC leader and civil servant herself. Malinská charged that singling out married women for punishment went against the ideals of democracy. For her, democracy was bound up with the right to choose one's own path in life, which was exactly what was being denied to married women. "Would it not be a moral paradox," she wrote, "for a democratic state to force a female citizen to decide between work and family life?"[42] Malinská also tried to set up a dichotomy between progressive "Czech" behavior and autocratic "Austrian" practices. Under the monarchy, she said, bureaucratic jobs had been nothing but secure, cushy paychecks and the *celibát* had been accepted practice. The new Czechoslovak state had changed that, reforming the civil service and lifting the *celibát* in the name of the modern values of efficiency and equality. When people denied these changes by regarding civil service jobs as pay without work and calling for a return of practices like the *celibát*, what they were really doing was "returning to the old, Austrian mentality." Those who proposed sanctions for married women, Malinská implied, were forgetting their true Czech heritage.

As the blitz of letters on this topic wound down, it was apparent that both those who advocated removing married women from the civil service and those who defended the right of such women to work were deeply entrenched in their views. Each side spoke its own language, which was almost unintelligible to its opponents. Those who believed the government should not employ wives, particularly wives of other civil servants, did so out of a fundamental conviction that it was husbands who were supposed to support the family financially and wives who had the task of maintaining the family's household and raising its children. While they acknowledged that this ideal was not possible for all families and that some wives were forced by financial need to take on paid employment, they continued to believe in it as the proper form of the family in society. Therefore, it seemed only logical to call for increasing employment opportunities for husbands by banning wives from choice government jobs. The women who held such jobs were not sympathetic victims, they were egoists who refused to be satisfied with their proper role as homemaker and mother, selfish beasts willing to sacrifice both their own family and the families of the unemployed for the sake of their personal intellectual or financial gain.

Those who defended the right of wives to work answered on a completely different level of argument. Their basic position was that the right of all citizens to work was sacred and protected by the constitution. They argued that since these women did their jobs, they had the same right to a salary as anybody else, regardless of their personal situation. They tried to convince the opposition that the right of personal choice was an integral part of democracy and that wives, like all persons, should be able to choose when and whether to work. But such arguments simply did not mean much to people who strongly believed that wives were not individuals and that their duties to their families outweighed any measure of personal freedom they might have. Such basic convictions about what civil equality meant and who was able to demand rights on what grounds were not easily changed and made a solution to the conflict appear to be impossible.

## The Austerity Measures of 1932 and 1933

Despite the efforts of groups like the WNC to defuse the situation, the venomous charges being bandied about in the media about working wives in the civil service continued.[43] At the same time, the government's financial situation was growing increasingly dire. In such an atmosphere, it was not surprising that prejudices against working married women soon found their way again into government policy. In June 1932, the government released a proposal for a package of austerity measures. The package called for a variety of cuts in employee benefits and salaries, amounting to as much as 10 percent of a worker's total wages. Some of these measures were directed specifically at married female workers and pensioners. The first of these concerned the *činovné*, or "active-duty supplement." In a plan reminiscent of the Christmas bonus affair, the government planned to reduce the *činovné* of married couples who were both civil servants. The supplement of the spouse who earned the least, presumably the wife, would be cut in half.[44] This was a significant loss: representatives from the Imperial Union of Czechoslovak Women Teachers estimated that women affected by this measure would lose an amount equivalent to between 6 and 10 percent of an experienced teacher's salary.[45] The cuts directed against female pensioners were even more dramatic. If the bill passed, many women would see their pension benefits reduced by half, and others would see them disappear altogether.[46]

Women's professional organizations were appalled and incensed by these proposals. The WNC collaborated with the Czechoslovak Association of University Women, the Syndicate of Public Female Employees, and the Action Committee of the Czech Community of Teachers to create a united campaign against the austerity package. The government went into its summer holidays shortly after the bill was made public, but these groups worked throughout the vacation to mobilize their members for the fight. The WNC instructed its member organizations to mount a protest stressing women's constitutional right to work and to receive equal treatment with men. The members responded to their leadership's call with a barrage of letters and pleas to officials at all levels of government, packing public protest meetings, and signing group resolutions.[47] They presented the government with arguments based on democratic principle, declaring that the proposed austerity package violated both Article 106 of the Czechoslovak Constitution, because it treated male and female employees differently, and Article 126, because it penalized married couples solely on the grounds of their marital status.

WNC leaders haunted the offices of the government ministries, looking for concrete proof that the changes they demanded would actually be made. Throughout the fall, they were reassured by officials that the austerity package was being reworked and that women's right to the same salary and pension benefits as men would be protected. But no written documents were ever given to supplement these verbal assurances, and the text of the revised version of the austerity measures was kept secret until the day it was presented to both chambers of the National Assembly. In this tense atmosphere of suspicion, rumors abounded, and the WNC struggled to follow up on every possible new threat with repeated personal interventions in the various ministries, new rounds of letters to the government and legislators, and new exhortations to its constituents to keep up the pressure.[48] In the end, despite many moments of uncertainty, the WNC campaign was largely successful in achieving its goals. Although many voices in the press continued to call for removing married women from the civil service, the government was persuaded by the WNC's arguments. The package of austerity measures that was finally passed by the National Assembly in December 1932 did not make active distinctions between men and women. It severely cut salaries and pension benefits, but did so for men and women equally.[49]

While acknowledging their "good fight won," the women in the WNC remained worried about the future. "The voices of doom have not been silenced!" fretted Ottile Malá in *Ženská Rada* in 1933. She cited several articles printed in major newspapers in early January of that year that still called for an end to married women in the civil service, and urged women to stay vigilant.[50] As it turned out, Malá's worries were soon realized. During the winter of 1932–1933, unemployment soared in Czechoslovakia. As the financial crisis became steadily more acute, the Finance Ministry again began to contemplate cutting employee salaries to balance the budget.[51] By the summer of 1933, married women in the civil service were again set on edge by persistent rumors that their salaries and even their jobs were in jeopardy. In response, the WNC demanded a meeting with the prime minister, Jan Malypetr of the Agrarian Party. During their July 20 meeting, Malypetr told WNC representatives that the government was not contemplating anything of the sort. He assured them that "they would be informed about eventual negotiations on this matter and consulted on their standpoint."[52] Despite Malypetr's remonstrations, however, the WNC remained suspicious, noting that personal surveys had been issued to all state employees requiring them to submit information about their spouse's occupation and income, as well as on their use of maternity and childcare leave. This could only mean trouble, warned an article in *Ženská Rada*. Even if the government did not mean to use such information to justify measures against working wives, the very existence of such statistics would "foster . . . among employees a spirit of spite instead of collegial feelings and benevolence—a vehicle for the breakdown of state society."[53]

In October, although nothing had been officially announced or released, the WNC succeeded in getting a copy of a draft proposal for additional austerity measures and found that their fears had been realized. The new proposal would reduce the pay of all married employees whose spouses also worked, whether for the state or in the private sector. Couples who lived together but were not legally married would also be subjected to extra cuts, as would single employees who lived with parents who were also government workers. Married pensioners would also face additional deductions from their benefits.

The WNC quickly condemned the proposal and began a spirited campaign to amend the proposed austerity measures before they could be put into effect. During November 1933 it launched a protest blitz, focusing its efforts on government ministers.[54] Františka Plamínková quickly arranged a meeting with Prime Minister Malypetr. Unfortunately, this conversation only served to strengthen the WNC's suspicion that the government was planning to make married working women into its sacrificial lamb. Plamínková asked Malypetr if he intended to hurt married women, and he replied that he did not. She then presented him with the WNC's position and demands, denouncing the special deductions for married couples as a social injustice. Instead of responding directly to her concerns, Malypetr countered that the public was demanding that married women be fired. Plamínková retorted that people had been making such demands since 1904 and that this was not a reason to give in to injustice, warning that "the future will judge us and we must never sell principles for financial gain." Malypetr replied, "Something had to be done with married women. . . . The public was so biased towards the employment of married couples in the civil service, that if he wanted to keep women at all, these pay cuts . . . had to be made." He went on to say that it was "impossible" for married couples to hold two jobs in such hard times. At the conclusion of their meeting, he denied that he had the authority to order any changes anyway, telling Plamínková that it was the Finance Ministry that would prepare the final draft of any new austerity measures and that the affair really depended only upon what that office decided.[55]

Malypetr's comments indicated that the WNC's worst fears had been realized. The government coalition had apparently decided that married women working in the civil service were too great a political liability to defend. Malypetr did not bother to debate Plamínková on the terms of her arguments about the right to work regardless of marital status or equal pay for equal work. He did not comment on her insistence that democratic principles should not be shelved for the sake of party politics, or address her concerns about the social effects of the proposed salary cuts. Instead he merely cited the outpouring of public opinion against wives in the workforce, claiming that the government's hand was being forced by these outside pressures. He refused to acknowledge that the government had any responsibility to respect the constitution or its democratic ideals (and did not contradict Plamínková's assertion that the new austerity package flaunted those ideals), but rather placed its duty with following the voice of "the people." He acted as if the government was only reluctantly following the public's demands, even claiming that cutting their paychecks was actually helping the married women who worked for the state. Malypetr implied that this sop to public opinion would enable the government to at least keep these women employed, even if it devalued their work. The WNC and its allies charged that the government was merely trying to make itself more popular at little cost by attacking this small and defenseless minority. Plamínková asserted that this action would only inflame the public's desire for further sacrifices from employed wives, remarking: "Without this *official* impetus, no one would have dared to doubt [married women's] equal right to bread in public offices!"[56]

With the government and the public arrayed against them, the WNC was unable to lessen the impact of the proposed pay cuts, which went through as planned.[57] The parallel tales of the WNC's fight against pay cuts for married civil servants in 1932 and again in 1933 show how rapidly attitudes were turning against wives in the workplace. In 1932, the media clamored for the government to stop the "double earners" from taking more than their fair share of the government's largesse, but large-scale protests by women's groups succeeded in convincing lawmakers that such a policy was discriminatory. In 1933, the media barrage continued and intensified, and this time, efforts by Czech feminists and working women to ameliorate these proposals failed utterly. Lacking an effective plan for attacking its economic problems and seeing its own standing decline, the Czechoslovak government began to see, as Malypetr's comments to Plamínková indicated, that sanctions against married women in its employ would at least give the public a sense that action was being taken to address the situation. Attacking double earners would help the masses feel that the state was behind them, even if such measures would not actually have an appreciable effect on unemployment or the budget. Protecting the rights of married women to work in an equal relationship to other employees was not worth endangering the government's position in the eyes of its constituents. Once this basic line had been established, there was little that groups like the WNC could do to change it.

## The Right to Work, the Duty to Stay at Home

The WNC, as well as other organizations of professional women, issued sharply worded protests in response to the new austerity measures, in which they claimed that these regulations violated their rights as free and equal citizens in a democratic republic. The WNC's official statement announced: "We protest as [female] citizens of this state, who feel that this government resolution has threatened the democratic principles by which the state was founded; we protest especially as women, for the spirit of this resolution has dangerously attacked the economic independence of working women and in this way impinged upon their human freedom and civil equality, values we are resolved to defend until the end of our strength."[58] However, the majority of the Czechoslovak population had little sympathy with the assertion that laws should deal with "citizens" and not with men and women. While there were a number of intellectuals and lawyers who agreed with the WNC on legal and constitutional grounds, most people simply could not conceive of work without reference to gendered norms of behavior. From this perspective, the scenario of married women with able-bodied husbands holding good office jobs during an economic crisis was a symbol of gross injustice. Although the constitution might have guaranteed such women their right to work, most people did not believe it was right for them to exercise it. At this gut level of right and wrong, they did not really think married women should be working, and the rights-based language of the WNC could do little to change their emotional reactions to working wives.[59]

Feminists and others who supported the cause of married working women realized that public opinion and attitudes were their biggest liability. As the leftist writer and commentator Otto Rádl remarked in an article in *Přítomnost,* the legal structures for ensuring women's equality were already largely in place, and changing attitudes was a more urgent matter than changing laws. In order for the rights granted to women on paper to become reality, opinions about women would need to undergo a radical transformation.[60] But this task was proving to be more than groups like the WNC could handle. As the economic and political pressures of the 1930s increased, prejudices against married working women received so much attention in the press that the voices raised in their support were largely drowned out. By 1935, an activist for the Federation of Czechoslovak Female Teachers reported that she was powerless to stop the unending waves of attacks on married working women appearing in the local and national press, which "came regularly during the period of equatorial rains and peaked during the autumnal equinox . . . then for a moment began to subside but did not completely disappear in any season of the year. Whenever there are spots on the sun, the flowers of these attacks open in all colors, sizes, beauties and with different powers of resistance." Her fruitless efforts to respond to these unceasing campaigns against working women began to make her feel as if fighting back was "a waste of time." While she still hoped women would win in the end, she also dispiritedly remarked, "the envy of these people is so great, that there is nothing they don't abhor."[61]

In the fall of 1935, the tensions grew even more pronounced. The impetus for the increase in venom against married working women was a plan for economic recovery released that September by Karel Engliš, who was now the head of the Czechoslovak National Bank. As finance minister in 1930, Engliš had proposed that the government lay off all of its married female workers as part of its solution to the economic crisis. Now he came out with another detailed plan for reviving the depressed economy in which he suggested that unemployment could be lowered by excluding married women from the work in the public sector, as well as by limiting the employment of single women under twenty-four to those whose parents could not support them. The Engliš plan, caused panic among the ranks of married female civil servants, who began to worry that the slightest misstep would cost them their jobs.[62] Their panic was exacerbated by further comments from leading government officials that seemed to point to mass layoffs for married women. The prime minister, now Milan Hodža of the Agrarian Party, remarked in May 1936 that he would "solve" the question of married working women as soon as possible. Even the new Czechoslovak president, Edvard Beneš, a protégé of Tomáš Masaryk and long considered by the WNC as one of their supporters, made comments in April 1936 to a group of labor leaders in which he admitted that "double-earning" married couples in the civil service were a "problem." He remarked to a group of students the following month that the government was trying to "solve this problem of married couples."[63]

The WNC continued to articulate its position that such policies were unconstitutional and against the democratic nature of the state and to lobby for support in these terms. Attempting to counter arguments that women should be willing to sacrifice their work for their family and the good of society, it declared that working women were willing to sacrifice for their nation, but that as equal citizens they should not be expected to sacrifice *more* than other sectors of the population. As the WNC wrote to Engliš, "In the Czechoslovak Republic, women are citizens with complete rights. . . . They would understand a just, *general* lowering of the standard of living for all citizens, they are not against lower living standards, if they are lowered in the same measure for all."[64] Its bottom line remained equality of the right to work for men and women, regardless of their civil status. At a protest meeting called in June 1936, they reaffirmed these principles and passed a resolution that demanded "that the government of the Czechoslovak Republic remember that each attack on married couples, however formulated, is really a restriction and assault on women's equal right to work . . . the foundation of democracy is also the free choice of a life-long career and the right of self-determination for all citizens, for women as for men."[65]

These calls for democracy and equality, however, continued to fall on deaf ears. The economic situation did not improve, and demands for wives to be ejected from their jobs did not abate. Talk of rights had little power, it seemed, when applied to working women. For those who clamored for eliminating married women from the labor market, wives had duties and responsibilities to their families and by extension to the nation, which far overshadowed any rights they might claim. The duties accorded to married women as wives came to overshadow their status as rights-bearing individuals, making possible the discriminatory policies leveled against them.

THESE ATTACKS against women in the civil service were not unique to the Czech lands. Keeping married women out of government jobs was a popular practice around Europe during the decades between the wars. Similar rhetoric against double earners was frequently heard in Weimar and Nazi Germany. The Nazi Party was particularly outspoken in its opposition to women working outside of the home, an ideology it put into practice when it expelled all women from the civil service in 1934.[66] That same year, the fascist regime in Italy allowed government departments to limit their female office workers (both married and single) to 20 percent of their total staff; this was lowered to 10 percent in 1938.[67] Public resentment toward double earners in France found its way into policy there as well, most notably during the Vichy regime.[68] Nor were such attitudes about women and especially wives in the workforce limited to authoritarian regimes, or even to Europe. As the historian Alice Kessler-Harris notes, they were quite the norm in the United States, where legislators and the public both condemned married women for taking jobs from male breadwinners. The Economy Act, passed by the U.S. Congress in 1932, mandated that married people whose spouses were also civil servants be the first dismissed if layoffs became economically necessary. This policy lasted until 1937.[69] The link in all these cases was a similar conception of economic fairness and a belief that this had precedence over a doctrine of individual rights. The basic economic unit was the family, not the individual, and the family's true provider was its male head. In this belief system, it was more just to economically favor the married man, using him as a way of spreading benefits to families. Throughout Europe and the United States, governments elevated this notion of economic fairness over their duty to protect the individual liberties and freedoms of their citizens.[70]

While this reasoning was not exclusively Czech, it is more striking in the Czech case because the Czechoslovak state clung tightly to its self identity as a democratic state and because its government, in other contexts, loudly proclaimed its respect for women's rights. The irony and contradiction in the government's self-congratulatory praise of its stance toward women, when compared with its legally sanctioned, discriminatory treatment of those females who worked, seemed to be recognized only by the increasingly beleaguered working wives themselves, their families, and a few ideological supporters. The feminists in the WNC and their allies envisioned democracy as composed of individual citizens, each of which had a right to equal treatment in all areas of society. In their eyes, it was a dangerous contradiction to limit the right of some citizens to something as basic as work in a declared democratic state. Such acts, they felt, brought Czechoslovakia uncomfortably close to its more authoritarian neighbors, who were busily dismantling the individual freedoms their citizens had previously enjoyed. As one anonymous writer remarked in response to the pay cuts directed against married women in 1933, the tendency to force women away from gainful employment and make them dedicate themselves to the family was manifested primarily in countries with a militaristic ideology, which expected women to bear children for future wars. He warned that Czechoslovakia should be careful about turning to such models.[71] Similarly, an article in *Přítomnost* exhorted readers to uphold the progressive example set by the Czechoslovak Constitution and not "fall into the trap of Germany."[72] These writers argued that the Czechs and the Czechoslovak state were different from the Nazis, but these differences were not fixed; without strict vigilance they too could lose their grip on democracy and freedom. They worried that the wanton disregard of individual rights exhibited by their government in its dealings with its female employees heralded a general movement away from the democratic foundation on which the republic had been based.

Those who sanctioned limiting women's rights to employment, which seemed to be the majority of Czechs and certainly the majority of their politicians, did not see their actions as antidemocratic. For them, the right to vote and the right to work were separate entities that did not immediately follow from each other. The basic organizing principle of political life was the individual citizen, who voted and was elected without regard to gender. However, citizens were not the basic organizing principle of social and economic life; that role went to the family, which was composed of the strictly gendered categories of husband and wife. Therefore, the rights or entitlements of individuals within those spheres were dependent upon their status within the family and tied to the "natural" roles of men and women in society. Since wives were supposed to exist primarily in the domestic realm, they did not need and were therefore not entitled to the same privileges as men in areas like work. Husbands were supposed to be the providers, thus they had greater rights to work and wages. The overtly discriminatory policies adopted by the state toward married women in the civil service after 1933 were based on this kind of reasoning. The eventual victory and acceptance of such policies within the democratic system showed how firmly traditional gender roles were embedded in Czech society, despite the fact women had achieved formal political equality.

# 5

## ABORTION POLITICS IN
## INTERWAR CZECHOSLOVAKIA

To be a mother is a very responsible task. A woman is predestined for this role from birth, but motherhood demands a woman not only be a mother, but also rear a healthy, strong child. . . . To do that under today's circumstances for a larger number of children is completely impossible. I think that no one should have the right to command a woman to have children if they can't or don't want to give her the standard of living she would need to fulfill her task as a mother.

J. Srbová, *Právo Lidu*, March 23, 1930

AT THE BEGINNING of the summer of 1932, a diatribe against abortion appeared on the front page of *Lidové Listy* (The People's Paper), the newspaper of the People's Party. It was written by the paper's editor, Jan Scheinost, who declared, "until last week, it was generally accepted in Czechoslovakia that October 28, 1918, emancipated not only all the Czechoslovak people, but especially its women, to whom it gave suffrage and otherwise essentially placed in public life on a level with men." According to Scheinost, Czech socialists had suddenly decided that women's emancipation was not complete and would not be so until they had access to legal abortion. Scheinost claimed that these unspecified "socialists" used a radical interpretation of individual rights as their primary argument for legalizing abortion, declaring that a woman had the right to control her own body, "even when there was another life beating inside of it." For him, this was a graphic illustration of how the idea of individual rights could be taken to outrageous and morally dubious extremes, used to sanction what he called the murder of an unborn child. He bemoaned the fact that abortion supporters thought only about their rights and disregarded their duty to their country, their society, and their nation.[1]

Scheinost implied abortion was not an issue in Czechoslovak politics before the summer of 1932, when it suddenly took over the front pages of major daily newspapers like his own. It was the republic's own Justice Ministry that had brought abortion into the limelight, by drafting a law that would have legalized the procedure in a few circumstances. But while the Justice Ministry's proposal certainly gave abortion a new visibility, this was not its first appearance in the public arena. Debates over abortion actually stretched back much further, almost to Scheinost's mythical moment of ideological consensus in October of 1918. Scheinost's essay was also misleading in its characterization of abortion politics in the Czech lands. Scheinost wrote that Czech supporters of legal abortion were most concerned with protecting a woman's individual rights, a schematic that fits in both with contemporary American notions of abortion as an issue based on rights (whether of a woman or a fetus) and with the typical concerns of the interwar Czech women's movement on other matters, like family law and employment practices. However, outside of Scheinost's rhetoric, only a small minority of Czechs saw abortion as a rights issue. Even amongst abortion supporters, legalizing abortion was usually talked about as a social matter, framed in terms of social justice and responsibility, not in terms of individual rights.

The conflict over abortion in interwar Czechoslovakia reframed the themes of equality, social responsibility, and familial duty that characterized other debates over gender and rights. Only a few of the participants in the battle over abortion used the language of rights so common to other areas of Czech politics. But even without this vocabulary, the debate over abortion formed a vital part of the larger discussion over the legal limits of individual freedom and the proper relationship between the family and the state. In the case of abortion, however, these questions became overlaid with notions of social justice and fairness that were heavily influenced by both class and religious convictions. Therefore, the issue of abortion found different constituencies than other conflicts over the meaning of women's citizenship. The leading opponents of abortion reform were Catholic activists. The leading proponents of legalizing abortion identified themselves more as socialists than as women or as feminists. While feminist groups like the Women's National Council had strong ties to the left in its leadership and intellectual orientation, the WNC found itself unable as an organization to wholeheartedly join this fight. In the hands of the political left, abortion became a topic bound up with the economic situation of the working class, tied to the issue of economic equality more than civil and political rights. Abortion politics in interwar Czechoslovakia operated at the intersection of class and gender interests, demonstrating how notions of family responsibility complicated ideas about citizenship and rights.[2]

## The First Challenges to §144

In interwar Czechoslovakia, laws regulating abortion were derived from Habsburg-era statutes that dated from 1852 and formed §144–148 of the Austrian criminal code. According to these paragraphs, abortion was a felony punishable by up to five years of hard labor. The same penalties applied to the woman who aborted and anyone who assisted her, whether a doctor, midwife, village healer, or friend. These laws, commonly referred to simply as §144, came under attack soon after the establishment of the Czechoslovak state. In October 1920, Luisa Landová-Štychová, a parliamentary representative then attached to the Czech (National) Socialist party, submitted a bill to the National Assembly for a new abortion law.[3] Landová-Štychová's bill, which was signed by twenty-one other members of her party, proposed removing §144 from the books, eliminating all penalties for abortions conducted through the end of the first trimester of pregnancy as long as the operation was performed by trained medical personnel. Under this bill, the ultimate arbiter of a pregnancy was the woman herself. If it became law, her desire for an abortion would be the only legal requirement needed to obtain one.

In the written commentary that accompanied the bill, Landová-Štychová presented her proposal as a public health measure designed to protect motherhood by saving poor women from shadowy back-alley abortionists. Trying to dispel beliefs that women who aborted did so for selfish reasons, she argued that the harsh realities of postwar inflation, unemployment, and housing shortages led women to consider illegal abortions. Landová-Štychová emphatically declared that the social problems that led to abortion "could not be solved simply by putting women in jail," which was all that current laws allowed. Indeed, she went on, laws that "forced [a woman] to become a mother without regard to her health or economic situation were an insult to women, for they degraded her as a human being and also worsened the situation." Instead, women needed to be allowed to choose when they would become mothers and permitted to have children when they were truly able to provide for them. This, she said, would enhance, not diminish, the "desire for motherhood" that every woman experienced.[4] She stressed that legal abortion was not the only answer to the problems facing working-class mothers and their families, but represented only part of what should be a comprehensive policy to support motherhood, including greater state support for women and children. In this spirit, Landová-Štychová paired her abortion bill with one calling for state-sponsored maternity insurance for all women.[5]

Landová-Štychová's bill to radically revise Czechoslovak abortion laws did not make it very far in the legislative process. It was accepted, printed, and dispatched to the National Assembly's legal committee in December 1920. After spending a few years there, it was formally tabled in 1922. But although it never made it to the floor of the National Assembly, it attracted some notice. Much of the initial reaction from the Czech press was very negative, even in women's publications. Those who wrote in support of abolishing §144 tended to be, like Landová-Štychová, from one of Czechoslovakia's socialist parties, but even among socialists the reaction was far from unanimous. A few leading women from the Social Democratic Party publicly came out in favor of the bill, including Betty Karpíšková, editor of the Social-Democratic weekly *Ženské Noviny* (The Women's News) and a future parliamentary representative. Karpíšková praised Landová-Štychová for defending a woman's right to freely decide whether or not to have a child and was particularly upset by those who claimed that women had a responsibility to carry pregnancies to term in order to increase the Czechoslovak population. In her opinion, women had a right to "self-determination" that outweighed any social or national duty to reproduce, especially since the considerable physical and financial burdens of childcare fell primarily on them. Like Landová-Štychová, Karpíšková claimed that poor women resorted to risky illegal abortions only when they felt they could not live up to these burdens. She championed such decisions to abort, remarking, "I don't think it is very heroic or moral to bring a lot of children into the world and then watch them die . . . from a lack of means." With statements like these, Karpíšková made an explicit distinction between the plight of poor women, who she claimed subjected themselves to dangerous procedures out of desperation and need, and the situation of wealthy women. Those who had the financial wherewithal to care for large families but instead used their money to purchase safe abortions in doctor's offices, flouting both the law and their own supposed social concerns and moral standards, received little support from Karpíšková. She portrayed abortion both as a universal issue of individual freedom and as part of the class struggle against capitalist privilege. Abortion was something all women should have access to *and* an issue that had special relevance for the working class.[6]

Politically active women outside the socialist camp tended to disagree with this assessment. Rather than seeing abortion as a manifestation of women's personal freedom or a socially just measure that would allow couples to decide when it was economically feasible to have children, they simply saw it as wrong. Writing in the Agrarian Party publication *Zvěstování* (The Annunciation), Božena Novotná called abortion "an evil epidemic," and defended tough abortion laws as society's defense against this pernicious infection. She claimed that most people, especially most women, saw abortion as a crime and would be offended by its legalization. This, she said, had nothing to do with party politics or political ideologies—it was about morality, a righteous "disgust with this violent attack on the laws of nature . . . a healthy disgust with human willfulness, which wants to destroy the most fundamental of nature's laws, the law of life and death." For her, abortion was quite simply murder, the killing of an innocent life. As Novotná saw it, this was a matter governed by laws originating outside the democratic state, in nature, or in God.[7]

Those with a less religious bent often still regarded abortion as an immoral act. Anna Honzáková, one of the first Czech female doctors and a woman with long-standing ties to Czech women's organizations, strongly condemned the idea of legalizing abortion. While allowing that promoters of Landová-Štychová's bill "were led by the best intentions to help economically disadvantaged women," she condemned their campaign as "a catastrophic mistake," saying it would "only lead to the complete moral deterioration of women and the destruction of their health." Honzáková warned that repeated abortions could lead to infertility, lessen a woman's ability to work, and cause lifelong pain and other medical difficulties. Like Karpíšková, Honzáková realized that having children placed a considerable responsibility on a woman's shoulders and was sympathetic to the idea that some might want to limit their family size. But the only method she recommended for doing so was abstinence, even within marriage. She proposed educating couples about the consequences and responsibilities of sexual life, urging men to "approach their wives with respect and seriousness, as the mother of a new generation and not their momentary plaything." She also urged women to realize that they had the right to refuse their husband's sexual advances if they were worried about having more children.[8]

Honzáková's position proved to be fairly representative of the Czech medical profession. Most doctors were soundly against abortion on a woman's own demand, though many (including Honzáková herself) thought it was acceptable in cases where the pregnancy presented a serious danger to the mother's health, or, less frequently, in instances of rape.[9] Dr. Milan Janů, who wrote and lectured to women's groups on the subject, described abortion as a "social and psychological disease" of epidemic proportions. Although he admitted that there was no hard data on illegal abortions, Janů estimated there were 80,000–100,000 abortions per year in the Czechoslovak Republic and quoted studies that claimed up to half of the patients at some gynecological clinics were there either to have abortions or because they suffered from the effects of one.[10] He maintained that this "abortion epidemic" not only endangered women's health, but also added to the moral decline of the entire nation and potentially undermined normal population growth. The extensive social fallout from this "evil of enormous dimensions" made it into a serious public health problem. Janů's proposal for a cure, however, differed substantially from Honzáková's endorsement of sexual abstinence. According to him, the high incidence of illegal abortion in Europe resulted from a complicated combination of postwar economic and moral declines, each of which fed on the other. Both needed to be addressed if abortion rates were to fall: moral education would only be effective if accompanied by state programs to reduce unemployment, end housing shortages, lower inflation, provide economic assistance and medical services to married and unmarried mothers, and guarantee paid maternity leave to all working women.[11]

Very similar opinions were on display at a series of meetings of the society of Czech doctors in Prague, which voted both in 1920 and in 1921 to endorse abortion only in cases where the mother's life was in serious danger.[12] At the 1921 meeting, however, Dr. Max Wassermann advocated legalizing abortion during the first trimester, albeit for different reasons than Landová-Štychová. Rather than emphasizing a woman's right to decide whether or not to continue with a pregnancy, Wassermann talked about the medical, eugenic, and social benefits of bringing abortion into the doctor's office. He claimed that legalization would help stamp out dangerous quack abortionists, make it possible to control the spread of genetic diseases, and give poor women relief from the burden of caring for ever-growing families. As he described it, abortion would be a useful tool for those who dedicated themselves to constructing a healthier, more socially just Czechoslovakia. Wassermann dismissed concerns that abortion led to moral decline or was simply murder, saying that at early stages a fetus was "no more than a piece of meat" that could be manipulated without qualm.[13]

Although they allowed Wassermann to present his rather radical views, the assembled doctors all emphatically disagreed with him on virtually every point. One, Jan Jerie, wondered if "destroying a germinating life" would really assist the poor. Like Milan Janů, he declared that impoverished women needed better state welfare and maternity insurance, not abortion. Jerie was seconded by others who advocated the use of contraceptives as an alternative to abortion. A number of speakers also expressed some general doubts about selecting people for eugenic "therapies." While they did not discount the potential social benefits of eugenics, many felt that abortion was not the best means for weeding hereditary diseases out of the population. These doctors also worried that eugenic science had not yet advanced to the point where it could reliably determine which conditions were in fact genetic or who was the true carrier of an undesirable disease or trait. Despite the fact that the other doctors at this meeting all apparently disagreed with Wassermann's conclusions, they shared his basic assumption that it was professionals—doctors, social workers, or eugenicists—who should determine whether it was necessary to abort a pregnancy. As Jerie remarked, "How would we look on a doctor who carried out an unnecessary surgical operation simply because a patient wanted it, or just because he wanted to make money? . . . We would consider him a monstrous manifestation of the state of the medical profession." Doctors, not patients, should diagnose a body and determine its cure, even in the case of something as intimate as pregnancy.[14]

Czech doctors may have been reluctant to sanction abortion except for serious medical reasons, but this was not the case for lawyers.[15] The issue was a major topic of discussion at a congress of Czechoslovak lawyers held in Brno in 1925. This congress took place as the Czechoslovak Justice Ministry was preparing to revise its criminal code, and those assembled understood that their debates would factor into that process. The chairman of the session, Professor Augustin Miřička, summarized reports by prominent lawyers Antonín Kissich, Ivo Halík, and G. Hubáček, which generally took the position that abortion was a harmful practice that injured a woman's health, took the life of the fetus, and threatened society with depopulation and moral decline. But Miřička, along with Hubáček and Kissich, also felt that there were a few cases in which abortion was just. For example, if a woman had been raped, then forcing her to carry the child to term and care for it would be, in Miřička's words, "indecent."[16] Or, as Kissich said, if a woman was very poor and had many children, "according to the unwritten laws of compassion she would not be culpable if she aborted," because having another child would bring severe hardship to her and her family.[17] Although a few of those present believed that the need to protect the "germinating life" of the fetus always took precedence over other social or eugenic concerns, the congress eventually passed a resolution that departed from that strict position. This resolution demanded that any new Czechoslovak criminal code insist that abortion was a criminal offense, but also proposed making exceptions to this rule in well-defined cases of medical, social, or eugenic need, as mandated by "rules of medical knowledge" or "the demands of reasonable social or criminal politics." Like many doctors, the lawyers of the congress emphasized that "the evil that abortion indisputably is" could not be "fought only with punishment." Instead, the state needed to take a hand in ameliorating the social factors that led to abortion, "particularly by organizing care for families and children, above all unmarried mothers."[18]

This was a far cry from Luisa Landová-Štychová's original idea to completely legalize first-trimester abortions, but it did point out a potential avenue for change. The 1920 abortion bill was too radical to gain the depth of political support necessary to actually become law. As Dr. Marie Svozilová, who worked with feminist groups like the WNC, remarked, the idea of "free motherhood" or unrestricted access to abortion was repugnant to most Czechs, albeit for different sets of reasons. For some, legalizing abortion sanctioned a practice they considered immoral, while for others, it represented a threat to the growth of the Czechoslovak population.[19] Although few Czechs accepted the idea of abortion as a woman's inalienable right, many were willing to allow that women, especially poor women, who chose abortion often did so under duress. Like the lawyers gathered at the 1925 conference in Brno, they believed that the state had a responsibility to try and alleviate this suffering and take the desperation out of motherhood. There was undoubtedly more enthusiasm for financial assistance for mothers and ending legal discrimination against illegitimate children, but a growing number also began to see "socially or eugenically indicated" abortions as a partial solution to the problem. In this case, however, abortion was not a right, but was something granted via dispensation, a procedure carefully administered by medical professionals and social workers, acceptable only because of what it could contribute to the greater social good. There was little support for abortion as an instrument of women's personal autonomy.

After her 1920 bill failed to go anywhere in the legislative machinery, Landová-Štychová herself realized that perhaps putting the issue in a different way might have a better chance of success. She offered a revised bill in 1922 and yet another version in 1926, both of which added the requirement that women have "medical, eugenic, or social reasons" for requesting an abortion, or be victims of rape, or younger than seventeen years old. This change was mostly cosmetic, since her proposed laws still emphasized legalization based on "a woman's demand" and relied on a woman's own assessment of the validity of her reasons for choosing an abortion. But Landová-Štychová's changes indicate the public mood around her, as did her written commentaries on each bill. In the introduction to the 1926 version, she felt compelled to write, "abortion is evil," although she continued by asserting that "the birth of a child to unhealthy parents and into unfavorable conditions is the bigger evil" and went on to claim that "the evil of abortion cannot be confronted like other criminal evils, with crude punishments." Her 1922 and 1926 efforts at new abortion legislation show Landová-Štychová trying to reach out to what she called the "third group" —those who didn't support complete legalization but approved of lightening or limiting criminal punishment. With their support for the idea of socially or medically indicated abortions, perhaps some changes to §144 could finally be made.[20]

This "third group" was perhaps more fully represented by yet another bill to revise abortion laws, submitted in 1926 by Fanni Blatný, a member of the German Social Democratic Party. Her proposal, which was signed by twenty-one members of her party, would have made abortion legal only with the written approval of special commissions, each composed of two doctors and a female representative. Women who wished to abort would have to make a formal application to their local commission, which was supposed to agree to all reasonable requests and keep the details of its work confidential. The idea, apparently, was to make abortion possible and safe for those who could demonstrate a need for it while appeasing fears of spiking abortion rates and population decline by giving a supposedly objective body the chance to vet all requests for abortion.[21] However, both these attempts at providing some sort of more limited legalization went nowhere. The legal committee of the National Assembly never publicly discussed them, nor did the press comment on them. Evidently, in the eyes of the Czech public, these measures were but mere sidenotes to

Landová-Štychová's original and unsuccessful bid to make abortion legal on a woman's demand.[22]

## The Právo Lidu survey

While Luisa Landová-Štychová's attempts to change Czechoslovak abortion laws in the early 1920s were noticed and reported on by the Czech press, the coverage they received was very moderate. But in the spring of 1930 the issue of abortion took over the pages of one major daily. That March, the newspaper of the Social Democratic Party, *Právo Lidu* (The People's Right), sponsored a survey of its readers to find out how they felt about §144. The survey, which ran in the paper's Sunday "Women and Family" section, was inspired by the results of an earlier write-in campaign entitled "What Do We Demand?" Many of the responses to that survey had demanded changes to Czechoslovakia's abortion laws, prompting the editors to devote their next survey effort to this topic. The response was overwhelming. Letters poured in and were printed in the Sunday edition of the paper over the next nine weeks, until the editors finally had to ask people to stop sending them. In their initial request for submissions, the editors rather obviously attempted to influence the kind of response they received, making it clear that they considered §144 a pernicious law that needed to be abolished. One of the questions they posed to readers asked: "Are you for public medical assistance and advice, or for secret abortionists who are the bane of proletarian women's health and lives?"[23] After making their own position clear, however, the editors presented the letters they chose to print without comment. To their credit, they included a wide variety of responses, including some that diverged quite strongly from their own standpoint. The letters came from a diverse mix of people: men and women, factory workers and professionals, Prague-based urbanites and small-town dwellers. Many recalled personal experiences, others presented scientific data or offered moral pronouncements. Although the readers of this particular paper were almost certainly politically inclined to the left and very possibly tied to the Social Democratic Party, the sheer volume and diversity of responses to this survey made it clear that ordinary Czechs were very interested in abortion laws and often thought about abortion in ways that were different from the pronouncements of politicians or professionals.

The majority of those who responded to the *Právo Lidu* survey were in favor of legalizing abortion in some fashion, whether they preferred unrestricted access or limiting legal abortion to cases that demonstrated "social or eugenic indications" of need. Quite strikingly, however, few of those who wrote in talked about abortion as an issue of women's bodily self-determination in the way that female socialist leaders like Luisa Landová-Štychová or Betty Karpíšková did. Instead, most saw §144 as part of a social system that oppressed the working class as a whole. Many respondents echoed Karel Ježek, a teacher from Cerekvice u Hořic, who described the struggle to revise §144 as having "wide social, national-economic, and moral significance." "The sooner we abolish this paragraph," he claimed, "the better it will be for human society." According to Ježek, one of the primary problems with keeping abortion illegal was not that it inhibited women's freedom to choose when to become mothers, but that it left the poor with families they could not support.[24] Families too large for the size of their paychecks were what kept the working class in such a desperate material condition. Many letters used this Neo-Malthusian argument, claiming that legal abortion was the one fail-safe method for limiting family size. As G. Braun from Liberec put it, "with less children [we will] raise the human value of the worker!"[25]

A poignant example of this attitude came in a letter from Josef Vištein, a miner from Kladno. Vištein said that in the past he had been against abortion, thinking that hard work would provide for his growing family. He and his wife had seven children and cared for them all without complaint. Even though they realized that their standard of living could not compare with friends who had smaller families, they continued to welcome each child as it came. But then, Vištein said, he lost his job at the mine. He pleaded with the management to keep him on for the sake of his children, but to no avail. Ever since, he had been out of work. Although his wife and children did their best to pitch in, without his salary the family just couldn't make enough to satisfy all those hungry young appetites. Bitterly, Vištein recalled that he and his wife "had worked for thirty years

. . . and now I wait, me, a proud miner, for someone to give me a piece of bread." The humiliation of this experience convinced him that large families were just not viable under the oppressive capitalist system, when workers could not be sure of what they would earn from year to year. He implored legislators to abolish §144 and "give couples complete freedom, not shed tears for the unborn. Our sainted duty," he declared, " is to protect the living, to protect the family and those children who have already been born, so they can be educated as healthy citizens of this republic, so that they don't go around scruffy and hungry."[26] As Vištein described it, the heart of the debate over legalizing abortion was social justice. He believed abortion should be decriminalized because this would ameliorate some of the factors that contributed to the material condition of the poor, not because it would help women gain a new kind of individual freedom.

For Vištein, §144 was above all a class issue: this was a law that specifically attacked the working class. This idea that abortion laws were unfairly weighted against workers was a persistent theme in survey responses. Many especially deplored the uneven way in which abortion laws were supposedly enforced. For example, František Šlégl, a worker from Žamberk, claimed that "if a poor woman disobeys §144, she is punished, not only by the back-alley abortionist, but with prison, sickness, and perhaps even death." However, he continued, "capital is relieved of these punishments because it has the ability to squander hundreds or thousands of crowns [to pay a doctor to perform the operation], and for this it is not punished."[27] Such comments were given additional weight by letters from practicing physicians. The pediatrician Kamil Neumann from Prague made no bones about the fact that gynecologists could be persuaded to ignore the law and perform an abortion for "some hundred crowns," a sum way beyond the reach of a working-class woman. So, while "women of property" easily evaded any medical or legal risk, poor women were "put in danger by various charlatans and crones (*báby*), paying for it with their health, and often their life."[28]

Although many respondents emphasized how abortion laws discriminated against the working class as a whole, others stressed the consequences of §144 specifically for proletarian women. A number of letters advocated abolishing §144 simply because back-alley abortions or home brewed abortifacients were such a threat to women's health. In an early letter often cited in later replies to the survey, a woman who identified herself only as "X.Y.," the wife of a poor smelter from Kročehlavy, told of how she had three children and found herself pregnant again at the age of forty-two. Desperate and without the three hundred crowns for "the woman who was said to know about these things," she "had to go where it could be done cheaper." Complications from what was done left her a bedridden invalid. This, she said, for a woman who "knew that her duty regarding her husband's poverty was not to have children." Lamenting the fact that she was now only a burden to her overworked husband, she said, "If only §144 didn't exist, then doctors wouldn't be afraid to help women who can't have children."[29] Another respondent, a man who wrote under the initials FR. H. N., related how a poor country woman came to him to purchase some nail filings (he must have owned or operated a hardware store or metal shop). As he wrapped them up, he asked the woman why she wanted them. When she gave him an evasive reply, he asked his wife, who matter-of-factly told him that the woman would drink them in a broth as a way of inducing a miscarriage. Horrified and unwilling to endanger the woman's health, he refused to sell her the filings. She burst into tears and "declared that she couldn't keep it and had to get five hundred crowns for the 'crone' (bába) or they wouldn't have anything to eat." This shocking incident helped convince him that "the first duty of our male and especially female comrade parliamentary representatives is to work for the reform of §144."[30]

Others, mostly women themselves, were more concerned with the consequences "involuntary" motherhood had on poor women's lives. A number of respondents emphasized the toll that motherhood exacted on working-class women and argued that women's well-being demanded that they limit their family size. Marie Hanusová from České Budějovice, for example, described the enormous amounts of work and financial sacrifice it took to properly raise children in a working-class household, or even just to keep their rapacious mouths full of bread. She firmly believed that all poor mothers "looked with horror on every new 'addition' and cursed the paragraph that made them a slave, because any mother who has four or five children is a true slave."[31] Another woman, Božena L from Brno, also made a sharp distinction between "the noble calling of motherhood" so often extolled in the press and its more sobering realities. For unmarried women, she said, pregnancy could mean the loss of a job, health problems, and lower chances of ever getting married (and hence finding respectability).[32] Similar feelings came out in a short manifesto sent by a representative of the woman's local Social Democratic organization from Plžeň-Doubravka. "We want less children," this writer emphatically declared. "Let there be in every family only as many children as the parents can decently support . . . !"[33]

The feelings these women had about abortion came from their own experiences and were expressed in those terms. They did not make complicated moral or philosophical arguments to support their position. Instead, they simply offered up their own lives as evidence, seeing the hardships they had endured as reason enough for legalizing abortion. They wrote of their desire to lessen their own suffering and toil and to give their children a better life. In this, they echoed the other survey respondents who portrayed the lack of safe, legal abortions as a "social" problem. But these women went further and decried §144 as an attack on their own personal autonomy. They railed against the "slavery" of forced motherhood and saw abolishing §144 as a means of liberation. These women demanded control over how many children they would have and when they would have them—echoing, in their own fashion, Landová-Štychová's calls for women's "self-determination" without using her language of rights. With J. Srbová, a worker from Prague, they complained "Paragraph 144 orders a woman: you will give birth! But it doesn't mention how to feed, clothe and educate two, three, or more children in today's bad economic situation. Being a mother is a very responsible task."[34] For women like Srbová, financial matters and social conditions were reasons to want access to abortion, but such concerns did not stand alone. They mixed with an equally strong desire to prevent the state from influencing a woman's decision about when to take on the considerable demands of motherhood.

Other letters, also from women, raised the issue of women's bodily autonomy in a strikingly different way: these women feared revising §144 because they worried that it would increase women's sexual exploitation by men. One respondent, a former midwife from Litomysl named Marcela K., charged that legalizing abortion would do nothing to solve women's real problem, men who refused to take responsibility for the consequences of their sexual activity. Legalizing abortion would only encourage men to sacrifice women's bodies for their own momentary pleasure.[35] Her fears were repeated in a rather more misogynist way by an author identified only as M. ST from Prague. M. ST was for a "revision" of §144, but not in favor of its complete abolition because, as s/he said, "I worry . . . that women would suffer much more than today, because the stupid or passive ones (which I take to be the majority of them), would be unscrupulously used by men."[36] In a similar fashion, Božena Janoušková of Dubeč worried that getting rid of §144 would not decrease the "green graves of young women destroyed by abortion." If abortion were legalized, men would just refuse to use contraception, despite the health risks abortion posed for their wives or girlfriends. A better strategy, Janoušková said, would be to sponsor a contest among doctors to see who could develop the most effective contraceptive device.[37]

Still other respondents to the survey were against abortion on the grounds that terminating a pregnancy was akin to murder. One of the first letters to bring up such concerns was from Ed Štorch, a teacher from Prague. Štorch called abortion "a crime, a sin against nature, a terrible barbarity and an abasement of women." Claiming to be "against the death penalty, against war, [and] against the exploitation of the working class," Štorch found abortion to combine elements of all of those things. He declared that aborted working-class fetuses were "sacrifices for capitalism," lost fighters for the proletarian cause. While he admitted that the contemporary situation was unjust, he advocated honoring and supporting mothers and children, and attacking the causes of abortion rather than the laws against it.[38] While Štorch's passionate defense of §144, which gave a socialist spin to attitudes more commonly associated with the Catholic right, was rather unusual for the readers of *Právo Lidu*, it did have its admirers. Božena Janousková, for one, specifically thanked Štorch for his contribution to the debate and agreed with his position.[39]

Other letters worried that legalizing abortion would hurt the growth of the Czechoslovak population or suggested that abortion was not the real solution to the problems of poverty and unemployment that faced working-class families. The feminist Mila Grimmichová, for example, claimed that abolishing §144 would only lead to more irresponsible sexual behavior among young people, seducing them away from the responsibilities of parenthood.[40] Similarly, Marie Rosolková from Lahovičky noted that the birth rate in the USSR had not dropped after it instituted legal abortion. She therefore advocated better contraception instead.[41] J. Kocman, writing from Opatovice nad Labem, had a slightly different perspective. He said the real problem was the sexual profligacy of modern society. Noting that animals mated only to have their young, he deplored the fact that "we want to misuse our sexual drive, given to us by nature for such a great purpose, only to satisfy our degenerate lusts." Whether abortion was legal or not was, for him, rather beside the point. If people would only lead decorous sexual lives, then whether the law admitted or prohibited abortion would be immaterial.[42]

By the time it concluded on May 11, 1930, the *Právo Lidu* abortion survey had certainly made it clear that "§144 was a very ticklish question."[43] Even though the survey only reached the readers of a Social Democratic newspaper, the letters that were printed certainly did not represent a united front. Dr. Max Popper claimed in his contribution to the survey that the majority of respondents did not seem to consider abortion a crime.[44] Paragraph 144 offended their sense of justice by punishing acts they saw as normal, if regrettable. It compounded this injustice by targeting the poor and unfortunate and contributing to the misery of the working class family. But the majority was not without its opposition. While the Social Democratic Party officially supported the repeal of §144, some readers of its own newspaper vocally dissented from the party line. A few called abortion a moral abomination. Others boldly declared that abolishing §144 would not help women or the working class. Even among those who opposed §144, there was no consensus about what should replace current abortion laws. Those who identified themselves as workers, and especially working women, tended to advocate unrestricted legalization of abortion, while most doctors, lawyers, teachers, and other white-collar workers favored legalizing abortion only in documented cases of financial or medical distress.

The thread that linked most of these varied responses together was the idea that abortion was a "social" issue rather than a question of women's rights as individuals. Few respondents to the *Právo Lidu* survey echoed the language of Social Democratic leaders like Betty Karpíšková, who wrote in an article published alongside one installment of letters that the "most just and correct argument for birth control is the right of women to be an entire person . . . not just a parent, when that would take from her all possibility for personal growth and would take from the child the chance for an educated mother."[45] Instead, letters both for and against the repeal of §144 ignored the idea of individual rights in favor of a more collective web of responsibilities that linked the family and the state. Those who advocated abolishing §144 wrote in terms of social justice, believing that the state should not outlaw a practice that might help alleviate family misery. Those who condemned abortion tended to frame the argument in a similar way, worrying that abortion would lead families to neglect their responsibility to add to the population, or lead to the moral degeneration of society. For those who responded to this survey, abortion was not an individual matter, but a practice that shaped families, classes, and society as a whole.

## Meissner's Draft

In 1925, at the request of a conference of health workers, the Czechoslovak Ministry of Justice began its own investigation into the prosecution of abortion cases. Its research, which covered the years from 1925 through 1930, showed that at least some of the assumptions made by *Právo Lidu* readers were true. On average, very few women were actually prosecuted for abortion: about 800 women a year were indicted and 180 of them were found guilty. As the ministry acknowledged, however, abortion was much more common than that. The small percentage who wound up in court did so because someone turned them in for personal reasons, or they terminated the pregnancy at a very late stage, or, more likely, because they had suffered a botched procedure at the hands of a midwife or quack abortionist, forcing them to seek medical attention. Most of these women, a full 68 percent of those indicted and 80 percent of those convicted, were, in fact, from the working class. Those who could afford doctors willing to perform the procedure were very rarely discovered, making up only around 5 percent of cases.[46]

Even more interestingly, the Justice Ministry discovered that judges were loath to actually send women convicted of abortion to prison. On average, 90 percent of the women convicted under §144 during the years between 1925 and 1930 received suspended sentences. Judges were more likely to imprison midwives convicted of assisting in illegal abortions, but only about half of those found guilty served their sentences, which were always less than six months. Seeing that the law did seem to fall most heavily on poor women who had the ill fortune of falling into the hands of back-alley abortionists, and that judges weren't usually keen on putting such women in prison anyway, the Justice Ministry decided it was time for a change.[47] Under the direction of Justice Minister Alfréd Meissner, a Social Democrat, the ministry began working on a revision of §144. It was completed in June 1932, and sent, along with an explanatory text, to the other government ministries for review. The proposal was also given to a number of other government organizations, medical associations, prominent doctors and lawyers, and a few women's groups for their comments.

Although the Justice Ministry did not seem to realize it, its proposal was somewhat revolutionary. The proposed new law continued to ban abortion in principle, but also created new exceptions to that general rule. Physicians in public medical institutes would be legally able to perform abortions under any of the following circumstances: the life of the mother was in danger; the pregnancy was the result of rape; the pregnant woman was under sixteen years of age; the fetus was severely mentally or physically handicapped; or the birth would render the pregnant woman unable to support herself, the baby, or her living children. Health insurance companies would have to cover approved abortions and the uninsured would be eligible for state assistance. In addition, the penalties for abortion offenders would change substantially. A woman convicted of having an illegal abortion would be charged with a misdemeanor rather than a felony, and face a heavily reduced sentence of one to six months in jail. However, a person accused of assisting her would continue to face felony charges and stiffer penalties. Sentences would be highest for those convicted of performing illegal abortions for money, reaching up to five years of hard labor.[48]

This proposal, which became known as Meissner's draft, showed the influence of a number of trends that had been emerging since the 1920s. It treated abortion as an occasional social or medical necessity, not as an absolute moral wrong or unqualified right, an approach similar to the one taken by many *Právo Lidu* readers, who emphasized what they called social justice. Meissner's draft lifted the abortion issue out of the arena of individual rights and treated it as something that could only be evaluated in the context of a wider social reality. The proposal also presented illegal abortionists as more culpable than the women who sought their services. In the lines of this draft law, women were portrayed as victims, while the true culprits were the shadowy back-alley figures who performed abortions without a physician's approval or guidance. The new §144 aimed to regulate these shady characters by allowing trained doctors to become abortion's new gatekeepers. Any legal abortion would have to be performed by licensed physicians, who would also be largely responsible for determining whether or not a woman was eligible for an abortion under the new legal guidelines. Although it was not clear from the draft who would determine whether or not an abortion was "socially indicated" by a woman's financial situation, doctors would certainly figure prominently in such cases, as well.

In Meissner's discussion of the draft, he tried to present it as a moderate and carefully considered piece of legislation that rested on a firm scientific basis. In an October speech to a group of women from his own Social Democratic Party, Meissner claimed that he was personally against abortion in all circumstances. But personal feelings, he said, did not direct laws, and moral convictions could not always determine which acts should be criminally prosecuted. Many Czechs might consider suicide, drunkenness, or promiscuity to be immoral, but few would say they should be illegal. The Justice Ministry had decided that abortion really belonged to this category of offenses. Meissner stressed that ministry officials had taken their lead from prominent legal scholars. He particularly mentioned the 1925 congress of lawyers in Brno, where the idea of using "social indications" as a legal justification for abortion had been approved by many prominent figures in the legal community. Meissner also noted that recent laws in Yugoslavia mandated even lighter sentences for those convicted of abortion, and even Catholic Poland had legalized abortion in cases of medical necessity or rape.[49]

Initially, Meissner's moderate approach seemed capable of finding broad-based political support. Most of the groups that had been sent the original draft proposal responded with at least qualified approval of the Justice Ministry's plan. Of the other government ministries, only the Agrarian Party–led Ministry of Agriculture was categorically against the proposal, and its opposition was based on the belief that the entire penal code should be modernized at the same time, rather than in piecemeal fashion. The General Prosecutor's Office and Highest Court both welcomed the changes as legally necessary. The reactions of the various medical organizations were more mixed: most favored legalizing abortion in at least some medically indicated instances. A number of doctors' associations, however, were dubious about social and eugenic exceptions to prosecution, because they did not believe that doctors were capable of deciding when an abortion would be justified in these cases. Different reservations were raised by the Finance Ministry, Budget Office, and insurance industry, each of which was concerned about the financial impact of the plan, especially since it required insurance companies to pay for properly "indicated" abortions. Most of the other interest groups polled offered some measure of support, with the exception of the Federation of Catholic Women and Girls.[50]

According to a survey of Czechoslovakia's political parties conducted by the *Prager Tagblatt*, only the various Catholic parties (the German Christian Socialists, the People's Party, and the Slovak People's Party) were strongly opposed to Meissner's draft. Most other parties indicated tentative support for the proposal. Both the German and Czechoslovak Social Democratic parties responded that they would vote for the measure, though they commented that the draft did not liberalize the law as much as they would like. The National Socialists wrote that while their legal commission had not yet formally taken up the matter, they expected that it would follow the prevailing opinion in the party ranks, which was favorable toward Meissner's changes to abortion law. Rather remarkably, the outlook of the National Socialists was echoed by the center-right Commerce Party, as well as the heavily Catholic Czech Agrarian Party, which claimed that the "mood in its ranks was for the proposal in principle," though it might demand amendments. Further to the right in the political spectrum, the National Democrats stated that while their party had not yet taken a definite position, local conferences of party members were leaning toward opposing a liberalization of abortion law. On the extreme left, the Communists simply declared that they were for the complete repeal of §144. They did not tell the pollsters whether or not this would lead them to oppose a partial measure like the one at hand.[51]

A surprising majority of parties seemed poised to accept Meissner's draft. However, they also refused to firmly commit themselves, perhaps waiting to be convinced that supporting Meissner was the appropriate course of action. In contrast, the Catholic parties were vocal and direct in their opposition. They would fight attempts to make abortion legal under any circumstances. Their determination might have set the stage for a bitter battle over §144, but the Catholics' fervor lacked an appropriately ferocious opponent. Most of the other parties polled indicated only a tepid approval of Meissner's draft. Like all compromises, for some it was a stretch, for others it did not go far enough. Not one seemed willing to take ownership of the proposal and fight for its survival.

In the end, Meissner's own Social Democrats stood behind him. Leading women from that party became the most vocal supporters of the ministry's proposals, even though Meissner admitted in speeches that he was against the idea of free motherhood and declared that a socialist who was personally against abortion could still be a good socialist. Betty Karpíšková was a particularly prominent proponent of Meissner's draft. While she admitted that a more radical proposal would have suited her better, she saw this proposal as a positive step, especially its offer of state assistance to help poor women pay for abortions if they qualified for them.[52] Karpíšková wrote pamphlets, held meetings, and tried to rally working-class women in support of the ministry's proposal. For her, this was still an issue that combined feminist and socialist concerns. As a feminist, she emphasized the evils of what she called the "biological yoke" imposed on women by current abortion laws. She supported legal abortion as a way of liberating women from this "forced motherhood," demanding that the state recognize a woman's right to choose for herself when to have children. While she admitted that motherhood was a social responsibility for women, she declared that "a mature mother would only give birth for her own happiness" and not "at the dictate of policemen, moralizers, or bigoted clerics."[53] Karpíšková admitted that Meissner's draft did not represent state support of truly free motherhood, but she urged women from all parties to recognize that it was probably all they could reasonably expect to achieve in the current political climate.

However, in other moments, Karpíšková abandoned the bipartisan approach, making legal abortion sound very much like a class and party issue. She claimed that the bourgeoisie was behind Czechoslovakia's restrictive abortion laws, "demanding that the poor bear many children so that they can have enough cheap labor and so that the nation can increase numerically." She soundly berated almost every political party except for her own Social Democrats for not supporting Meissner strongly enough. She scoffed at the Agrarians, the Commerce Party, and the National Socialists for "only waiting" and not speaking out on behalf of Meissner's draft. "They are careful," she said, "either for bourgeois reasons tied to capitalism, or for reasons of population fanaticism." She also attacked the Communists, who finally decided to oppose Meissner's draft because it was not radical enough. Karpíšková's greatest ire, however, was reserved for conservative Catholics. Though she made a small attempt to reach out to religious women who might still be in favor of abortion, she mostly inveighed against the "stupid, medieval opinions of the Church on motherhood and the fetus." These attacks on the Church, other political parties, and the middle class undermined any attempt to bring a diverse group of women together in support of Meissner's proposal.

In fact, the strong link Karpíšková made between support for abortion rights and socialism only fueled the opposition. Catholic groups, who tended to react strongly to "godless" socialists, quickly characterized their drive against Meissner's draft as a fight against socialism as well as a battle to save the unborn. Legal abortion had already been popularly associated with the Soviet Union, which was the first and only European nation to have allowed abortion on demand. The newspaper of the People's Party labeled the Ministry's proposal "bolshevik" from its inception and urged its readers to combat this "Soviet legislation."[54] One Catholic commentator, Jan Richter, used this fear to make a rather surprising argument about how allowing abortion would hurt women's personal freedom. He complained that legal abortion could usher in a socialist totalitarian population regime, in which central offices would decide who could have children and when. He assumed that all women wanted to be mothers and was afraid that new abortion laws would create a reality in which they could no longer freely realize that dream. The revision of §144 threatened to undermine what Richter contended was the fundamental basis of democratic society: free will. In a democracy, a woman could decide for herself "if she wants to work her whole life, or have a family, or only a dog." Under socialism, the state threatened to make the choice for her. As a Catholic, Richter did not see abortion as something a woman might choose, just as he assumed she would have to pick either a career or a family. A woman used her free will up until the moment of conception, but not after.[55]

Karpíšková's pronouncements also got her into a battle with the Catholic philosopher and essayist Emanuel Rádl, who penned a number of articles and pamphlets against Meissner's draft. In stark contrast to Richter, Rádl criticized Karpíšková and her allies for emphasizing women's individual rights too much. A true socialist, Rádl said, should realize that all free individuals lived in a society and sometimes had to modify their personal desires to accommodate the needs of the collective good. To promote personal freedom above all else was anarchism, and, he remarked, "anarchists were the fundamental enemies of Social Democracy." Women, Rádl said, had a social duty to bear children that was "'more inalienable' than their personal rights." Rádl also attacked the socialist-feminist idea that women alone had jurisdiction over their unborn progeny. If women wanted men to have any responsibility for their living children, he noted, they had to admit that men had rights over the fetuses they carried as well.[56]

What troubled Rádl most, however, was the idea that women's rights over their bodies were more sacrosanct than the rights of fetuses to live. As a practicing Catholic, Rádl considered the fetus to be a living being from the moment of conception and characterized abortion as murder. For this reason, he was strongly against the idea of allowing "socially indicated" abortion, a term that he said merely put a "humanitarian cloak" over what was really just killing.[57] The idea that abortion in some circumstances could contribute to the greater social good was ridiculous to him. In his view, the real way to improve the life of the community was to combat the sexual immorality that had infected society, leading people into the thrall of their baser instincts and spawning approval for inhumane practices like abortion. Fighting Meissner's draft was working to cure this "social disease." It was, therefore, more than just a battle over a law. To oppose changes to §144 "was about progressive ideals, justice for the weak, faith in the power of the soul over the body and holding on to the natural foundations of life."[58]

Rádl's defense of fetal rights and his moral condemnation of abortion was popular among Catholic activists, all of whom loudly denounced Meissner's draft. Catholic women's groups like the Federation of Catholic Women and Girls exhorted their numerous members to fight against any changes to §144.[59] A typical appeal in a Catholic women's magazine declared, "abortion was a low act on a defenseless being," and charged that it violated the unborn child's right to life. But even here the concern was not only with the fate of the individual fetus, but also with how abortion would affect society as a whole. The author warned that legalizing abortion could have dire consequences, since "even great empires have fallen because of bad laws." Abortion threatened society by tempting women away from their natural responsibilities as mothers and wives. Women tried to deny their maternity by using contraception and having abortions, but only received "cancerous inflammations" and "psychological tortures" in return. Instead of the poor, desperate housewife held up by the Social Democrats, here was a woman who pursued ease and freedom, hoping to "use the world and not slave for a family." She was not a helpless victim who needed state assistance. Rather, she was a self-serving schemer who ignored her own social responsibilities, threatening "national honor, humane behavior, and pure, sacred marriage."[60] In this kind of rhetoric, abortion was reframed as a threat, not merely to one fetus, but to motherhood itself. By giving women the opportunity to reject the identity of wife/mother, abortion represented an attack on the entire gendered structure of society. It was a blow to a lifestyle and set of values that many, if not most, Czechs considered to be the natural order of things.

In the end, Catholic resistance proved decisive for the fate of Meissner's draft. The People's Party was part of the government in 1932 and it had enough weight to make sure that the proposal never left the interministerial commission to which it had been sent for review. The newspaper of the People's Party implied that tabling the draft had been relatively easy, and that members of the government coalition were secretly pleased. In fact, the article charged, Meissner had never wanted or expected to see the law changed; he only authorized the draft of a new §144 to appease the women in the Social Democratic Party.[61] Whether or not this was the case, abortion law was obviously not a large priority for the non-Catholic parties in the governing coalition, which included the Social Democrats, German Social Democrats, and Agrarians. While each of these groups initially indicated that they might have been willing to support the proposal, none proved willing to press their case with the Catholics.

The Justice Ministry's failure to liberalize abortion law in 1932 did not mean that the issue died. Socialist women, especially Social Democrats, continued to agitate for legal abortion. Betty Karpíšková, in particular, remained a firm champion of abortion rights and often wrote about §144 in *Ženské Noviny*. She also founded a society to promote birth control and abortion. However, it became clear even to these women activists that they could never reach their goal as long as Catholic parties remained a strong presence in the government. As one article declared, "poor women will remain the victims of back-alley abortionists as long as the political influence [of Catholic bishops] is not broken."[62] After seeing the fracas caused by Meissner's draft, no Czechoslovak politician from within the governing coalition was willing to try loosening the legal restrictions on abortion. Paragraph 144 remained as it was throughout the lifespan of the First Czechoslovak Republic.

## Abortion and the Czech Feminist Movement

Many of the loudest voices in the debate over Meissner's draft belonged to Social Democratic women and Catholics, and each group did its best to shape the debate over §144 into a fight between "bolsheviks" and "clericals." Through all of this, Czech feminist groups like the WNC remained uncharacteristically silent. The WNC's journal scarcely mentioned Meissner's draft. The group did not sponsor petitions or letter-writing campaigns either for or against changes to §144. Outspoken WNC leaders like Františka Plamínková made no speeches on the issue. As Božena Trávníčková noted in the journal *Ženský Obzor* (Women's Horizon), Meissner's draft had "awakened far less interest in women's circles than government attempts to balance the state budget by firing married female state employees." Trávníčková put this down to hard economic times, which made the "fight for a piece of bread . . . take precedence over all other questions, even those more personally relevant, as women's maternity undoubtedly is."[63] But this reason was not very convincing, considering that women's groups were still concerned with changing the Czechoslovak civil code, an issue that had little to do with women's access to employment opportunities.

A more plausible reason was that groups that had come together to work on issues like women's right to equal employment and equality in civil law simply did not agree on §144. The socialist-feminist argument that women had the right to bodily self-determination shared an intellectual foundation with Czech feminist calls for women's equality in Czechoslovak state law. Yet many women who supported women's rights in other areas did not agree with the more radical conception of individual freedom put forth by socialists like Betty Karpíšková and Luisa Landová-Štychová. Trávníčková, for example, was against legal abortion in all cases except where the life of the mother was in danger. In her article on §144, Trávníčková blended themes of equality and responsibility when it came to family life and sexual relations. She believed that women should have equal rights within their families and recognized a wife's right to "liberate herself from unending maternity, that racks her body and absorbs all elements of her life." However, she also exhorted women to remember their unique responsibilities to their nation to bear and raise children and to maintain the moral standards of the community. The latter concern precluded using abortion, which Trávníčková equated with murder, as a means of limiting family size. In her opinion, the only morally responsible method for that was sexual abstinence. She endorsed sublimating the sexual drive as a way of bringing the soul to a higher, more cultured, and more refined plane. Her views paralleled those of Tomáš Masaryk, who rejected sexual liberation and advocated abstinence instead of abortion. They also echoed Emanuel Rádl, who wrote that the fight for women's equality was supposed to bring men up to women's higher moral level, not give women the license to take on men's vices. Feminism was about freeing women to do good for their country, not freeing their sexuality.[64]

Many of the organizations in the WNC federation adhered to similar views. The WNC was initially asked by the Justice Ministry for input on Meissner's draft, and its central office sent out a questionnaire to some of its member organizations, primarily those that worked on women's health issues. Those who responded were split. Only one response (and the only one from an individual rather than a group) was in favor of legalizing abortion in all circumstances. Some groups, like the Organization of Midwives from Moravian Silesia and Slovakia, were against all abortions because they felt they lowered national health and threatened the stability of the population. Others, like the Czechoslovak Association of University Women, accepted Meissner's draft in principle, but had quibbles with it. The Association of University Women did not like the stipulation that legal abortions would be covered by health insurance, which they felt would only encourage an essentially immoral practice. Instead, they wanted to see contraceptive information and devices covered by insurance policies.[65]

The head of the WNC's legal committee, Milada Králová-Horáková, had her own problems with Meissner's draft. As a lawyer, she felt that the idea of vetting abortions according to some ill-defined set of social indications was ridiculously vague and she wondered how anyone would determine the criteria for judging the cases. But Králová-Horáková's bigger objection was that the new law did not consider women capable of judging for themselves what was right for their bodies. She noted that there were only two legal instances in which citizens were denied the right to freely control their bodies and both were gendered: the law requiring military service for men, and §144. While she did not give her opinion on military service, she did argue for completely abolishing §144, and for establishing publicly funded family planning centers that would dispense contraceptives.[66] WNC president Františka Plamínková did not condone abortion as a moral practice, but she was a pragmatist and believed that getting women out of the clutches of back-alley abortionists was the most important goal. Only fully legal abortion would make women comfortable enough to see a doctor if they feared they were pregnant and did not want to be.[67]

However, as Králová-Horáková realized, in this case the views of the WNC leadership did not match those of their member organizations. Considering this, she thought it best to put off legal abortion for "a future time in our evolution."[68] As a compromise, the WNC legal committee sent a statement to the Ministry of Justice that accepted Meissner's draft and offered suggestions for some minor amendments. The letter noted that a "substantial minority" within the WNC wanted a more complete legalization of abortion and believed that only free motherhood could lessen the numbers of children who suffered from poverty or the lack of a loving home. But it could not present this position as the opinion of the organization as a whole. Because the issue was so contentious, the WNC also decided to invite its member organizations to submit their own suggestions to the Justice Ministry if they had a substantially different viewpoint.[69] This was quite a concession, since the group generally discouraged this in order to present a strong, united front. This indicates that §144 was an issue that confounded the WNC, and hints at the reason they failed to do much in the battle over Meissner's draft. They simply saw no way of building a consensus between members who had such different ideas about abortion, and did not want to dissolve their coalition over it. In any case, to the mostly middle-class, professional women whose organizations dominated the WNC, abortion laws may not have seemed worth the fight, especially since professional women were rarely prosecuted under §144.[70] If the members would not support the action, the WNC presidium could not initiate it.

THE FIGHT OVER §144 reveals, most of all, how deeply the tropes of family, duty, and responsibility were embedded in Czech political culture and how these ideals clashed with competing discourses of rights and equality. In this instance, the rights-based arguments that Czech feminists used in other venues found few adherents, even among the feminists themselves. Women like Betty Karpíšková, who advocated abortion as a woman's right to control her own body, found themselves marginalized, even among their own socialist allies. For women to talk about individual rights in the context of pregnancy was seen as either immoral or selfish, a radical refusal of womanhood that threatened the very basis of the social order. Even women who had fought for changing the civil code to reflect the status of women as equal citizens found themselves unable to transfer those concepts to a pregnant body. Legalizing abortion as a woman's right went much further than granting women the same civil rights as men. The latter gave wives and mothers an equal standing within their families, but the former had a much more radical potential. It would have enabled women to refuse motherhood at will, even within marriage, and to place their own individual interests even more firmly above their family's.

The debates over abortion in the Czech lands show most Czechs favoring the collective interest of the family and the state or nation over the interests of individuals. Quite strikingly, this holds true across the political spectrum. The majority of those on either side of the struggle over §144 argued in terms of abortion's effects on a larger social good. From medical professionals who feared abortion's impact on public health and nationalists worried about a falling population to workers who believed that large families were oppressing the working class and left-leaning bureaucrats in the Justice Ministry concerned about poverty, the emphasis was placed on the needs of society over the needs of individuals. Even many Catholic activists, who decried abortion as murder, spoke in terms of the moral degradation that would come from legalization and the potential impact of abortion on women's willingness to perform their appropriate roles as wives and mothers. It was a similar social concern that motivated Alfred Meissner, who personally opposed abortion, to advocate its legalization where it could promote the formation of strong families. This indicates that these categories of family and nation were pivotal in people's thinking about what was politically right and just.

In this, the Czechs were also not so far away from other Europeans. Czech attitudes toward abortion seemed close to those of many Germans —both the Social Democrats who called abortion a scourge of the working class and the doctors and social workers who argued for or against abortion in terms of its effects on the national body.[71] However, as in the case of Germany, such attitudes also had a problematic side. While they were not, of course, inherently pernicious, they also showed a set of points where democratic ideals became vulnerable. In the case of abortion, the waters were muddied. Since it was a case where the rights of the individual were themselves debatable (who was the rights-bearing individual in a pregnancy?), it seemed a fair compromise to defer to the needs of some larger collective. But if the nation or the family was indeed more important than the individual, then there might come a time when other rights might be sacrificed for the common good.

# 6

## WOMEN AND POLITICS IN THE
## CZECH LANDS AFTER MUNICH

Democracy is not easy. Democracy demands the re-education of all of us: it demands internal discipline so that we—individuals in a family, in society, in a political party, in a nation or a state—can restrain ourselves from that which irritates or upsets others, so that as a society we can create the preconditions for calm, genial understanding! And over this all, in the depths of our convictions must be: that everyone has the same right to life and that no one can take this right, that would mean to sin against the principle of life itself. We are all, all of humanity, on one ship, which either we will all steer together—or we will all drown.

Františka Plamínková, *Ženská Rada*, 1938

In MARCH 1937, readers of the political-cultural weekly *Přítomnost* were treated to an exposé on the fate of German women under Nazism. The author, Bedřich Pilč, claimed that large numbers of women had initially been drawn to the Nazi Party precisely because Nazi leaders declared they would deprive them of all the rights they had gained under the Weimar regime. These women leapt at the chance to trade equality in public life for the opportunity to be "sovereign queens" in their own domestic realm. However, they soon discovered that they had been tricked into a situation that spiraled rapidly out of their control, leaving them the powerless subjects of the male-dominated state. Their roles as mothers and nurturers were systematically undercut by the party, which forced children into the Hitler Youth and League of German Girls. At the same time, the state tried to manage their domestic activities by forcing them to participate in endless campaigns to collect everything from metal and rags to vegetable peelings. It put their homes under surveillance, urging their servants, landladies, and even children to monitor their willingness to comply with state directives. Pilč described women who felt like virtual prisoners in their own homes, chided by nosy neighbors for wasting national property when they peeled the potatoes too thickly and threatened by their children when they neglected to greet them with an enthusiastic "Heil Hitler."[1]

The world Pilč described was a horrible dystopia, where the reality of gendered inequalities turned out to only be oppression. It was a world, however, that he characterized as a peculiar aberration of Nazism, quoting Heinrich Mann to note that the Third Reich was the only state that had "dared to treat women in this manner." While Pilč did not make direct comparisons between Germany and Czechoslovakia in his article, the Czechoslovak Republic was silently held up as counterexample, a state where women could still practice their professions, educate their children as they saw fit, and not worry about being imprisoned for their political views. His essay is less a warning to Czechs about the dangers of attacking women's rights than a condemnation of foreign barbarity. But the idea that had attracted German women (and men) to the Nazi Party—a social order that traded equality for stability and abandoned universal individual freedoms for the good of the family and the nation—was one that also had considerable appeal for Czechs. In some instances, such as the fight over the civil code and in the battle over the double earners, Czech support for what Pilč rather contemptuously called "the anti-emancipation movement" had legal consequences, which limited Czech women's access to the benefits of citizenship. While this had certainly not reached the levels it had in Nazi Germany, it did show a certain ideological connection between the political thinking of Czechs and Germans, particularly those on the political right. While this connection was very muted in 1937, it would come to the fore much more forcefully after the Munich Conference of 1938.

## How to Build a Second Republic

In the late 1930s, the Czechoslovak Republic faced a long list of political and economic troubles. In the face of a weak economy, problems between the country's different national groups grew in intensity. The animosity was particularly bitter between Czechs and Germans. Czechoslovakia's large German minority had been a political pressure point since the founding of the state in 1918, but the situation became increasingly serious during the 1930s, when many Czechoslovak Germans drifted politically toward the radical right, influenced by the spread of ultra-nationalism and fascism throughout Europe. They manifested their political sentiments by supporting Konrad Henlein's Sudeten German Party (Sudetendeutsche Partei, or SdP). By 1935, the SdP had emerged as the single most popular party in all of Czechoslovakia, winning 67 percent of the total German vote in parliamentary elections and gaining forty-four seats in the National Assembly.[2] The rise of the SdP highlighted the inherent instability of a Czechoslovak Republic that tried simultaneously to be both an egalitarian and a national state.

The country was not, however, actually ripped apart from within, but from without. With the active support of Nazi Germany, Henlein and his supporters mounted international protests claiming that Germans forced to live in the Czechoslovak state were being unfairly oppressed. He demanded that those areas of Czechoslovakia with a German majority (the region known as the Sudetenland) be allowed to secede and join the German Reich. In the fall of 1938, Hitler responded with an ultimatum requiring Czechoslovakia to surrender the Sudetenland to Germany. At a conference of European leaders in Munich, he managed to convince France and Britain, Czechoslovakia's West European allies, to support him in this demand. Czechoslovakia was presented with a completed agreement and pressed to agree to its terms. Czechoslovak president Edvard Beneš reluctantly signed the Munich settlement rather than go to war without the support of his Western allies, and on October 1, 1938, the Sudetenland became part of Germany.[3]

It was the diplomatic defeat of Munich that shattered the Czechoslovak Republic. The surrender of the Sudetenland, which not only ceded territory but left Czechoslovakia militarily open to attack from the west, turned the masses against their government. Beneš, forced to resign, fled the country, while the democracy he represented was jettisoned in favor of something that would do a better job of protecting national interests.[4] As George F. Kennan, then Secretary of Legation for the United States in Prague, wrote in a letter of December 1938, "Everything which had any powers of cohesion went by the boards. Nothing was left in the popular mind but bitterness, bewilderment, and skepticism. Every feature of liberalism and democracy, in particular, was hopelessly and irretrievably discredited."[5] Many thought that the only hope for their state lay in some kind of radical political change, believing, like the historian František Kutnar, that Czechoslovakia "must be [made] new in every way—this is the only path out of the crisis."[6]

In October 1938, it seemed to most Czechs that only the political Right could possibly achieve the kind of regeneration Kutnar envisioned. Riding this wave, the conservative wing of the Czech right, led by Agrarian Party chief Rudolf Beran, quickly took power. To symbolize their distance from pre-Munich Czechoslovakia, the Beran government announced that the Czechoslovak Republic of 1918 was dead, and declared the beginning of a Second Czechoslovak Republic, which would be built upon a completely new ideological foundation. Its primary political task would not be to promote democracy or to protect the equality and freedom of its citizens, but to defend the Czech nation against further threats to its sovereignty. Czechoslovakia's new leaders regarded the national community with an almost religious devotion and pledged themselves to its protection at all costs. As Rudolf Halík, the editor of the Agrarian Party daily *Venkov* (The Countryside) declared, the Czechs needed get rid of "partisanship, class prejudice, ideology, broken forms of thought. We will cast off oversensitive humanism and consideration for foreigners. We are a national state and we will cleanse [our] sacred nation from foreign elements. We will only take care of ourselves, we will not suffer encumbrances in our national sanctuary again."[7] For Czechoslovakia's new leaders, the state was now primarily a mechanism for serving the Czech (and/or Slovak) nation(s), and the rights it granted its citizens became dependent on their place in the nation.[8]

Czechoslovakia's new leaders did not believe that liberal democracy had the power to defend the nation, but they did not advocate turning to fascism. Instead, they proposed a Czech "third way" that would merge elements of both systems in something they called "authoritarian democracy."[9] The proponents of this paradoxically named new system claimed that their plan was merely to create a different democracy, one that worked. Halík presented the "authoritarian" character of this new political ideology as a benign way of streamlining government, declaring that it would have nothing in common with "totalitarianism."[10] However, when Beran and his Agrarian Party allies began to thrash out the specifics of this new approach to government, it became clear that this new politics took significant inspiration from fascist regimes. An article entitled "How to Build a Second Republic," published in *Brázda* (The Furrow), the mouthpiece of a group of young Agrarian intellectuals, clearly indicated the tone and direction of the new regime.[11] This article was not an official policy proclamation, but it was certainly taken as such by contemporaries. Most major Czech dailies and political journals published some response to its proposals. Almost all were approving.[12]

In the *Brázda* program, authoritarianism was the only way to save the Czechs from national extinction. "We must," the authors declared, "concentrate [our] positive national strengths to create a single national will, on which it will be possible to base an authoritarian government, socially just and controlled, so that we can quickly, thoroughly and efficiently realize the program of national renewal."[13] The first step was, as Halík had also noted, to purge the nation of "foreign elements." As the authors wrote, "the smaller the living space of a people, the more pure its cultural forms and public activities must be." They therefore recommended expelling all (legal and illegal) aliens and revoking the citizenship of anyone who had been naturalized since 1918. While the authors stated that Czechoslovakia's German, Hungarian, Romanian, and Polish minorities should retain their citizenship rights, they recommended that the state direct these groups toward developing more exclusive relations with their own national communities. Jewish citizens would also be allowed to stay, but would be excluded from participating in "non-Jewish" media or politics.

In pursuit of national regeneration, the *Brázda* program advocated a number of policies commonly associated with the European radical Right, including disbanding the Czechoslovak National Assembly, banning political parties, and centralizing nongovernmental groups and organizations under state or national auspices (a process even the Czechs referred to as *Gleichschaltung* or *"zglajchšaltování"*). Their ideas for social policy were also directly inspired by the radical Right elsewhere in Europe, especially Germany and Italy.[14] The *Brázda* group demanded a social politics that was national in focus, concerned primarily with protecting a specific form of family life that they judged crucial for the survival of the Czech nation. This concept of "the family" was grounded in a traditional notion of masculine-feminine relations: a heterosexual couple and their offspring, whose communal life operated according to a gendered division of labor. To encourage the proliferation of such families, the *Brázda* authors demanded that the state guarantee a proper "family wage" to male heads of households and ban wives from the labor market. They also suggested encouraging marriage by levying special taxes on single adults and using the revenues to fund low-interest loans for couples who wished to marry and establish a family—with the proviso, as in Germany, that after marriage the new wife would agree to be supported by her husband. Other financial incentives, like subsidized housing, would encourage women to fulfill themselves by working for their families instead of for wages. The educational system was to take a hand here, directing girls into schools of domestic education to prepare them for their roles as wives and mothers. The numbers of women admitted to university study would be strictly limited. Schools and the media would play a key role in enforcing this family policy. Anything "which undermine[d] the moral basis of the family [would] be removed from the school system, legislation and public culture."[15]

Though the *Brázda* article was only a political wish list, the new government of the Second Republic (dominated by *Brázda*'s Agrarian Party), would indeed move to implement a number of its demands, and, more importantly, to adopt its political philosophy.[16] Czech politicians signaled their acceptance of this set of political values by agreeing to a radical transformation of the party system and allowing the powers of Czechoslovakia's legislative institutions to be sharply curtailed in favor of the executive branch. Two new mass parties were created: the government-sponsored National Unity Party, which most parties voted to join, and the opposition National Labor Party composed only of the Social Democrats and a few renegade Czech National Socialists. In addition, the Communist Party was banned and an Enabling Law, which allowed rule by emergency decree, was rammed through the National Assembly.[17] Beran also hoped to neutralize the largely unofficial power of the presidency by installing Emil Hácha, an elderly jurist with no political experience, in that office. Other areas of public life were also affected. Cultural organizations, professional groups, and national societies were asked to liquidate and merge into new mass organizations allied with the state, gathering their strength for the nation's defense.[18]

## The Realities of the New Regime

With the birth of the Second Republic, the egalitarian language that had been prominent in Czech political discourse before 1938 gave way to a politics more exclusively based on difference. In place of Masaryk's humanism, the Second Republic emphasized a more collective philosophy, in which the needs of the nation took precedence over the rights of individual citizens. This shift had enormous ramifications for all Czechoslovak citizens, who could now find their political and civil rights means-tested against their benefit to the nation. Czechoslovakia's Jews were among the first to find that their citizenship no longer offered them the same protections it had in the past. Whether out of sincere conviction or to prove to the Nazis that they could be ideologically correct neighbors, the Czechoslovak government initiated its own anti-Jewish legislation in January 1939. All Jews employed in the civil service were fired or pensioned off and Jewish access to universities was limited.[19]

These acts were justified by locating Jews outside the Czech(oslovak) national community, but national priorities could be used to attack the rights of Czechs as well. As the *Brázda* program made clear, the Second Republic was founded to protect a nation that was deeply gendered. Czech women did not belong to that nation as equal citizens; they served it as wives and mothers. This increased emphasis on gender difference was even included in founding program of the new Party of National Unity, which stated, "The family will become the reliable basis of national life. We will return women to their occupation, maternal happiness, a quiet home, and a working husband."[20]

Shortly after Munich, the Beran government made plans to finally put a new civil code into effect, using the new Enabling Act to present it as a government decree. However, as Jaromír Sedláček, a former member of the super-revisory committee, noted in a letter to the Ministry of Justice, it was important that some revisions to the old version be made first. In particular, he said, the family law sections of the code should be updated to fit the "radical turn-around" that had occurred in the way the state regarded the position of women in the family. Evidently in agreement with this turn of events, Sedláček was especially concerned that wives who wanted to dedicate themselves to their families receive more legal protection. Because, as he reminded the ministry, "the family is a matter of serious significance for us and the future of our nation depends on a proper solution."[21]

Before the civil code could be finalized, however, the Beran regime moved to settle another long-standing dispute: the issue of the double earners. On December 21, 1938, the government passed two resolutions that revolutionized the place of married women in the civil service. According to the first, married women would be given the opportunity to voluntarily leave their jobs or go into retirement before January 16, 1939.[22] Those who left of their own accord would receive severance pay or pension benefits. After that date, all married female civil servants whose husbands earned anything over a set minimum could be fired.[23] Women whose husbands' assets did not reach this minimum could possibly retain their jobs, but their cases would be evaluated by a special commission. Women whose salaries were not considered necessary for the basic maintenance of their family could also be dismissed, regardless of the income level of their husband. Finally, all single, female employees who got married would be given a month's notice, without exception. The second of the resolutions cut the pension benefits of married female retirees in half if the woman had a spouse who received any pension or salary from the state, no matter what its amount.[24]

For the feminists of the Women's National Council, the implementation of these resolutions represented an utter betrayal of their beloved democracy and the Czech nation. In a draft of a protest letter penned by Horáková at Plamínková's direction, the WNC declared that only the democratic ideals of the First Republic could reinvigorate the severely tested state. The authors charged that undermining these principles was not just a politically suspect act, but a national crime, and that the Beran government had proven itself to be even worse than the Habsburgs. Not only had it instituted a *celibát* more restrictive than anything the Austrian state had ever produced, it was, they said, "murdering the pioneering work of the best Czech men and women and destroying their legacy, which should have been protected for your daughters." But the women of the WNC were clinging to a set of values that had fallen from public favor, and their reaction was not remotely typical of the rest of the population. In the political and spiritual climate of the Second Republic, the good of the national community carried much more weight than ideals of equality. Even those who criticized the Beran government in other areas, including the editors of the staunchly democratic *Přítomnost,* supported firing married women from the civil service.[25] In the largely anti-Beran journal *Sobota* (Saturday), an anonymous author bemoaned attacks on Jewish civil rights as a "loss of national civility," yet advocated restrictions on married women's right to work as a form of social justice.[26] Few seemed concerned with protecting the right of women to work unless the resolutions affected them personally. It was a far cry from 1919, when politicians and public alike, regardless of their personal situations, acclaimed the democratic principles behind lifting the *celibát.* In 1938, most people believed that wives should not be working, and that the government was right to force them not to do so.

Many people did write to their government to protest the resolutions, but most of these letters only objected that many married women *had* to work, complaining that the loss of the extra income would create financial disaster for them and their families. These writers showed little concern for how the resolutions would affect others, much less how they might harm something intangible like rights. As one woman, who identified herself only as "a desperate mother" wrote, "In a large majority of households where the wife is in state service her husband is also gainfully employed or the family is otherwise economically secure. In this case, firing women from the state service is quite proper and will not have any great consequences, even if they [the family of the fired woman] would sometimes have to scrimp." She went on to explain that this was not the case for *her,* and that her family really counted on her paycheck to pay the rent and not just to purchase luxuries.[27] Like many others who wrote in, her assessment of who should be allowed to work was based solely on a criteria of need. Many prefaced their appeals to be allowed to remain on the job by remarking that they would be embarrassed or ashamed to work if they did not truly need their earnings to feed their families. Very few would admit to believing that some women might find more personal fulfillment on the job than in the home.[28]

This attitude that the right of women to work was contingent upon their need for the money they would earn was so prevalent that it was even shared by Milena Jesenská, a Czech journalist and member of the avant-garde scene in Prague, perhaps best known as Franz Kafka's friend and Czech translator. Covering the subject for the journal *Přítomnost*, Jesenská presented objections to excluding married women from the workforce, but based them largely on financial grounds. If wives were not allowed to work, she wrote, most couples would not be able to afford to marry, and marriage would become a luxury available only to the wealthy. She dryly commented that such a state of affairs would not have the hoped for effect on public morality. Even for an "emancipated" woman like Jesenská, the question in 1938 was simply a question of need—a modern marriage needed two incomes to survive—and not a matter of rights. "There was a time," she recalled in her article, "when people spoke of women's emancipation, about the equality of women and fighters for women's rights. But those times are long gone."[29]

## The Czech Women's Movement in the Post-Munich Era

For the feminists in the Women's National Council, the shifting ideological climate in the newly truncated Czechoslovakia was cause for despair, but other groups within the spectrum of the Czech women's movement saw the Second Republic as an opportunity. Although the Women's National Council had achieved a leading role in the Czech women's movement, it was never the only voice on gender issues. Throughout the First Republic there had been disputes between what might be termed the "separate" and the "equal" camps of the Czech women's movement, as those who espoused a more maternalist ideology clashed with those who advocated a more classically liberal version of equality. While the groups sometimes worked together, differences over divorce law, family law, and policies toward working women remained, exacerbating the divisions between the different sides. The feminist wing headed by the WNC initially had the upper hand in these battles, but support for policies that would protect traditional gender roles increased as the economic and political crises facing Czechoslovakia began to deepen.

During the First Republic, policies that limited women's individual rights in deference to their gender achieved only limited government support, despite their large popular base. This was due in no small part to the determined lobbying efforts of the WNC and the amount of influence its leaders enjoyed in political circles, especially their strong relationship with presidents Masaryk and Beneš. The fall of that regime, however, gave other women's groups reason to hope that their demands might be realized. In the opinion of these more "difference oriented" women, the Munich defeat justified their agenda of supporting the traditional family. Munich had discredited the old regime, and with it its feminist allies. Certainly, in the view of these women, the feminists' emphasis on rights and equality had not been successful in guaranteeing the security of the family. WNC leaders, like other First Republic officials, should step down from their positions so that their organization could be "reoriented" to the new realities of the Second Republic.

The move to revamp the WNC was led by women who had been active in the world of secular women's organizations and who had worked in groups that were part of the WNC federation. The campaign was headed by Marie Tumlířová, a parliamentary representative for the Agrarian Party and the long-standing president of the Czechoslovak Association of University Women. Tumlířová had a long record of cooperation with the WNC in both of these capacities, though she had never served as one of its functionaries. In the 1930s, Tumlířová had pressed the Association of University Women to work closely with the WNC on the issues of protecting women's right to work and equal opportunities for professional advancement.[30] Although she and Františka Plamínková came from different sides of the political spectrum, Tumlířová had publicly expressed respect for the WNC leader, calling her the "speaker of the history of the women's movement of her era" as well as the "teacher of a generation," and wished that "her vibrant example would continue to teach for a long time and that the burning sparks of her pure flame would ignite the souls of many members of the next generation with the same pure flare in the fight for the victory of justice."[31]

But the tragic events of 1938 convinced Tumlířová that Plamínková's legacy would be better left with the past of the women's movement and not associated with its future. In the weeks after the Munich decision, she and some other members of the Association of University Women, notably Alžběta Birnbaumová and Růžena Bednáříková-Turnwaldová, decided to oust Plamínková from her post and take over the leadership of the WNC. Initially, they tried to convince the executive board of the WNC to ask Plamínková to step down, but the members of the WNC presidium refused and instead demanded that she stay in her post. After other attempts to force Plamínková to resign also failed, Tumlířová's group decided it would be better to start a competing organization, which they hoped would replace the WNC in Czech politics.[32]

Tumlířová and her friends immediately contacted Prime Minister Beran, writing in the name of the Czechoslovak Association of University Women. They explained that they wanted to create a new organizational center for the Czech women's movement and asked for the government's assistance.[33] The government encouraged the group to form a new "Women's Center" within the auspices of an existing organization, the Czech National Council (Ústředí Žen při České Národní Radě). This Czech National Council was not formally part of the state, but the Beran regime had quasi-officially assigned it the job of "coordinating" national life during the process of *Gleichschaltung* it sponsored in the weeks after Munich, making it, in effect, part of the cultural arm of the regime. Ensconced within the Czech National Council, the founders of the new "Women's Center" could easily envision their new group as an "official" sort of institution that would have a direct influence on state policy. They pictured themselves working in concert with the Beran government to mold women's place in the new state, developing programs and policies to shape a new woman's sphere within the reinvigorated Czech nation.

While the founders of the new Women's Center supported the rhetoric of national defense promulgated by their leaders, they definitely had their own agenda. These were not docile housewives, but educated professionals, experienced politicians, and veterans of the women's movement. They had not retreated to their houses, but acted decisively to position themselves in what they hoped would be an authoritative place from which to direct women's participation in the new regime. Early policy statements make it clear that the women behind the Women's Center believed that Czech women had a strong and positive public role to play in the project of national renewal. They described their mission as enabling women to "develop their personalities in biological, economic, social, and intellectual respects for the good of the nation."[34] Such remarks indicate that, like the democratically oriented women's movement it sought to replace, the Women's Center's goal was to create a powerful space for women in public life. But unlike the feminist movement of the First Republic, the Women's Center fought for women's participation in national life on gendered terms. The new group urged women to concentrate on their own special qualities and talents, helping them to develop their own distinct feminine sphere within Czech society. As its leaders declared, "Women and men are two different beings and must follow two different paths to the same goal . . . the protection of national self-determination." Their declaration added that, "in the present era, woman must present herself in a truly feminine way, that is, to be able to support the male part of the nation in the moment of eventual despair and loss of courage. Thus woman must start from the framework of her family, so that she can carry her maternal calm into public life."[35]

Statements such as this show the delicate balancing act the leaders of the Women's Center attempted to play. Although they rejected egalitarian ideals in favor of glorifying gender difference, they still believed that women deserved an equivalent status to men. They exhorted women to act like women: to develop their "natural" talents for caring and nurturing and concentrate on helping their families, raising their children, and supporting their husbands rather than competing with them. Yet at the same time, they did not see these feminine talents as inferior to men's capabilities; indeed, they declared that the comforting, nurturing qualities of women were the most crucial asset the nation possessed. And while the members of the Women's Center glorified maternity as the essence of a woman's being, they never characterized motherhood as something that should keep women closeted at home. Instead, they looked at the capacity for motherhood as a woman's point of entrance into public life. As mothers, women would bring something special to politics. They would keep political dealings moral, and their special insight could be used to ensure that only the policies best for the nation's future would be enacted.[36]

In contrast to the *Brázda* program, the Women's Center refused to accept a subordinate position in society and vigorously demanded that women receive equal status and social value for the work they did, even as it agreed that women's work should be distinct from men's. This attitude was very apparent from the way in which the group organized itself and defined its tasks in the late fall and winter of 1938–1939. Its work would be broad in scope, with sections devoted to (decidedly unfeminine) political and "national-economic" concerns, as well as social and "cultural-moral" matters. The mission statements of each section made it clear that the Women's Center did not see women's place in the new state as bounded by the kitchen and the nursery. The political division declared that its primary goal was "to make new efforts so that women, as the larger half of the nation, will retain their political rights of representation in all public/legal bodies and institutions."[37] While it was implied in this statement that it would be the Women's Center that would have the job of representing women politically, it was also clear that its leaders did not intend for women to be powerless in the political sphere.[38]

In a similar vein, the economic section also emphasized policies that would maintain and not undermine women's independence. Its goal was to increase the value accorded to women's work, both within the household and outside of it. Part of this division's mandate was to find and promote occupations that seemed especially appropriate for women, "suited to their mentality and in agreement with the needs of the state and the nation."[39] Housework and child-rearing were prominent among these occupations, but the Women's Center also took seriously the problem of finding employment opportunities for women and developing "feminine" industries where women could be dominant and not compete directly with men.

The fields they suggested were usually related to domestic tasks and included things like midwifery, the production of luxury goods (such as porcelain or glass), confectionery, cooking, nutrition, massage, and hotel administration.[40] Not surprisingly for a group composed mostly of highly educated women, they stressed providing women with formal training in their sphere of work. They wanted to see women treated as skilled professionals and not as cheap labor or powerless wives, whether those women worked for wages or in their own homes.

The economic program of the Women's Center vividly illustrates the ways in which Czech women of the Right both accepted and challenged the ideological basis of the Second Republic and its new version of citizenship. The leaders of the Women's Center explicitly declared that men and women were not equally suited to the same jobs, and so agreed, to a point, with the regime's policy of firing married women from some professions to make way for unemployed men. Their acceptance of gender difference, however, did not translate into acceptance of economic dependence or subordination. The leaders of the Women's Center hoped that the national crisis might lead to a reevaluation of tasks often denigrated as "women's work," giving women's occupations an equivalent power and status to those of men. In a manner reminiscent of rightist women all over Europe, their hope was that acceptance and glorification of women's difference from men would finally bring women an equal position in society.[41]

WNC leaders found out about the new group when some of their colleagues were asked to join it. As the WNC went over its options during the turbulent spring of 1939, its leaders initially considered cooperating with or even joining the Women's Center. As political circumstances rapidly changed in the Czech lands, it was not clear what kind of organizational activity would be allowed, and some members of the WNC board worried that the organization would have to join the Women's Center in order to remain legally operational. Indeed, noises from government officials seemed to indicate that as a likely possibility. But others expressed concern that cooperating with the Women's Center would mean selling out the ideals and mission of the WNC. Among the latter group was Milada Horáková, who declared that the WNC should "remain pure" at all costs and that it would be better to disband if they could not work on their own terms. Others, like Irene Malinská, thought that the WNC should struggle to exist, even if it had to do so within the confines of the Women's Center. Tumlířová and other leaders of the Women's Center were known and trusted by Czech women, she said. While the WNC might not agree with their views, they might be doing useful work. It would be best for the WNC, Malinská argued, to continue to help women in whatever way it could. Františka Plamínková was not optimistic about joining with the Women's Center, which she feared would inevitably lead to compromising the democratic values of the WNC. If the WNC managed to gain influence within the new group, she declared, then it would also take on the moral responsibility for whatever acts the Women's Center might undertake, some of which would undoubtedly clash with the WNC's ideology. Plamínková was not willing to bear the psychological burden of encouraging Czech women in directions she did not think they should go.[42] In the end, Horáková attended some exploratory meetings in the summer of 1939 with Tumlířová and Jan Kapras, head of the Czech National Council, but nothing came of them.[43] The WNC continued to function independently, and the Women's Center, for its part, refused to publicly attack the WNC for refusal to cooperate.[44] The circumstances in which both organizations operated, however, changed dramatically.

## Gender and Politics during the Protectorate

Tumlířová and her colleagues at the Women's Center had hoped to create a new kind of women's movement for a new era. They accepted the Czech experiment with "authoritarian democracy" as a chance for a new beginning and sought to build a strong place for women within that rubric. However, their plans never had a chance to come to fruition. The Beran government's attempt to transform Czechoslovakia into an ideologically compatible neighbor for Nazi Germany did not appease Hitler any more than the surrender of the Sudetenland. On March 15, 1939, German troops entered Prague and ended the Second Republic, only a few short months after it had begun. The Germans split Czechoslovakia in two, replacing the Czech lands with a new entity they called the Protectorate of Bohemia and Moravia and establishing an independent Slovakia.[45] Under this scheme, the Czech lands lost their sovereignty, but they were not directly annexed to the Reich; the Protectorate was a subject territory with its own special legal status. Although political authority in the Czech lands ultimately rested with the occupiers, the Czechs retained a significant amount of local autonomy. President Emil Hácha remained in office, as did most of the government ministers. The one casualty from the Cabinet was Beran, as the only member with a significant history in Czechoslovak politics. Thus, the government of the Second Republic continued to function, although its role was much more limited and its subservience to the wishes of Berlin was no longer a matter of choice.[46]

The invasion made the form and substance of Czech politics an open question once again. While the bureaucracy continued to function, the National Assembly was dispersed and political parties banned, leaving the relationship of the administration to the population unclear. It was actually President Hácha who took charge. On March 16 he had already proposed a means to fill the gap, in the form of a new, mass association called the National Partnership (NP or Národní Souručenství), which was billed as the single political outlet for Czechs in the Protectorate. First and foremost, the NP was conceived as a way to keep things firmly in the hands of the "good" (i.e., conservative, rather than radical) Right, limit the influence that Czech fascists had on Protectorate administration and policy, and ensure that "the protection of national matters would be in the hands of decent people."[47] But the NP's mandate went beyond taking the place of political parties and providing a forum for Czechs in public life. Its creators envisioned the NP as a Czech shadow-state, which would administer the internal affairs of the nation and concern itself with the general welfare of Czech residents by sponsoring social welfare programs, supervising economic and cultural life, and generally "caring for the nation."[48] However, although it was designed to replace national government, there was nothing democratic about the National Partnership. It was headed by a committee of fifty men appointed by Hácha himself and all of its local leaders were also appointed rather than elected.[49]

Nonetheless, the National Partnership was presented to the public as the only officially sanctioned space for Czechs to work together on social and national issues: a new, if highly structured, kind of public sphere. It was in this sense that it was "political," since it did not have any direct legislative power or official links to the Protectorate government, except through the person of President Hácha, who stood at the head of both. Still, the idea of the organization struck a chord with the population; the membership campaign begun just after the plan was announced was spectacularly successful, as demoralized Czechs strained to show their patriotism in this one permitted manner. At the end of the week-long drive, a total of 98.4 percent of all adult men living in the Protectorate had applied for membership.[50] Women, however, were excluded from this process. The requirements for membership in the National Partnership were Czech nationality, integrity, adulthood, Aryan origin, and being male. The National Partnership was the only forum for political life allowed in the Protectorate and women were simply not welcome in it.

In the occupied Czech lands, voting was not a right given to anyone. There were no elections and there was no other way for the public to be directly involved in the legislative process. In one fell swoop, the NP governing committee (itself an appointed body) had deprived Czech women of the political equality they had gained in 1918 and thrust the legal standing of women back to where it had been during the Habsburg Monarchy, when they had been prohibited from joining political organizations. The National Partnership claimed that it was doing this to "protect" women. However, while it was true that being involved with public life now did carry with it an element of danger, it was also not the case that the Gestapo was hot on the trail of every member of the NP—this was patently impossible, since virtually every adult Czech male belonged to it. The amount of danger women would have faced by applying for membership was negligible. In addition, the NP leadership contended that women did not have strong enough nerves to be involved in politics during such a time, when hard decisions involving many lives might have to be made. Ironically, the lack of democratic process within the NP was also brought up as a reason for excluding women. Women were supposedly too inclined to debate and argumentation to sit on decision-making bodies in which there were no democratic procedures or voting. Decisions needed to be made quickly and without fuss, hence, there could be no female representatives.[51]

The decision to bar women from participation in the National Partnership shocked and horrified Czech women from all sides of the political spectrum, from the leaders of the WNC to those involved with the new Women's Center. Though their responses were muffled by severe controls on the press, they did not hesitate to make their views known to the men in charge of the NP. The woman's section of the National Unity Party, led in part by Women's Center president Marie Tumlířová, immediately sent a sharp protest to Adolf Hrubý, the man who had been appointed by President Hácha to head the National Partnership. Tumlířová, like the other leading women of the National Unity Party, had been involved in party politics for decades. They had never dreamed that their male colleagues would get together and secretly decide to kick them all out of politics, or what would now pass for politics in the occupied Czech lands. In their attempts to grapple with this betrayal of trust, however, rightist women like Tumlířová found themselves stymied by their own logic and beliefs. They had long before adopted the position that men and women were essentially different. This meant that while they could argue that women's difference did not preclude them from political participation, they had to allow that some activities suited men more than women and vice versa. How, then, could they counter the argument that the occupation had radically changed the political playing field, making public life too dangerous for the feminine sex?

In its protest letter to Hrubý, the women's section of the National Unity Party professed shock that the executive committee of the National Partnership could express such utter disregard for over half the nation's population. The letter's tone, however was more muted than indignant. Its authors merely emphasized their will to serve and registered their dismay that women had been denied the opportunity to help their nation in its time of need. The nation needed its women, they declared, if it was going to survive the current crisis, and it needed them not only in domestic sectors. Based on this assessment of the nation's needs, they demanded that the NP revoke its decision, accept women as equal members of the organization, and place women on its executive committee and other commissions. The letter writers did not mention that the exclusion of women from the only permitted political organization in the Czech lands infringed upon the rights of Czech women to participate equally in society. Instead, they simply begged to be allowed to contribute to the national community, as if they were supplicants asking for a great favor rather than citizens demanding their due. They tried to position themselves as reliable supporters of the regime, stressing that women would only assist the aims of the NP, not dispute them. In the end, they simply pleaded with the men in the National Partnership, writing "We don't know where we are going and so we cry out again—don't disperse the nation's strength, don't reject the collaboration of women, who have always been the carriers and maintainers of order and of the conservative regime. . . . Correct the mistake that you have made."[52]

Plamínková responded to the situation somewhat differently, calling upon Czech politicians to remember their nation's tradition of supporting women's political rights. In a personal letter of protest sent to President Hácha, she reminded him of the long-standing feminine presence in Czech politics. She emphasized how Czech women with voting rights to the Bohemian Diet had used their votes to support Czech national interests and pointed out that Czech nationalists had enthusiastically joined the fight for women's suffrage in Austria. Moreover, she argued that Czech historical and legal precedent supported political rights for women, implying that to deny that precedent was to deny Czech heritage. Appealing to the old legal scholar's sense of justice, Plamínková asked Hácha not to deprive women of political representation and destroy the historical political equality of Czech women and men.[53] Since the occupation had made more public forms of protest impossible, many other formerly politically active Czech women also sent letters of protest to leading Protectorate figures. Like Anna Mrskošová, a former parliamentary representative from the Agrarian Party, they raged that the leaders of the National Partnership had ranked women behind "(male) drunks, gamblers, and good-for-nothings, and just because they are women!" Mrskošová claimed that "thousands of rural Czech women think like me. But there are few of us who have the courage to express the matter publicly."[54] In March 1939, no one knew how the new German authorities would react to such protests, or how Czech officials might respond, now that they had the means of Nazi repression at their disposal.

While those who wrote letters seem to have suffered no immediate consequences, the results of their protests were discouraging. Writing in response to WNC letters of protest, NP head Adolf Hrubý stated that the National Partnership was willing to permit women's collaboration in its programs, but only on its own terms and not from a position of equal power.[55] Finally, on March 6, 1940, a delegation of women, including Marie Tumlířová and Milena Šmejcová, a former parliamentary representative from the National Socialist Party, met with President Hácha to discuss the matter of women within the National Partnership. Those present agreed that women would finally be allowed to apply for membership in the NP. However, their activities in the organization would be limited to areas that were deemed appropriate for women, such as welfare programs and cultural life. Women would not be allowed take part in any of the more political functions of the NP and would not have any representation in its leadership, either on the national or local level. What was being offered was a very limited form of citizenship. The NP, functioning as substitute Czech state, would recognize women as members in the national collective, but only up to a point. Women would be set apart from "normal" members, cordoned off into a special category that had strictly defined parameters.

This news caused an uproar amongst those who had been active in the Czech women's movement. The spectacle of two former female members of the National Assembly publicly agreeing, in the name of all women, to a lesser status in politics incensed those who had given their lives working to erase just such distinctions. Antonie Maxová, a prominent leader of several women's professional organizations, expressed the thoughts of many others when she wrote in a personal letter to Šmejcová that she was "dumbfounded and deeply upset by the fact that independent women, among them two former deputies, could actively participate in destroying the principle of equality for women in political activity in our state." She charged that Šmejcová had gone against her duty as an elected representative to uphold the constitution and her party's own program (Šmejcová's National Socialist party had always supported women's equality). According to Maxová, acting against those principles "was unjustified, irresponsible, and inadmissible, all the more so because [their] action today could have fateful consequences in the future."[56] Would it set a precedent that could not be overcome once the Germans had left the Czech lands?

Such concerns were also heard inside the Women's Center. Although the delegation to President Hácha had been led by Tumlířová, she had not informed the rest of the group about her participation in advance. In fact, at a Women's Center board meeting a few weeks prior to her audience with Hácha, she presented a report about the process of negotiations with the National Partnership that demanded women be allowed into the NP (only) as equal members; this was the position the Women's Center executive committee believed it had endorsed.[57] At a meeting of the executive committee shortly after the news about the agreement with Hácha was made public, at which Tumlířová was conspicuously absent, the members expressed their dismay over what had happened. One, Marie Provazníková, was furious with Tumlířová's duplicity. She declared that it would have been better for women to remain outside the NP than be admitted on the terms negotiated by Tumlířová. Another member of the committee, Božena Krchová, seconded Provazníková's position and worried that the public would think that the Women's Center was behind the whole affair, since Tumlířová was widely known as its president. Provazníková proposed that the Women's Center issue a public statement declaring that it had nothing to do with the delegation and did not support its work.[58]

But this was too radical a step for most of the other members. They deplored the situation, but shrank away from public declarations. To come out against the delegation could be construed as being against the National Partnership, and that would be counterproductive, as well as possibly dangerous. The important thing was to keep working and support the nation. Even the angry Krchová did not consider public protests to be appropriate. "We cannot answer a wrong with a wrong," she said, "our only duty is to defend the nation's existence."[59] Another member of the committee, Bohumila Smolařová-Čapková, agreed, saying that "today is an exceptional era and what concerns all of us is that the whole nation stands behind the NP. Surely we all want the nation to be united and thus we must contribute to this ourselves." Working for the NP, rather than against it, was what the situation required. As one of the Women's Center's vice-presidents, Dr. Růžena Bednaříková, declared, the way to make change was by participation; once the leaders of the NP saw the work that women could accomplish, they would open other doors to them. At the end of the meeting, Provazníková was not convinced, but the others agreed to forsake protest and work with the National Partnership on its terms rather than their own.[60]

This decision guaranteed the Women's Center a place in the life of the Protectorate. The organization continued to meet and carry out its activities through 1944. However, its leaders were forced to curtail their original plans quite significantly. After March 1940, when Tumlířová agreed to support women's entry into the National Partnership on gendered terms, the Women's Center's agenda was gradually influenced by the men in charge of the Czech National Council, officials from the National Partnership and the Protectorate cultural ministry—figures who were increasingly identified with German occupying forces. The organization's emphasis slowly shifted away from promoting a relatively powerful "women's sphere" to glorifying domesticity. Time and resources were directed primarily toward cultural projects that celebrated self-sacrificial motherhood, such as a lecture series on the mother and child, or to activities designed to help housewives deal with the hardships of war, such as printing recipe books on making the most out of available rations. The group continued to stress the necessity of schooling women for work as well as domestic life, and developed projects to assist working women with childcare and domestic responsibilities. However, these activities were only instituted after the German declaration of total war in 1941 had put the onus on Czech leaders (as well as their German counterparts) to put women into the factories. They were directly sponsored by Josef Drachovský, the president of the Czech National Council after 1941, and Emanuel Moravec, the Protectorate Minister of Public Enlightenment, men later reviled for their Nazi ties. Thus the Women's Center wound up promoting women's work only when it suited the Protectorate regime as part of a general effort to help Czech women shoulder the double burden of working for the Reich and raising new generations of healthy workers.[61]

## Staying Alive by Keeping Silent

The Women's National Council was unwilling to accept this kind of compromise. The organization steadfastly resisted publicly accepting the plan to bring women into the National Partnership on an unequal basis with men. At the same time, its leaders decided against an openly critical response, judging it to be both possibly dangerous and potentially alienating to the masses of Czech women, who for the most part just wanted to join the NP on any terms in order to express solidarity with their nation.[62] However, WNC leaders Plamínková, Horáková, Maxová, Mrskošová, and Zdeňka Patschová met privately on April 29, 1940, with then head of the National Partnership, Jan Nebeský, and its general secretary, Dr. Mrazík, to discuss their concerns about the unequal position women were being offered in the NP. Nebeský claimed to understand their position, but then demanded that the WNC publicly endorse the entry of women into the National Partnership, hinting that the future of the WNC depended on its willingness to "work well" with his organization. By their own account, the women present did not crack under this substantial pressure. Instead, they declared that they could not publicly invite women to join the NP, because such an act went against their status as a nonpartisan institution and their principles. They informed Nebeský that they could only remain "loyally silent," and not openly condemn the manner in which women were being inducted into the NP. The demand to work with the NP they accepted, and in the spirit of immediate cooperation pulled out a set of suggestions they had prepared on how to moderate the ill-effects of the government resolution that had banned married women from the civil service and asked for Nebeský's help in realizing them.[63]

While we do not know Nebeský's response to their audacity, it is clear that WNC leaders kept their word and tried to remain "loyally silent." They also steadfastly refused to openly support women's participation in the National Partnership. Protectorate leaders, some of whom still had sympathies for the WNC, initially did nothing more to force them, finding their nonconfrontational stance adequate.[64] Others, however, found their silence to be suspicious behavior. On February 6, 1942, Karel Werner, a journalist notorious for supporting the Germans, attacked the WNC and Plamínková in the newspaper *Polední List* (The Midday News). During the First Republic, Werner claimed, the WNC was conspicuous for its frequent and noisy protests, and "Now for three years the WNC has been as silent as a grave." Werner charged that Plamínková was stifling the voice of the WNC by refusing to give up her leadership of the organization or change its ideological basis to conform to the times. In his view, Plamínková and others from the interwar period who did not declare their support of the new order or go quietly into private life were "obstacles on the Czech nation's path to a new future, whose silence caused more damage than they knew." He demanded that Plamínková cede the presidency of the organization to someone who was "more appropriate for the new conditions," and wished her a pleasant and relaxing retirement.[65]

Plamínková was furious about the article, perhaps even more so because, while it was directed against her, it cast a spotlight on the WNC and placed the whole organization in jeopardy. It was only by keeping out of public notice that the WNC had managed to stay alive while making few concessions to the regime. In her anger, she went to the offices of *Polední List* and demanded redress from the editor. He asked her what the WNC was doing with its time, since it had disappeared from public view, and inquired why the WNC had not participated in other public causes like collections for the German army and the anti-Western propaganda campaign. Irritated, Plamínková snapped that the National Partnership had said that women were not fit to take part in politics and so the WNC was staying out of them. The editor responded that, even if this was the case, such programs were not politics. Plamínková apparently then said that by having published the article, his newspaper might have brought about the demise of the WNC. To this the editor replied that if *Polední List*'s article resulted in a change of leadership for the group, it would be saving it and not destroying it.[66]

Plamínková's unfortunate, if understandable, remarks, which *Polední List* published, set off a wave of bad press for the WNC. Journalists accused them of being against the regime and anti-Czech, and demanded that they actively collaborate with Protectorate authorities. Several of the daily papers ran articles about the incident, some of which were very critical of the WNC, as well as personally insulting to Plamínková. In *České Slovo* (The Czech Word), one author cattily remarked, "the WNC is one of the institutions which spoke frequently and about everything during the previous regime, but has now fallen into a deep sleep. The president of the WNC was the former Senator Plamínková. Who of us would have thought that this woman would ever be denied the gift of her tongue?"[67]

The publicity also forced the National Partnership to publicly take a stand against the WNC. As a part of the Protectorate system, it could not appear to be in sympathy with groups who did not enthusiastically support Nazi rule over the Czech lands. In an interview with *Polední List*, the NP took pains to distance itself from the WNC, claiming that just because it called itself the Women's National Council did not mean that the group had any real connection to the Czech nation or the National Partnership, both of which were enthusiastically behind the German war effort. In addition, the NP's representative, Jan Fousek, firmly denied that it had issued any sort of directive limiting women's participation in public activities. He stated, "For women who truly want to work, there is a wide field of activities available. The participation of women is not denied, on the contrary it is welcomed."[68]

Despite the claims made by *Polední List*, the Women's National Council had not been idle since the establishment of the Protectorate. The goal of its activities, however, was to cling to its beliefs and to feminism, both to mitigate the effects the Nazi occupation might have on the situation of women in society and to prepare for the future. WNC leaders firmly believed that the occupation would be only temporary, and they wanted make sure that any steps taken against women's rights in the meantime would also be temporary. As Plamínková said to the assembled WNC board in a meeting during the early months of the Protectorate, "We cannot remain dead. We want to meet and to do what is possible and we must do that very intensively." She realized that the occupying forces would severely limit their ability to act, but emphasized that "while we cannot make extensive plans, we can never give up trying to get back to where we were."[69]

This was a tall order. The kinds of gender policies begun during the Second Republic had been very much in step with those in Nazi Germany, and they remained and intensified during the Protectorate. The media, the schools, the policies and programs of the National Partnership and the Protectorate government all emphasized the idea that men and women had different paths in life, mandated by their biological natures. Because these courses were directed by nature, there could be no deviation, and no denying them. In this ideological climate, political rights for women were regarded as unnatural; they went against women's genetically-based disposition and hindered their ability to fulfill their sex-linked functions as wives and mothers. The reversal in public discourse around women's suffrage was particularly startling, considering that during the previous regime even Czech conservatives and Catholics had welcomed and encouraged women's participation in the political process. Now, the right of women to vote was characterized as the single most pernicious influence on women during the First Republic.

A 1941 article printed in *České Slovo* claimed that political rights only made women think they could be like men and had brought grief to them and those around them. These "viragos," created out of the false sense of equality brought on by women's suffrage, had lowered the moral standards of the nation, left behind a mountain of broken marriages, and severely weakened society's most important institution: the family. The new order, inspired by Nazi ideas but reworked for Czechs, would reject all of that. Its system would not be built on dubious ideas of gender equality, but would "come from the unadulterated laws of nature, directing women above all to their basic function in national society: maternity and running the household." In fact, returning women to the family and keeping their functions completely divorced from men's was the path to "true freedom." The right to vote had merely brought competition between men and women, taking it away had eased that tension and enabled both to realize their own abilities for the good of the nation. At the time that this article was published, women had been absent from Czech politics for three years, and, in the author's view, the results had been good. He concluded, "it will always be better to have women without politics than homes without women." Clearly, for this author, women and politics had an essentially antagonistic relationship; contact between them could not but contaminate both sides.[70]

The opinions expressed in this piece were consistent with the general slant of the media toward women during the Protectorate. Although the Czech press was severely compromised during the occupation and became known as a haven for the most ardent collaborationists, its work did not simply draw on an imposed Nazi ideology; rather, it elaborated on themes of family crisis and moral decay that had been present in Czech political culture for decades. The content of the press did not change during the

Protectorate as much as the way attacks like the one above came to dominate the discourse on gender. During the First Republic, the cause of gender equality had defenders as well as detractors, even in the popular press, and every attack could be followed by a counterattack. In the occupied Czech lands, this was impossible. The mass media did not allow for rebuttals and the authorities did not take kindly to opposing points of view. The WNC was not allowed into the mainstream press at all, even to advertise its lectures. The editor of the WNC's journal, Věra Urbanová, complained that "they don't accept us in any newspaper, no matter what we do. So, it is a difficult matter. Radio is also impossible."[71] The single voice in the press, then, was calling for women's return to the home, and this—combined with the already long-standing ambivalence among Czechs about women's rights—could not but have a profound effect on the way people in the Czech lands thought about men, women, and their roles in society.

The WNC certainly took the matter seriously. The biggest fear of its members was that, tracked into schools devoted to the household arts and deprived of access to other ideas, women would be transformed into little more than servants, incapable of even imagining more for themselves. One way of preventing this was to provide an ideological center for those who did not approve of the new regime's approach to gender issues. In order to be able to provide this kind of spiritual and intellectual home for Czech feminists, however, the WNC's leadership had to reach women directly, including those who might be far from Prague. Therefore, they began to attract more individual (as opposed to institutional) members and to extend their own system of WNC clubs. Since its founding, the WNC had been primarily a federation of independent associations, acting as a center and a focus for the combined concerns of its member organizations. But it had also established a network of WNC clubs, open to both men and women, which served mainly as discussion groups and provided an institutional setting from which to offer public lectures and other events designed to influence public opinion. Now, especially with many other groups choosing to disband rather than risk running into conflict with Protectorate authorities, these clubs took on new importance. Incredibly, in an era in which associational life was rapidly imploding from within, the WNC managed to found several new clubs during the first years of the Protectorate. In 1940 alone it attempted to found twenty new groups.[72] These were mainly located in smaller towns such as Přerov, where there were few other outlets for women to meet. The clubs provided "spiritual sustenance for those who were appalled by the tenor of the regime's attitudes toward women and gave them a venue to reach out to others in their community.

The WNC central office urged the clubs to educate women about their own capabilities, teaching them the history of the Czech women's movement and engaging in other consciousness-raising activities. A circular sent to all of the clubs in October 1940 reminded them of the need to build women's solidarity against the hostile climate being created by the press and Protectorate authorities, and stressed the importance of cultural programs in this effort. "Culture" was one of the few arenas in which it was possible to organize public events in the Protectorate, and if clubs planned events for people other than their own members, they had to take place under this rubric. In addition, programs such as an evening honoring women writers whose work positively portrayed female self-reliance and independence, like Božena Němcová and Eliška Krásnohorská, were an effective means of bolstering women's confidence.

It was with a similar goal that the WNC began a campaign against so-called "women's literature"—insipid romances that were being marketed as appropriate reading for women. The WNC saw an attempt to lower or suppress women's intelligence by discouraging them from reading works that would require them to think. WNC leaders were particularly worried about the effect these novels were having on the minds of young girls, who were growing up in a period of increasing hostility towards independent, smart women, and might be easily seduced into believing that their life could or should mimic the path of a cheap romance.[73] The WNC clubs were asked to mount protests demanding that publishers print intelligent books for everyone to read, and form their own reading groups. The WNC central office could even supply reading lists and provide commentary on works chosen.[74]

Creating a reading group of women in a provincial Czech town to discuss the classics of Czech literature may not seem like a significant intervention in the totalizing policies of an oppressive regime, but the WNC correctly realized that, in an occupied nation in the middle of a continent at war, such projects were the only possible venues for intervening in public discourse. More overtly radical public projects would have been forbidden by the police or censors. In private, the WNC central office continued to negotiate with Protectorate officials on matters such as women's education and on further state support for women financially devastated after being laid off from their state jobs.

Additionally, a number of WNC leaders, including Plamínková and Horáková, were involved with the Czech resistance loyal to the exiled Czechoslovak government in London. It was undoubtedly in their interest to keep the WNC alive and out of the public eye as a cover for these illicit activities. Horáková later claimed to have used WNC clubs as a way of organizing the production and distribution of underground newspapers, illegal border crossings, and the gathering of news for the London government.[75] However, little evidence of the scope or nature of these activities exists. It is certain, however, that many WNC leaders were arrested for their involvement in resistance groups, and this eventually played a decisive role in the fate of the WNC. Plamínková was initially arrested during the first weeks of the occupation as part of a sweep of former politicians and other prominent individuals who had had influence in the Beneš government. She was released after a few weeks, but remained under the watch of the Gestapo. Milada Horáková was arrested in August 1940 and remained in prison until the end of the war. The same was true of a number of other WNC functionaries. More significant, however, was the second arrest of Plamínková in June 1942. She was taken by German forces as part of a wave of retaliatory arrests that followed the assassination of Reinhard Heydrich, the head of the German occupying administration. She was executed shortly afterwards.

The loss of Plamínková proved too much to bear for those functionaries left in the WNC. Without her drive, her vision, and her certainty, they found themselves adrift in a sea of despair and fear. The terror that followed Heydrich's death shocked and cowed many Czechs, who until then had not known the extent of the Nazi capacity for random violence. The *Heydrichiáda*, as it is known in Czech, was in many ways a turning point for those in the occupied Czech lands, including the members of the WNC.[76] In August 1942, unable to see how they could meaningfully affect the future, the WNC board members that were left decided to dissolve the organization. So the WNC died a quiet death, unnoticed by all but a few faithful adherents. Tied inextricably to the Czechoslovak Republic that had spawned it, the group was unable to survive in the new atmosphere of the Nazi Protectorate.

# 7

## THE LIMITS OF CITIZENSHIP IN
## THE PEOPLE'S DEMOCRACY

Under the new concept of law we are called traitors, but we still know
that if we had freedom of action again we would act no differently
than we have acted all our lives, truly serving the noble ideals of liberty,
democracy, social progress and humanity. That loyalty is now considered
treason. In this most trying moment, we take strength from the realiza-
tion that we were not alone in our actions, that our cause will not die with
our going.

Milada Horáková, courtroom speech, June 1950

AFTER HER ARREST in 1942, Františka Plamínková met Milada Horáková
once more, in the women's camp for political prisoners in Terezín. During
the days they spent there together, she urged Horáková to continue their
struggle for women's rights, making her promise that she would take the
lead in reconstituting the WNC after the war's end. Horáková assured her
friend and mentor that she would never relinquish their common goal of
creating a democratic society for both men and women. A few days later,
on June 30, 1942, Františka Plamínková was shot in the Prague suburb of
Kobylisy. Milada Horáková, however, escaped her teacher's fate. Initially
arrested in 1940, Horáková endured two years in Prague prisons before
being transferred to the concentration camp at Terezín. She was kept there
for a further two years, often in punishing solitary confinement. Throughout her imprisonment, she steadfastly refused to divulge information about

the Czech resistance and just as tenaciously held on to the hope of a better future for herself and for her country. Finally, in October 1944, she was put on trial before the People's Court in Dresden, where the Nazi prosecutor recommended a death sentence. An accomplished lawyer, Horáková presented her own defense before the German judges. While she was found guilty, her efforts persuaded the court to deny the prosecution's call for her execution. She was sentenced instead to eight years in the prison of Aichach outside of Munich, where she was held until liberated by American forces on May 20, 1945.[1]

Shortly thereafter, Horáková was back in Prague and intent on returning to her former public activities. True to her promise to Plamínková, one of her first priorities was rebuilding the Czech women's movement. She founded a new organization to be its guiding force: the Council of Czechoslovak Women (CCW, or Rada Československých Žen), which she hoped would continue the legacy of the WNC. Elected the group's first president, Horáková tried to implement a program based on the goals and methods of the interwar feminist movement. But, as Horáková herself realized, a simple return to the prewar First Republic was impossible under postwar circumstances. The experience of Munich, occupation, and liberation had fundamentally changed Czechoslovak politics, creating a new set of basic assumptions about the nature of the state, the relationship of the state to the individual, and the country's place in Europe. Like 1918, 1945 was a revolutionary moment, one that would set the terms for a new era in the region's history.

## The People's Democracy

Soon after he fled post-Munich Czechoslovakia for the University of Chicago, former Czechoslovak president Edvard Beneš began to ponder what would make democracy work, both in his country and in Europe as a whole. In his 1939 book *Democracy Today and Tomorrow,* he suggested that future democratic politicians would need to think about citizenship differently. Social and economic equality would take on greater importance, and individual freedoms might even have to be limited in order to pursue these new standards of social justice.[2] During the war years, Beneš after he had left Chicago to head the Czechoslovak exile government in London, Beneš transformed his ideas into a program for a completely new Czechoslovak Republic, one that married democracy with socialism. If he returned to power, Beneš declared, he would enact a social revolution by nationalizing major industries and breaking up large estates in the countryside. He would create national unity by expelling German and Hungarian traitors, and pursue alliances with the Soviet Union as well as with the West.[3]

In many respects, Beneš's plans for a new postwar Czechoslovakia dovetailed with the hopes of the Czechoslovak Communist Party (Komunistická Strana Československa, or KSČ). After they formally split off from the Czechoslovak Social Democratic party in 1921, the Czechoslovak Communists had, unlike other Communist parties in Central and Eastern Europe, legally participated in parliamentary politics. In their electoral debut in 1925, the Communists had achieved the second strongest showing nationally. In later elections their popularity dipped somewhat, but the KSČ retained a significant share of the electorate throughout the interwar years, gaining around 10 percent of the total vote in both the 1929 and 1935 elections. However, the party never participated in a governing coalition and was always relegated to the ranks of the opposition.[4]

The KSČ's influence grew dramatically during the war years, as the party began to assert a leading position both at home and abroad. Its increased strength was the result of many factors, including the disorganization of other Czech parties after Munich and during the war, the KSČ's uncompromising resistance to Nazism at home, its bold vision for a new future that had no ties to the First Republic, and its association with the Soviet Union. Its Soviet ties served the party in several respects. A Soviet alliance appealed to the many Czechs who had lost faith in the West after Munich. It also certainly bought the Czechoslovak Communists a much more substantial role in creating a postwar government than they would have had otherwise, because the Soviets, as the military power in most of Czechoslovakia at the end of the war, could demand a Communist presence in any new regime. And, in fact, plans for a postwar Czechoslovak government were laid in Moscow during the spring of 1945, just as the Red Army began to enter the Czech lands.[5]

In Moscow, the Soviets hosted a meeting between the KSČ and representatives from the Czech exile government in London. Beneš invited representatives from four Czech parties to join the negotiations, where they were met by a Slovak delegation. Three of these parties were socialist: the Communists, Social Democrats, and Czech National Socialists. The centrist People's Party, formerly Catholic but now of a nondenominational Christian orientation, was also present. One of the first decisions made in Moscow was to effectively eliminate the right wing of the former political spectrum by banning all rightist parties, including the previously dominant Agrarian Party, for collaborating with the Nazi regime. The remaining four parties then agreed to work together as the National Front and jointly formed a provisional government. They accepted a common political program, later called the Košice program after the Slovak town in which their government formally took power in April 1945. The KSČ was the primary author of this document, but, after some negotiation, it was accepted by all of the parties in the National Front.

The Košice program indicated a fundamental shift in Czech politics, including a new set of assumptions about the meaning of citizenship. It created the blueprint for what would be called the "people's democracy," proclaiming, "the people are the single instrument of state power," and urging citizens to take charge of their own communities by forming "National Committees" to serve as their local government. These National Committees were encouraged to root out Germans and collaborators and take their property for the state. Citizenship would now be limited to those who could prove their national and patriotic credentials; Germans, Hungarians, and collaborators would find that their personal rights and property were no longer legally guaranteed.[6] However, in the new people's democracy, those who could claim citizenship would find that their list of rights had expanded considerably. The Košice program declared that Czechoslovak citizens were entitled to a long list of social rights, including the right to employment, vacation, medical care, and old age insurance.[7]

The Košice program provided the basis for what was later called the "national revolution." This "revolution" was really a set of presidential decrees promulgated by the Beneš administration between May and October of 1945. The Beneš decrees set out to nationalize the new republic by establishing special courts to try wartime collaborators and authorizing the expulsion of millions of German and Hungarian-speaking Czechoslovak citizens and the redistribution of their property to Czech and Slovak families.[8] The decrees also took a firm step toward "socializing democracy," most significantly by nationalizing major industrial enterprises. Although the standards varied by industry, all businesses over a certain size were subject to nationalization, effectively making the state the new authority in the realm of big business.[9] These revolutionary measures had the broad support of both the population and the parties of the National Front, as all agreed that a radical break had to be made between the present and pre-Munich Czechoslovakia.[10]

Although they technically formed a united coalition, the parties of the National Front soon began to viciously compete with each other for a greater share of political power. Each began a concerted drive to gain new members: by 1946 an unprecedented 40 percent of the population had joined a party. While all of the National Front parties made tremendous gains in their membership, it was the Communists who were able to present themselves as the true driving force of the revolution and to assert themselves as the party of the moment. With its engaging message and amazing organizational machine, the KSČ increased its membership from about fifty thousand individuals at the end of the war to over a million one year later.[11] As the party's leader, Klement Gottwald, declared in a speech shortly before the first parliamentary elections in May 1946, the Communists were the party of acts and deeds, not empty words and promises. The KSČ presented potential voters with a clear and confident plan of action, a blueprint for economic prosperity and national security.[12] Its vision was definitely directed toward a socialist future, but Communist leaders insisted on their commitment to democracy as a significant part of their Czech national heritage. In fact, the Communists styled themselves as the true defenders of democratic Czech national values. They even claimed to be the real inheritors of Masaryk's legacy, declaring that Masaryk would have recognized the value of scientific socialism.[13]

Through this platform, the Communists managed to set the terms of postwar Czech political discourse. The other parties were forced to operate on their terms and scrambled to find a way to answer the Communist challenge. Since none of them could produce a coherent plan that substantially differed from the Communist program, they were quickly reduced to attacking the idea of Communism, or fighting over who was the real descendent of Masaryk.[14] By the time of the first postwar elections in

May 1946, politics had devolved into increasingly bitter partisan warfare. The KSČ tried to tag the National Socialists as reactionaries who wanted to renege on the revolution and claimed that they harbored dubious elements from the banned Agrarian Party. The National Socialists and the People's Party darkly intoned about the dangers of the "totalitarian" Communists. The National Socialists derided the Social Democrats for merely being Communists in poor disguise, and the Social Democrats responded by calling the National Socialists "a party without action, without a program, and without character."[15] Unable to stay above the fray, the People's Party also attacked the National Socialists—even though they were its most likely allies against the KSČ—and mocked them for claiming to be both socialist and for private property.

In the midst of all this vitriol, the KSČ gained the advantage by moving beyond attacking its competitors and focusing the public on its positive message of social change. While the National Socialists and the People's Party both complained about the Communist Party's relentless campaigning—the National Socialist newspaper even ran a cartoon of a man covered in KSČ election stickers, telling his surprised wife in a caption that he had only stopped for a moment on the Charles Bridge when rabid Communist campaign workers confused his still form for a statue—it was they who had not been able to adequately adapt to new political circumstances.[16] The KSČ won a decisive victory, gaining 38 percent of the vote and the prime minister's chair for Klement Gottwald. Its closest rival, the National Socialist Party, won only 18.3 percent of the votes, trailed by the People's Party (15.6 percent), the Slovak Democrats (14.1 percent) and the Social Democrats (12.1 percent). With just over half the votes going to explicitly Marxist parties, it seemed that Czechoslovakia had indeed started down the road to a socialist future.[17]

## The Postwar Women's Movement

The government that took charge of the liberated Czechoslovakia promised its citizens a new beginning. The bright future that all the parties of the National Front hoped to offer, and which the Communists articulated especially well, rested on a new kind of equality: instead of a liberal state dedicated to protecting the freedom of people to do as they pleased, the trend after 1945 was toward a more interventionist state that would actively engineer the social and economic equality of its citizens. While the leaders of the "people's democracy" continued to concern themselves with a citizen's individual freedom, they placed a striking new emphasis on his or her material condition. This not only affected their thinking about the rights of citizenship, which were expanded to include the rights to sustenance, health, and relaxation, but also changed the way they conceived of a citizen's responsibilities. Postwar social rights did not come free; they were awarded to nationally reliable citizens on the basis of their work, not their humanity. It was only by actively contributing to the community that a citizen earned the benefits of belonging to that collective. The way that the new government approached the issue of women's citizenship was no exception to this attitude. The Košice program, like the Washington Declaration of 1918, proclaimed that women could expect equality in the political, economic, and cultural realms. But unlike the authors of the Washington Declaration, the framers of the Košice program pledged to "carry this out consistently." Perhaps more significantly, they specified that women would have the same rights to employment as men and be paid the same wages for the same work. Like men, women would earn rights through their labor.[18]

As in 1918, the politicians of 1945 loudly declared that women's equality was a fundamental part of the people's democracy. In a manner reminiscent of the earlier debates over women's suffrage, the National Front parties all claimed to champion women's rights. They proudly displayed their egalitarian credentials and tried to show women how they would work to realize their equality. As the parties openly admitted in their appeals to female voters, women were a majority of the electorate and the party that could command their support would be the victor.[19] Among the socialist parties, this spawned a contest to prove which party was the true friend of women's rights.

In their attempts to win women over to their camp, the Communists and Social Democrats emphasized their concern for the practical realities of women's lives. The Social Democrats mentioned prewar concerns like changing the civil code, but their basic answer to the "woman question" was to enable women to become independent and productive workers.

Capitalism had forced women into an oppressive economic dependence on their husbands that made any legal changes in their status meaningless. "Scientific socialism" would give them the economic wherewithal to actually utilize their legal rights. Both Marxist parties claimed that they would work to make women's lives easier materially, by providing them with washing machines, central heating, and day care facilities. The Communists also stressed that they were the only party with a real plan capable of accomplishing this, inviting women of all classes to come and "build a happy home with us." "Away with the old times!" the KSČ suggested to women, Communism will give you a prosperous new world." Under a picture of a smiling young woman worker and an older female peasant, the party newspaper, *Rudé Právo* (Red Right), seductively added, "our plan has bowls full of goodies for all good and upstanding people," if only they were willing to work with the Communist Party to achieve this bright future.[20]

The National Socialists and their leader, Petr Zenkl, also tried to sell themselves as the party most devoted to women's rights. In this area at least, the National Socialists could present a concrete program of demands, including giving women adequate access to training and education, providing childcare for working women, and looking after the rights of housewives in a worker's democracy. While the Communists and Social Democrats emphasized relieving women of domestic chores so that they could be workers like men, the National Socialists talked about legally recognizing housework as valuable work. They held up the record of their female representatives in the provisional National Assembly, which had been formed in the fall of 1946, a group that included Milada Horáková and longstanding party leader Fraňa Zemínová. The party noted that these women had been instrumental in recognizing housewives as workers in certain government programs.[21] Although the National Socialists emphasized their commitment to socialism and the Košice program, they tried to carve out a moderate position that emphasized women's ability to choose either a traditional or modern path, so that "able women could fully and actively take part in the building of the new republic," but marriage, motherhood, and the family would remain viable institutions.[22]

The People's Party also made attempts to attract women, and even placed women on its candidate lists for the first time. Its overtures to them used markedly different language from the prewar Federation of Catholic

Women and Girls. Female party leaders claimed that they would fight to see that women got their "just share" in public life. They declared that the People's Party was dedicated to "a democratic state as Masaryk understood it," emphasizing that a vote for the People's Party was a vote in support of freedom of expression, freedom of enterprise, and the free choice of profession and education. Yet, it was also in its appeals to women that the party most forcefully emphasized its Christian orientation—which was otherwise fairly muted in its election campaign—claiming that it would fight for Christian values in the schools and in family life. While women from the party did not return to prewar Catholic demands for a decidedly gendered household, they still assumed that women were particularly concerned with family and morality. In this way, they mimicked the National Socialists by attempting to capitalize on women's fears about how the socialist emphasis on wage work might affect family life and the job description of the housewife. Unlike the National Socialists, though, they also played up the atheism of the socialist camp, reminding women that only the People's Party had a firm moral standpoint dedicated to traditional values.[23]

With all the parties of the National Front doing anything they could to present themselves as favorable to women's rights, the immediate postwar era seemed like a real opportunity for women activists to push their own agenda and perhaps win some of the battles they had been fighting since 1918. However, the intense politicization and partisanship that began to develop after the spring of 1945 also affected the ability of women to work together for these goals. Shortly after the liberation of the country, female leaders from each of the parties in the National Front created their own coalition, which they called the National Women's Front (NWF). While it remained a partisan organization, the group later included representatives from the Council of Czechoslovak Women, the successor to the Women's National Council. But although the parties in the NWF had pledged to work in the interests of national unity and not personal political advantage, they found this difficult to achieve. Instead, partisan factions competed with each other and used the NWF as a forum for their own ends, which created more conflict than cooperation. For example, after the first NWF rally, held in Prague's Lucerna hall in September 1945, the Communist representative Julie Prokopová complained bitterly that some speakers had brought up subjects that had not been approved by the group. Prokopová particularly rebuked Fraňa Zemínová for paying tribute to her fallen National Socialist comrade Františka Plamínková without including any reference to women from other parties who had been killed by the Nazis. Prokopová was also upset that the Soviet flag was not among the decorations and that Soviet hymns were not sung. To resolve the dispute, the group agreed to work jointly on all speeches to be given at public gatherings in the future.[24]

The members of the NWF managed to work together on some issues. In one of their first projects, they attempted, albeit unsuccessfully, to convince the government to rehire the married women fired from the civil service in 1938. Beneš overturned the resolution that had authorized the layoffs, but refused to require the reinstatement of those who had been affected. The women could return to their old jobs, but only if their former offices wanted them back.[25] The NWF also worked toward greater parity for women in politics, organizing formal meetings with leaders from all parties to encourage them to place more women high on their candidate lists during the 1946 elections.[26] However, such moments of cooperation were relatively rare by mid-1946. After the KSČ triumphed in the elections, relations between the members of the NWF deteriorated, severely hampering the effectiveness of the organization.

Communist women hoped to use the NWF to bring more women into the workforce, which would have been a great boon to the new Gottwald government's economic program, known as the Two-Year Plan. However, they found their efforts at least partially blocked by the National Socialists and the People's Party. Female Communist leaders claimed in internal party documents that Zemínová attempted to stymie their plan to create women's work brigades in the countryside and that People's Party leader Marie Trojanová tried to prevent the NWF from encouraging married women's employment outside the home altogether. Both these women, they charged, were trying to use the NWF and its magazine, the very widely printed *Československá Žena* (Czechoslovak Woman), to spread "reactionary" ideas. On the other side, the National Socialists and People's Party members saw the Communists pushing a Two-Year Plan that was more a priority for their party than for the country as a whole. For the People's Party, plans to move women into the labor force in record numbers were especially problematic, because they pointed toward a new relationship between work and rights that they did not support.[27]

The conflicts within the NWF were especially evident during the group's 1946 congress, held in Prague on October 26–28. The speeches given by NWF leaders were vetted, in a rather contentious series of meetings, by the entire group. Although they eventually agreed upon the texts to be presented, the way the topics were distributed and discussed still captured the ideological differences between the parties. Speaking on the subject of the Two-Year Plan, Communist leader Anežka Hodinová stressed the need to increase industrial production, creating "rows of new tractors and machines, locomotives and railway cars, millions of meters of material and millions of pairs of shoes." The key to achieving this happy industrial future, where there would be no more lines for necessities like bread and potatoes, was the labor of women as well as men. Women, she said, had to be made to realize that their work was not only the basis of their own independence, but the foundation of the new republic. In her opinion, getting women to work was the NWF's biggest and most important task.[28]

The National Socialist leader Fraňa Zemínová took a very different tack in her speech, which covered the topic of the new constitution (then in the process of being written) and women in public life. She spoke of women gaining their freedom through law, rather than work. Harkening back to the language of the prewar era, she demanded that any new constitution address the long-standing concerns of women left over from the First Republic: legal equality within marriage and the family. In her notoriously spirited manner, Zemínová challenged Czech politicians to keep their promises to women once and for all, noting that even after the 1946 elections, only twenty-four out of three hundred representatives in the National Assembly were women, and there was not a single female minister. "We are half the nation," she declared, "why aren't there more of us in positions of responsibility?" Even women politically allied with the KSČ could accept this demand. Zemínová's call for women to unite in defense of national freedom as something more fundamental than the individual freedom granted to them by the constitution was more controversial.

Considering her deep suspicion of the Communists, she undoubtedly meant this as a plea against excessive Soviet influence in Czechoslovakia, even if her words could be read in multiple ways.[29]

In the last part of her speech, Zemínová remarked that the people's democracy was founded on the basis of partisan contestation and that women could not expect the National Women's Front to be like a party. However, while she and the other leaders of the NWF wanted to advance women's interests generally, they soon began to see that goal as inextricably tied to their own party's future. Zemínová herself clearly did not trust Communist women, even within the NWF. In March 1947, Zemínová wrote to a district-level leader in the National Socialist women's organization to complain that, against her explicit instructions, the Communists had "lured" National Socialist women in several towns into joining NWF celebrations in honor of International Women's Day, which she charged was a Marxist holiday that should not be endorsed by the NWF. According to Zemínová, the Communist women were "double crossers" who were only interested in using the NWF for their own partisan agitation. She warned the district leader to "keep the NWF at arm's length" and charged her with working to keep the Communists from organizing Czech women in a federation that was really under their umbrella, as she claimed they had done with unions and were trying to do with farmers.[30]

In 1947, Zemínová began to lead her National Socialist women's organization in an active struggle against the Communists. She launched a major campaign to bring women into the party and convince their male colleagues to take them seriously. As she explained to the party's male leaders, all of the other parties were strenuously engaged in competing for women's allegiance. While the National Socialists had a history of having the strongest women's movement, they were in danger of losing that advantage due to neglect. Even many of the wives of party members were voting Communist or Catholic, she charged. There was no excuse for not winning them over to the National Socialist camp. To begin, she announced a plan to register one hundred thousand new women and found one thousand new local organizations.[31] She also worked tirelessly to focus local leaders on the fight against the Communists and bring up party morale. In a letter to one of her district officials, she declared that the National Socialists were holding the line in their fight against Communist agitation, confiding that the Communists were beginning to worry about losing support in the next elections. Although she admitted that events in neighboring Poland and Hungary were troublesome, she held fast to the conviction that the Communists would not be able to stifle opposition in Czechoslovakia as they had done in those places, at least as long as Beneš was president. Zemínová urged her correspondent to throw herself into party work because the "biggest battle for democracy and the independence of the state lies in front of us."[32] As she wrote in another letter to the head of the party's women's group in the town of Horní Litvínov, the Czech nation did not take kindly to terror and would not easily submit to Communist domination. It was in resistance to such terror they had "broken up Austria, fought Hitler to the death, and believe me, we will also disperse this red cloud over our borders."[33]

Although Zemínová exuded confidence, the Communist Party's Central Women's Commission, led by Julie Prokopová and Anežka Hodinová, was ready for a fight. Their plan for 1947 was essentially the same as Zemínová's: to aggressively recruit more women. They hoped to make their members the backbone of every event or organization concerned with Czech women, and envisioned Communist women fanning out into every local community, where they would "help shape the opinion of Czechoslovak women in a positive relationship to the government and Gottwald."[34] Like the National Socialists, Communist women launched a major membership drive in 1947, but their effort seemed to be better supported by their men. Writing for the magazine directed at female party functionaries in May 1947, KSČ leader Rudolf Slanský declared that that the membership campaign would explicitly focus on women and young people. At that moment, he said, 30.5 percent of KSČ members were women, which was already the highest percentage of any Czechoslovak party, reflecting what he called the party's leading role in fighting for women's equality. But, said Slanský, the party's goal was to have half of its members be women. To achieve this, the Communist Party needed to show Czechoslovak women that it could transform the promises of the Košice program from words on paper into reality.[35]

Apparently, the KSČ did quite well in convincing women that it was committed to their interests: about 40 percent of those who joined the party in 1947 were women, and this number swelled to 50 percent in the cities of Prague, Kladno, and Brno. This was a marked improvement over previous efforts. In all, the Communists added 46,148 women to their membership rolls over the course of the year, giving them the impressive total of 446,148 female members. To put this number into perspective, in the fall of 1947 there were just under 600,000 people registered with the National Socialist party as a whole.[36] Despite their success, the Communists were, as Zemínová implied, increasingly nervous about their position. The leaders of the Central Women's Commission constantly referred to enemies who wanted to sabotage the Two-Year Plan: "The reaction is concentrating" they claimed, "looking for ways to strengthen the reactionary front and disempower us" by blaming the KSČ for problems with food distribution and low living standards. They vowed to put all their energy into fighting this conspiracy.[37]

In this poisonous atmosphere, building a truly nonpartisan women's organization like the old WNC was an incredibly difficult task. Former WNC leaders attempted to do so, however, through the CCW, which was modeled on its predecessor and dedicated to realizing women's equality "not only theoretically, but practically."[38] Like the WNC, the CCW was a federation of independent women's groups with a central core of officers and "expert" working groups dedicated to following the interests of the entire membership. In the intensely politicized atmosphere after the Second World War, however, an organization that purported to represent the interests of all Czechoslovak women could not exist without partisan involvement. The four parties of the National Women's Front conceded the need for a "professional" group dedicated to women's interests and distinct from their own "political" organization, but they still demanded representation on the CCW presidium.[39] From the beginning, the CCW struggled to maintain a place between the NWF and the individual parties. Its leaders continually emphasized their role not simply as feminists or advocates but as experts in women's affairs, a special group of skilled workers who could perform a distinct service for Czechoslovak women. The CCW created working groups to tackle a number of different issues, including old priorities, like revising citizenship regulations and family and marriage law, and new concerns, like ensuring that women were not disadvantaged in new national insurance schemes and arranging shop hours to benefit working women. The CCW also worked diligently to give women a voice in the writing of the new Czechoslovak Constitution, which began in earnest after the 1946 elections.[40]

But although a matter like the constitution was certainly one in which women had an interest regardless of party, partisan infighting made work within the CCW increasingly torturous. CCW president Milada Horáková had followed in Plamínková's footsteps by becoming a National Socialist representative to the National Assembly in 1946. Her political activities did have their benefit for the organization; she was appointed to the Assembly's constitutional commission and managed to arrange a meeting between its members and CCW representatives, which was impossible during the debates over the old constitution.[41] However, her link to the National Socialists also caused difficulties. Leaders of the Communist Party's Central Women's Commission in 1946 discussed their problems with the CCW. They recognized that the CCW could do good work and represented a truly "progressive" viewpoint, but were afraid that it was too identified with Horáková, a National Socialist. They called her "aggressive" and "ambitious" and were wary of supporting the CCW if it remained under her leadership. They planned to try and undermine her control of the group by placing their own comrades closely around her, so that they could influence the work of the CCW and perhaps even gain popularity with women alongside Horáková.[42]

Making things more difficult was the fact that many of the Communists were not foreigners to the Czech women's movement, but some of its veteran practitioners. Numerous members of the Czech intellectual elite joined the KSČ right after the war, and women were no exception. Indeed, frustration with the slow pace of progress for women's rights in the First Republic may have motivated many feminists to consider aligning themselves with the Communists, who not only had a long history of supporting gender equality but, as a former opposition party, also could not be blamed for the wrongs of previous governments. According to Vilma Součková, many of those left after the liquidation of the WNC came to realize that "a global socialist view" was the best way to achieve equality even before the end of the war, and quite a number of old WNC functionaries became Communists.[43] As tensions grew sharper between the Communists and National Socialists, work in the CCW grew harder to accomplish, and friendships began to fray under the strain. Horáková was particularly hurt by the antipathy she now felt from her old WNC colleague, the judge Zdenka Patschová, who tried to get her to join the KSČ and threatened her when she refused, saying "if we win, we must arrest you, and if you are brought into my court, I must sentence you to death for all you have done to undermine the regime."[44] But Milada Horáková was not one to go back on her convictions, and she was convinced that the Communists were bent on attacking democratic government. According to one story, when a colleague complained that the Communists seemed to be gaining the upper hand, Horáková replied that they were not going to gain the upper hand on her, adding, "a lot of people will still find me a hard nut to crack."[45]

This viciousness brewing inside the Czech women's movement shows how much politics had changed in Czechoslovakia since 1945. As in the interwar years, many politically active Czech women shared many of the same goals. They wanted to see the promises of the Košice program fulfilled, giving women and men equal access to social security, education, and economic opportunity. But, in the postwar era, consensus on such issues quickly ran aground on ideological differences. Each party began to see itself as the home of the righteous, and its opponents as the representatives of evil. As politics became polarized along the lines of good and evil, the possibility for dialogue disappeared, and the chance for building a workable consensus faded.

## February 1948 and Its Aftermath

From mid-1947 on, conflicts between the parties of the National Front escalated to a fever pitch, influenced at least in part by the poisonous atmosphere of the early Cold War. The steadily growing animosity between the United States and the Soviet Union made the idea of acting as a bridge between East and West untenable. Now, it seemed, everyone would have to choose sides. Inside the Czech lands, the idea of a unique Czechoslovak road to socialism began to fall apart. As the KSČ moved to solidify its power within the police force and the unions, the façade of the National Front quickly disintegrated into open battle between those who supported the Communists and those who did not.[46]

Things came to a head at a government meeting on February 13, 1948, when the National Socialists tried to make a stand on what was a relatively minor issue involving personnel transfers within the police force. Their decision to hold firm stemmed from a wider fear that the Communist Minister of the Interior, Vacláv Nosek, was using his position to turn the police into a KSČ institution. So the National Socialist ministers in the government announced that they would refuse to participate in government meetings until the transfers were reversed. When their demands were not met, they resigned, and took the Cabinet members from the Slovak Democratic and People's parties with them. The resigning ministers obviously hoped that their action would bring down the government and necessitate early elections, which they hoped to win. However, their plan was compromised by the fact that they had neglected to consult the Social Democrats in advance. By themselves, the National Socialists, Slovak Democrats, and People's Party did not form a majority of the government. Unless the Social Democrats joined them, there was nothing that could legally force Gottwald's government to fall. And he decided to make sure it would remain standing.[47]

Although the National Socialists had been the ones to resign, it was the KSČ that took the initiative. Communist leaders immediately decried the resignations as a reactionary attempt to break the National Front, divide the country, and destroy the revolution. Calling the resigning ministers traitors, Gottwald created what he called the Central Action Committee to root them and their supporters out of the National Front, leaving behind a new coalition of Communist fellow-travelers. At the same time, the KSČ mobilized its membership, about one and a half million strong, bringing them out into the streets to protest against this "attack" on the people's democracy. The other parties were paralyzed by this show of force, reduced to looking on in horror as hundreds of thousands of workers in Prague participated in a one-hour general strike in support of Gottwald's government. In the end, enough members of the National Assembly, whether out of conviction, fear, or opportunism, agreed to support the government for it to retain its majority.[48]

The matter now rested with President Beneš. If he accepted the resignations of the opposition ministers, Gottwald would be free to replace them with his own supporters. If not, the opposition would remain in the government. Under immense pressure, he yielded, and a Communist-dominated government was installed on February 25, 1948. This was ostensibly a legal transfer of power, made possible through the ill-advised actions of the opposition parties. However, Communist-sponsored violence and intimidation were crucial in determining the final shape of events. Much of this work was carried out by the so-called Action Committees. These ad-hoc groups of KSČ supporters formed throughout the country, fanning out from the Central Action Committee into every nook and cranny. In government ministries, public offices, within the other political parties, inside factories, businesses, and mass organizations like unions and clubs, Action Committees took root on every level and in virtually every public body. Their goal was to foil the "reactionary conspiracy" against the people's democracy, which generally involved identifying people who did not agree with the government's position and kicking them out of their positions. It was the Action Committees that performed the job of wrecking the opposition, purging anyone who refused to publicly support the government and driving them out of public life.[49]

The women's movement could not remain outside this process. The Council of Czechoslovak Women was invited to send delegates to the initial meeting of the Central Action Committee of the National Front, held on February 23, 1948. The CCW's governing committee agreed to send representatives, armed with a resolution declaring that the CCW "stood on the progressive front, but insisted on free elections." But the committee also decided, by a vote of twenty to thirteen, that the CCW would not formally join the Action Committee. The next day, Milada Horáková received a phone call from one of the Council's secretaries, telling her that CCW vice president Julie Prokopová, a high-ranking member of the KSČ, had demanded that Horáková agree to the organization's participation in the Action Committee. If she would not do this, Prokopová said, Horáková should surrender the Council's official stamp and some of its stationery so that Prokopová could join on behalf of herself and the thirteen members of the executive committee who had voted for inclusion. Horáková angrily replied that she was still the president of the CCW and would not allow the vote of its committee to be undermined in a blatantly undemocratic violation of its bylaws. "I am," she said, " a person who is used to closely adhering to laws, regulations, and rules." Instead of permitting Prokopová to have her way, she agreed to call a special emergency meeting of the governing committee the next day so that the entire group could revisit the issue. The meeting was called, but not before Prokopová had already acted on her own, writing (without the proper stationery or stamp) to ask that the Council of Czechoslovak Women be included as a member of the Central Action Committee, with Prokopová as its official representative.[50]

Speaking to the assembled committee members the next morning, Prokopová defended herself by saying, "the things that are developing around us are of the type that the true women's movement represented by the CCW cannot remain outside of them." If she had not taken charge, she contended, the CCW would not have been on the list of groups that had agreed to participate in the Action Committee, which had already been given to Gottwald. After she finished justifying her actions, the meeting was interrupted by women who had been delegates at the recently held Congress of Factory Councils. Since these women-unionists represented the largest organization within the CCW federation, they demanded that the CCW follow the lead of the unions and join the Action Committee. The women proclaimed: "women unionists will always be on guard against any threat to the Republic and its path to socialism and will not allow other forces within the CCW to devalue the progressive women's movement with their passivity." One of the women added, "if Ms. Plamínková was among us she would not stand by negatively but would be inclined toward working women, toward the strength of progress." Hearing Plamínková's name used as justification for joining the Action Committee angered her old friend (and former leader of teacher's unions) Antonie Maxová, who heatedly defended socialism but decried the events of the previous few days. She concluded by saying, "I remembered Senator Plamínková today as well, and she would certainly be on the side of progress, but not for a minute would she move off the path of democracy."[51]

After Maxová's outburst, the unionists were asked to leave, and the members of the committee discussed what the proper reaction of the women's movement should be. Quite a few of those present seemed unsure and perhaps afraid, asking for clarification on what precisely the Action Committee was and what joining it would mean. There were a few very vocal KSČ supporters (including Prokopová, Netušilová, and Augusta Müllerová) who presented the Action Committee as a new National Front "with the task of perfecting the reconstruction program." They presented the decision to join a vote in favor of "socializing democracy," arguing that not participating in the Action Committee would mean rejecting the Košice program and all that it stood for. They also reasoned that many other mass organizations, including the unions and the cooperatives, had already joined. This kind of talk seemed persuasive to women like Irene Malinská, who said she felt that the decision represented an enormous responsibility, but that it was clear that "the CCW cannot go against the people." But some of those present resisted the way the Communists characterized the Action Committee. Božena Kubičková insisted that the debate was not about "socializing democracy," because all the parties were in favor of further socialization, national insurance, and maintaining Czechoslovakia's Soviet alliance. "The difference is," she said, "that we want to take the democratic road and we reject methods in which someone autocratically does something that has not been voted on, even if they did it with the best intention." Her argument was not enough to win over the majority of the members, however, and the committee agreed to join the Action Committee by a vote of thirty to seven, with five abstentions.[52]

After the vote had been taken, Milada Horáková rose to speak. She had been mostly silent during the debate, she said, because she did not want her views to overly color the proceedings. But now she had to vent her own feelings. She was against joining the Action Committee because, in her opinion, it was not "the constitutional and democratic path." No one, she said, really knew what the Action Committees were, but it was certain that they were taking on enormous power and acting without real legal authority or oversight. They were, without mincing words, the shock troops of a revolution, and she vehemently opposed this kind of attack on the parliamentary system. She also strongly objected to those who contended that the CCW was not "progressive" or "radical" enough. The point of the CCW, she said, was not to be radical, but to create a coalition between

Czech women from both sides of the political spectrum that could span different opinions. To move away from that was to exclude some people from participation, and she rejected that path.[53]

As she finished speaking, Horáková acknowledged that her own opinions put her on the wrong side of the vote, but declared that this was no reason she could not stay in her post as president. "Maybe you think that I don't feel strong enough," she said, but "I will stay in charge until a plenary meeting removes me or until revolutionary circumstances force me to go." In fact, as soon as Horáková finished speaking, Julie Prokopová proposed that she be immediately removed as the head of the organization. However, Horáková's point that only a plenary meeting had the power to elect a new president carried some weight with those present. The committee did not vote to replace her out of hand, but instead agreed to call a new plenary meeting as soon as possible. This turned out to be just a temporary reprieve, as bylaws and regulations were soon cast aside in the name of political expediency.[54] The very next day, Horáková found herself suddenly locked out of the CCW offices. A self-proclaimed Action Committee of Czechoslovak Women declared it was taking over both the CCW and the National Women's Front in order to purge them of enemy elements that threatened to harm the people's democracy. Those who had voted with Horáková against joining the Action Committee were removed from the CCW. A similar process occurred in the central office of the NWF, where Fraňa Zemínová, the Catholic leader Marie Trojanová, and others were stripped of their posts. The leaders of the Action Committee urged women all over the country to form their own committees and take over local branches of the CCW and NWF. These local Action Committees would then purge unreliable elements out of the lower levels of both organizations and "help in the cleansing of the nation."[55]

At a meeting of the KSČ Central Women's Commission on February 26, Julie Prokopová defended all that had happened, saying that she and those who assisted her had acted in a completely correct manner. "The CCW, " she said, "had feigned a progressive orientation against fascism on the outside, but in reality it was governed by reactionary elements that hindered every positive effort." Horáková and the National Socialists were responsible for this untenable situation, and they had to go. Now the Commission members had to decide what they would do next. As Prokopová noted, they had an opportunity to put themselves in a strong position to "direct the education and mood of women." They decided right away to use the situation to liquidate the Czechoslovak Association of University Women, because of its "reactionary orientation," and promote a complete shakedown in the Housewives' Union, which they considered a nest of National Socialists. The NWF would also no longer be needed and could be disbanded. The Council of Czechoslovak Women they would keep, after cleansing its branches of women like Horáková. In fact, they later planned to expand the CCW and make it into a mass organization for Czechoslovak women. This was done and, its name changed to the Federation of Czechoslovak Women, the CCW lived on during the Communist regime as the official public outlet for women in Czechoslovakia.[56]

## The Trial of Milada Horáková

For Milada Horáková, being removed from her place at the head of the Council of Czechoslovak Women was only the beginning. Amongst themselves, female Communist leaders spoke of the need to publicize an attack on Horáková as a "warning sign" to others who might consider opposing them. They publicized her expulsion from the CCW and denounced her as a reactionary element in the Czech women's movement.[57] Within a few days, Horáková had been removed from her other positions in public life and even found herself ceremonially thrown out of some associations she had never joined. She lost her job with the Social Office of the City of Prague, and soon her husband, Bohuslav Horák, was fired as well. A few weeks later, she completed the cycle by resigning her seat in the National Assembly as a form of public protest against the events of February. She turned in her resignation on March 10, 1948, just after the mysterious suicide of the foreign minister, Jan Masaryk, son of Tomáš Masaryk.[58] Although she had given up her place in the National Assembly, Milada Horáková did not retreat into private life, nor did she leave the country, as a number of her colleagues did. As she wrote to some of them, she felt strongly that her place was at home, where she could work toward ending the Communist domination of politics. She knew that such work was dangerous, but she chose it anyway, remarking to one of her friends abroad, "one who has been imprisoned in German concentration camps like me . . . no longer fears what a man can do to another man. In any case, my own countrymen cannot be worse that the Germans."[59]

Horáková's activities during the months after February 1948 are difficult to determine. She certainly had strong ties to a number of leaders within the National Socialist party, including party chief Petr Zenkl and former government minister Herbert Ripka. She visited both men a number of times before they fled abroad, and then secretly corresponded with them. Evidence indicates that after they left the country, Horáková became a member of a group know as the " political six," a secret association of National Socialist loyalists who met to discuss what was going on in the country and report on events to their colleagues in exile. Horáková's biographer, Zora Dvořáková, called her a "master at gaining and gathering information" that she would then send abroad. For well over a year Horáková's reports to Zenkl gave the exiles a vivid portrait of the place they had left behind. They might not have always liked what they heard. Horáková quite emphatically told Zenkl that people were suspicious about hearing that the banned Agrarian and National Democratic parties had been reconstituted abroad. They did not, she wrote "want to substitute a leftist dictatorship with a rightist one." Instead, they wanted to be sure that most elements of the Košice program, including the nationalization of major industries and state-sponsored rights to employment, vacation, and a pension would be maintained.[60]

Besides corresponding with those across the border, Horáková was interested in creating a positive alternative political program to have ready for the time when an opposition party could openly function again. She firmly believed that any useful opposition needed to be clear about what it was for as well as what it fought against. Therefore, she devoted her energy toward working out the ideological basis and policy framework for an alternative regime, and not toward an armed revolt against the KSČ. Her efforts consisted mainly of organizing or attending meetings with people from different partisan backgrounds to construct a workable program. Besides meeting with other National Socialists, Horáková was in contact with a number of people from other opposition parties and tried to create a common organization between them, although this idea did not go anywhere. Despite her network of contacts, however, she was not by any means the center of opposition activity, but merely a member of one group among many.[61]

Horáková's clandestine activities suffered setbacks almost immediately, as some of those involved were detained by the State Security Services (Státní bezpečnost or StB). Drawing on their investigation of these individuals, the police decided to question Horáková as well. She was taken into custody at her office in late September 1949. Her husband, Bohuslav Horák, barely escaped from the agents that also showed up at their home, running in his house slippers out through the garden. After finding out that his wife had been arrested, he managed to slip across the border to Germany, where he stayed for over five years before finally getting permission to emigrate to the United States.[62]

Horáková was arrested just as a Cold War–inspired paranoia started to sweep over Eastern Europe. The search for traitors and class enemies intensified, heavily encouraged by Stalin, who hoped to create satellite Communist parties that would be too cowed by fear to take an independent line from the Soviet Union. In their quest to create more reliable political partners, Soviet advisers to East European Communist regimes introduced the phenomenon of the show trial, where political opponents were publicly tried for treason in heavily publicized and intricately staged events. Such trials had already begun in Hungary, and the Soviets hoped to bring them to Czechoslovakia, as well. Soviet advisers were sent to Prague to assist the StB in organizing trials there. When Milada Horáková was taken into custody, her captors did not know exactly what purpose she would serve. But as they began to investigate her and her associates, they began to envision a trial of a vast conspiracy to bring down the Communist regime, led by none other than Milada Horáková. The trial that they eventually created was the first of its kind in Czechoslovakia, and it provided the basis for many future show trials.

It is not entirely clear why the security agents responsible for designing the trial eventually settled on Horáková as their ringleader. Both Dvořáková and the historian Karel Kaplan suggest that, in the end, she was simply the one in custody that best fit their requirements. The trial planners had decided that they wanted a scenario that warned of a global conspiracy to overthrow the People's Democratic regime and they had proof that Horáková, a publicly known figure, had not only corresponded with prominent exiles like Zenkl and Ripka but had tried to acquire information about the true state of the economy to send to them.[63] In addition, as the former head of the National Assembly's Foreign Affairs committee and the CCW, it was easy to show that she had extensive contacts with influential people in Western governments.

Horáková did not prove to be a very cooperative subject, especially at the beginning. In her first set of recorded interrogations, conducted after she had been in prison for about six weeks, she readily admitted that she had a critical view of what had happened in February 1948 but steadfastly denied being involved in any illegal activity and claimed that the meetings she had attended all rejected the idea of forming illegal cells to actively oppose the KSČ. Even after several more months of relentless interrogations, she still refused to agree with her captors' version of events. One of the StB agents who questioned her remembered her later as an "absolute and ardent anti-Communist fighter," an impression that is borne out by some of her interrogation records.[64] When asked in a confrontational questioning session conducted in late January of 1950 if she had plotted to overthrow the people's democracy and return Czechoslovakia to the "subjection of Western imperialists," she firmly replied that she could never bear to see her country subjected to any form of imperialism. By this point in her captivity, she was willing to admit on the record that she wanted to oust the current regime, but insisted on adding that this was because she considered it "a sure form of dictatorship, not as democracy or the government of the people, but the government of one party." She declared that the goal of any punishable offenses she may have committed was only to establish a regime that was truly based on the "will of the people, expressed in free elections."[65]

But by her last set of recorded interrogations, taken in late April and May 1950, Horáková was more willing to adopt the role her interrogators prepared for her. Although no sure record of her treatment in prison exists, others incarcerated with her variously remembered being interrogated incessantly at all hours of the day, woken at odd times to see if they remembered the testimony that had been prepared for them, threatened with the arrest of spouses or family members, beaten, or forced to walk incessantly up and down the halls all day long.[66] Whatever physical or psychological pressures Horáková endured, she was finally convinced to sign some statements that fit the character the trial planners had decided she would play. For example, when asked what side she would take in a war between West and East, she agreed that she would take the side of the West, in order to use the situation to bring down the Communist regime in Czechoslovakia. When the questioner then demanded to know if this meant she wanted to create a fifth column in the country, she replied, "yes, it could be called that, or the actions of our subversive group would have to lead to this result."[67] Even though Horáková stressed in later portions of the interrogation that her activities were focused on passive resistance and not armed conflict, the mere suggestion of war in the newly nuclear standoff between the United States and Soviet Union was precisely what the trial organizers planned to use to convince the population that dangerous elements were in their midst. Milada Horáková was ready for her trial.

Just a few weeks later, the Justice Ministry published its indictment in the case they called "Milada Horáková and Associates." Twelve others were indicted along with her: six from her National Socialist party, along with two Social Democrats, two People's Party members, and two former Communists. Interestingly, three of the National Socialists on the dock were women; the others were Fraňa Zemínová and National Assemblywoman Antonie Kleinerová, who had known Horáková from their shared time in German prisons.[68] The indictment accused Horáková of organizing the others to work under the direction of exiled National Socialist leaders Petr Zenkl and Herbert Ripka. The group's goal was "to work for the return of capitalism and pre-Munich relations" via foreign intervention. According to the indictment, the exiles abroad ordered the conspirators to commit espionage; support terrorist acts, including attempts on the lives of KSČ leaders; and create "passive resistance" in industry to sabotage the economy. Their ultimate aim was to form a fifth column of reactionaries who would fight against the people's democracies of Eastern Europe and their Soviet allies in a war to bring all of Europe under imperialist domination.

With this kind of heated rhetoric, the indictment painted a picture of a vast international conspiracy that was plotting to plunge Czechoslovakia into a devastating nuclear war.[69]

The trial began the day after the indictment was published, on May 31, 1950. Like the indictment, the trial was carefully planned and scripted beforehand to create the sense of imminent danger facing the country. All the participants, including the defendants, learned their parts in advance and generally said their lines as directed. Kleinerová recalled later that the only deviation she allowed herself was to begin answers before the prosecutors had finished asking the questions, as an oblique form of protest.[70] Some historians have asserted that several of the accused, including Horáková, deviated more substantially from the script, but at the time, few would have been able to tell. Live radio transmission of the trial was halted after the first day (the trial was still broadcast, but not live), and the transcripts that were published daily in the papers were corrected to reflect the prepared text.[71] What people heard from the trial was what the regime wanted them to hear: those elements in society that claimed to support democracy and the legacy of the First Republic were really only in favor of war, annihilation, and the triumph of the bourgeoisie over the masses.

According to the published transcripts, Horáková freely admitted to working toward the overthrow of the current government and the establishment of a new one based on "bourgeois principles." She claimed that she knew the information she sent abroad would be used to destabilize Czechoslovakia and assumed it would help lead to "armed conflict" in the world. Even more alarmingly, she was asked if she realized that the atomic bomb might figure in to such a conflict, and replied that she had "reckoned even with that." The most quoted bit of her testimony, however, was the last question asked by the prosecutor. He inquired whether she had considered that Prague might be hit if war broke out. According to the printed text, she replied, "If there is a war, we have to expect that all targets might be hit." To which the prosecutor added, "Even Prague? Isn't your sixteen-year-old daughter in Prague?" And Horáková ended her testimony simply by answering, "Yes."[72]

This testimony was used to make Horáková seem like a cold and calculating monster who was willing to sacrifice even her own daughter in her fight for Western imperialism. In articles published during and just after the trial, Horáková was constantly described in such a way as to make her seem as unfeeling and unfeminine as possible. She was referred to as "proud," "cold-blooded," and "uncontrollably ambitious and conceited," primarily concerned with her own personal advancement.[73] One book openly portrayed her as a perverted specimen of womanhood, titling its chapter about her deeds "Mother," as an ironic comment on her failure to embody ideal feminine values. The authors noted that she had seen some of the destroyed cities of Europe during the Second World War, had met women who had lost children to bombs, and was a mother herself. Yet, they wrote, "she helped those who wanted to drop bombs on the cities where tens of thousands of Czechoslovak children live, where even her own daughter lives?"[74] Contemporary commentators thus presented Horáková, who had let her maternal instincts be swallowed by her hatred for the people's democracy, as a woman who had betrayed her gender—and therefore could not expect any leniency on behalf of her sex.

Implicit in the drive to present Horáková as a ruthless warmonger was a comparison with the new regime's recent relentless association of women and peace. Shortly after Horáková's expulsion from the Council of Czechoslovak Women, the group had begun to concentrate its activities around a government-sponsored campaign for peace, which was an attempt to simplify the growing animosity of the Cold War into a fight between those who wanted war (Western imperialists) and those who believed in peace (the Soviet Union and its allies). This project had culminated in the weeks before the trial, when seventy thousand women gathered in the Old Town Square in Prague to declare themselves ready to "fight for peace and the happiness of our children."[75] Millions around the country signed petitions declaring themselves "women-mothers for peace" who were against atomic weapons. Next to this, Horáková and her companions in the courtroom did indeed seem "inhuman," as one of Horáková's former colleagues from the CCW wrote, wondering what kind of woman would want "war to destroy the blooming land and growing towns, to betray defenseless children, who would want their death?" Obviously, said Julie Prokopová, the current president of the CCW, Milada Horáková was motivated only by hate.[76]

On the last day of the trial, the defendants were given the chance to address the court and explain their actions. By several accounts, Horáková took this opportunity to deviate from the script and defend herself. She claimed that she had not been a traitor, but had always held onto her convictions and remained true to the legacies of Masaryk and Beneš.[77] By this point, however, her words, which were expunged from official transcripts of the trial, could have little effect. Even if the judges had believed her, they had departed from a system in which the truth carried legal weight. This trial was more political theater than legal forum, and the play had to be played out to its conclusion. As a spectacle, the trial had already been tremendously successful in evoking an emotional response from a frightened public worried about the possibility of nuclear war. As the week of testimony wore on, thousands of resolutions had poured into the prosecutor's office from factories, schools, clubs, and associations all over the country, condemning the accused and demanding they receive the strictest sentences possible.[78] The whole nation seemed to be screaming for the blood of the conspirators in an outpouring of hysteria that surprised trial officials. The prosecutors even referred to it in their closing statements, demanding that the judges listen to the wishes of the working class and punish the traitors severely. It only took three hours after the trial had been concluded for the judges to reach their verdict. All of the accused were found guilty of treason and four of them, including Milada Horáková, were sentenced to death. The others received prison terms ranging from fifteen years to life. International figures from Einstein to Churchill protested Horáková's sentence, but to no avail. Within a few weeks, all appeals for clemency had been denied and the executions were set for June 28, 1950.[79]

Milada Horáková had beaten the Nazis in court, but in Dresden she had been tried as an individual and able to use the law and the rules of evidence in her own defense. In her own country, she was tried as the symbol of the former regime, the representative of an ideology that had become an enemy, in a court where laws had given way to theater. As she realized at the very end, in this kind of situation, there was nothing she could do. In the days before her death, she wrote a series of letters to her family detailing her thoughts and trying to come to terms with her fate. In the first letter, she likened her situation to that of an industrial worker who looks away from his machine for a second and turns back to find himself being crushed to death. The same thing, she wrote, can happen to political actors who fail to notice what is really going on around them; their inattention also often ended in death.[80] In the last letter, written in the final hours before her execution, she urged her loved ones not to despair at her passing, declaring that she felt calm and clear in her conscience. She ended the letter as the dawn was beginning to break, knowing that with it would come her death, saying "I am going with my head held high—one has to know even how to lose. It is not a disgrace. Even an enemy won't lose respect if he is true and honest. In battle one falls, and what is life but a battle?"[81] With that, she bid her loved ones farewell, put down her pen, and was led to the courtyard of the Pankrác prison to be hanged.

The Communist regime intended Horáková's death to be a symbol. In the minds of those who planned the trial, she would represent the true character of those who opposed Communism: a traitorous demon who was so attached to the values of Western imperialism that she hardly blinked at the thought of destroying her own daughter in a nuclear conflagration. This caricature, however, clouded the true symbolism of her execution. When it tried and killed Milada Horáková, the Communist government of Czechoslovakia was silencing her vision of Czech democracy and the feminism that was so closely intertwined with it. With her death, the feminist hope for liberation via democracy was definitively silenced.

AFTER 1945, the Czechoslovak Communists came to power promising a new form of democracy, one that would finally fix the inequities that had persisted during the First Republic. Their people's democracy would combine the basic legal equality of all individuals with a universal standard of living that would guarantee all Czechs a new level of material prosperity. It would not, they claimed, move completely away from the legacy of Masaryk's ideology, but would add to it the power of scientific socialism. After living through the indignities of Munich and German occupation, many Czechs gravitated towards the KSČ, and with good reason. Not only did the Communists have fresh ideas and a positive vision of the future, they seemed to be getting results. This was particularly true in the case of gender equality. During the First Republic, equality between the sexes was accepted as a general principle, but rarely enacted into specific policies, especially in the realm of the family. The Communists actively set out to change that.

Indeed, even in the first months after February of 1948, those feminists who had supported the KSČ could consider themselves to have been on the right side of the struggle. Politically, the Communists were far better than the other parties at bringing women into public office; fully half of the women elected to the National Assembly in 1946 represented the KSČ. And the party supported them in their efforts to legislate equality for women. With speed and ease, the KSČ managed to achieve most of what the interwar Czech feminists had struggled in vain to win. In the realm of women's employment, the Košice program had explicitly promised that women would receive the equal pay for equal work, and as early as 1945 the KSČ sponsored legislation to make that a reality. By 1947, the Gottwald government had passed a new citizenship law that allowed women the ability to control their own national allegiance, ending for once and for all the problem of statelessness for married women.[82] Much more importantly, the Constitution of May 1948 was a clear improvement over the old Constitution of 1920. Following the suggestions of advisers from the CCW, the writers of the new constitution removed the ambiguities that had dogged Article 106, especially when it came to women's place within the family. The 1948 document used much more specific language and declared that "men and women will have the same position in the family and in society and they will have the same access to education, to all professions, offices, and ranks."[83] This statement of principle provided the legal basis for a new set of family and marriage laws, finished a year later, which finally gave men and women equal rights and responsibilities in the family and as parents to their children.[84] In 1955 the Soviet Union re-legalized abortion, and Czechoslovakia soon followed with a law that allowed abortions during the first trimester with the approval of a local commission.[85]

Going by such measures, or by state support for working families in the form of day-care centers, cafeterias, and laundries, the Communist regime certainly was a substantial improvement over the First Republic. But, as Milada Horáková knew only too well, the kind of equality offered by the people's democracy meant little, since it was conditioned on accepting a society where individuals did not have the freedom to pursue their own paths in life, and where they could be persecuted and tried in courts that made a mockery of the very legal system that supposedly guaranteed their equality. As Horáková saw it, democracy rested on the twin pillars of equality and freedom, guaranteed by the rule of law. Without those elements held in some sort of balance, it would collapse. This ruin, she saw, was the reality of the people's democracy, which would quickly evolve into a hierarchically organized party dictatorship. As such, the Communist state could engineer some things that would benefit its citizens, as women who had safe, legal abortions, or wives who no longer had to worry that their husband might die and deprive them of custody over their own children could attest. But, as in any dictatorship, these benefits came at the pleasure of those in charge; they were not something citizens could easily demand by virtue of their constitutional rights, even if they technically had them. This was something even female Communist Party functionaries soon discovered to their chagrin, when the Central Committee of the Party decided, in 1954, to disband its Women's Commission, leaving party women without their own power center or a way to formally protect their own interests. By then, though, they had no means of expressing their opposition, and had, in fact, seen all too vividly what public opposition could bring. They had discovered that Horáková was right, but it was too late.

AFTER A DECADE or so had passed, the "thaw" of the Khrushchev era finally began to be felt in Czechoslovakia, leading the Czechs to rethink the Stalinist excesses of the early 1950s. By 1963, all of those who had been imprisoned as a result of the Horáková trial had been quietly released. After the liberalization of the Czechoslovak regime during the Prague Spring of 1968, the verdict of the case was formally overturned, and the "conspiracy" was denounced as an "artificial construction."[86] But this rehabilitation was cut short by the Soviet invasion of August 1968 and the hard-line regime that followed it. Milada Horáková's last letters to her family languished somewhere in a file in the Ministry of the Interior. Although her family knew of their existence, they were never allowed to see them. It was only after the fall of the Communist regime in 1989 that they were finally found, delivered, and eventually published. Time now fully revised its judgment and Horáková was no longer a traitor, or even a patriot who had been mistaken about the proper path for her country, but a courageous martyr who had given her life fighting against an oppressive regime. She was given a memorial in the Slavín cemetery, where many of the Czech nation's honored figures are buried, and a boulevard in Prague now bears her name. Although Horáková has been resurrected, she has been remembered almost exclusively as a "victim of anti-democratic iniquity."[87] Few recall her as a feminist leader who spent a lifetime working for women's rights. That story, along with the rest of the history of the egalitarian Czech feminist movement, remains a largely overlooked aspect of the history of Czechoslovakia.

# CONCLUSION

As long as people are people, democracy in the full sense of the word will always be no more than an ideal; one may approach it as one would a horizon, in ways that may be better or worse, but it can never be fully attained. In this sense, you too are merely approaching democracy.

Václav Havel, Speech to the United States Congress, February 21, 1990

IN HIS BOOK about the European twentieth century, the historian Mark Mazower challenges the contemporary assumption that democracy was somehow destined to succeed in Europe. Europeans, he reminds us, did not "naturally" take to democracy and, in fact, often fought against it with surprising zeal. It was only during the years after the First World War that democracy gained more than a toehold on the European continent, and this initial experiment did not turn out well. After only twenty years, European democracy looked utterly defeated on all fronts.[1] Revived on the Western half of the continent after the end of the Second World War, stable democracies are only just beginning to form in contemporary Eastern Europe.

The Czech experiment with democracy during the first half of the twentieth century was one of Europe's more successful efforts during the interwar years, and yet it, too, failed on multiple occasions, sliding into "authoritarian democracy" in 1938 and the Communist people's democracy in 1948. While many factors led to these events, including a global economic crisis, a devastating war, and pressure from Czechoslovakia's powerful neighbors, the demise of the Czech democracy cannot be laid so neatly at the feet of others. Helping to tie all of these other factors together was a profound sense of ambivalence from Czechs themselves, many of whom began to wonder if democracy was something they really wanted or trusted.

Democracy began with great fanfare in the Czech lands, brought into being by a wave of popular approval that was unusual in Central Europe just after the First World War. The Czechoslovak Republic was engineered, for the most part, by men and women who were enthusiastically tied to their cause. These Czech democrats, as described by their compatriot, the first Czechoslovak minister of justice, František Soukup, pictured themselves as revolutionaries, fighting "for the self-determination of the nation, the Czechoslovak Republic, democracy, and social justice."[2] As Soukup's words attest, the "democracy" they struggled to achieve was a far-reaching concept, intricately connected to a number of objectives that went far beyond parliamentary government. They were motivated by a utopian vision of a socially just and mutually supportive community of citizens, linked to a state that tied national sovereignty to individual freedom. Public support for the new republic made these democrats think that the society they sought had been won, simply by declaring it so. In fact, the kind of transformation they wanted could not be engineered via a few new laws and the introduction of regular elections. Once the initial euphoria had died down, it became clear that writing a new Czechoslovak Constitution did not "establish" democracy. The constitution was a blueprint for the process of democratization, not its endpoint. In actual practice, Czechoslovak democracy turned out to be a work in constant progress, as Czechs struggled amongst themselves to define precisely what they wanted from their government. Not even the most ardent of Czech democrats were adequately prepared to deal with the fact that many of their countrymen had different, conflicting ideas about what democracy should look like.

Women's citizenship was a field on which the process, and the progress, of democracy could be debated and enacted. Women's equality emerged early in 1918 as a symbol for the victory of democracy; it was hailed as the means by which the Czech nation would fling off its "backward" past as part of the Habsburg Empire. As such, it was not seen as a threatening concept, but could even represent the bright future facing the nation as it moved into modernity. But decreeing "women's equality" turned out to be a more difficult thing than even its proponents had realized. Equality was not an easily defined value, and figuring out how it applied to women in the Czechoslovak Republic was a torturous task. Meant to be an accomplishment that democrats could neatly tick off on their political checklist, the cause of women's rights became a source of constant questions and argument. It forced Czechs to consider how they wanted to define citizenship and rights and made them think about the potential social and cultural ramifications of their political ideologies.

It is in some ways remarkable that there could be so much discussion around women's place in the Czech democracy at all. This was in part due to the work of Czech feminists, who had helped to create enthusiasm for women's rights by tying the issue to Czech nationalist concerns. Charging that freedom for both men and women was necessary for the Czech nation to realize its full potential, they were able to fashion a wide-reaching consensus around the issue of women's suffrage that lasted for two decades. However, this consensus was limited to voting rights. Efforts to link support for women's political rights to campaigns in support of women's civil or social equality were not very successful. Many feminists found it difficult to comprehend how some could support women's equality in the political sphere and reject it in other aspects of life. The root of this disjuncture lay in the very way in which suffrage had become acceptable to many Czechs: its tie to the national good. Women who voted were not seen as threatening to the nation; indeed, they strengthened it by showing their public commitment to the state. But this did not mean that gender difference was no longer crucial to national stability. Gender difference within the family was perceived by many Czechs as the crucial glue that held Czech society together. For the family to be comprehensible, it had to conform to a gendered structure that divided tasks and powers differently among men and women.

When Czech feminists from the Women's National Council tried to bring democracy into the family, the public effectively saw them as attempting to destroy this beloved model of family life. Fear that progress might mean changing even their most intimate lives brought men and women out against the feminist project to revise Czechoslovak family law, set society against the double earners, and inspired resistance to changing the doctrine of family unity as the basis for citizenship law. Although lifting women's legal subordination to their husbands would not have mandated any changes in the ways people lived their lives, it was seen as having a potentially shattering effect on family life. As Marie Tippmannová remarked in a 1923 article cautioning married women against working for wages outside the home, a woman could not "serve two masters."[3] The real problem, however, was a woman's presumed desire to serve herself rather than her family.

One effect of this anxiety over women's right to self determination was that Czechs began to disassociate the language of rights from democracy. Although in 1918 democracy and equal rights seemed inseparable, by 1938, only democracy, bereft of its tie to rights, was essential to the health of the nation. This was a gradual process, observable in the ways in which Czechs began to argue against feminist demands for women's legal equality. Opponents of the feminist program found it difficult to combat the argument that democracy, as defined by the legal standards of the Czechoslovak Republic, required granting all citizens the same rights. So they stopped trying to respond to this point directly, and instead worked to change the terms of the argument itself. Sidestepping the issue of legal rights, they emphasized women's social responsibilities as mothers and wives. Like those who wrote angry letters to *Přítomnost* decrying the existence of the double earners, or demanded legal abortion in the name of social justice, opponents of the feminist agenda closely connected a woman's acceptance of her socially appointed role as wife and mother, the health of the Czech family, and the good of the Czech nation. It was in this way that women's legal rights, and the egalitarian brand of democracy that underlay them, seemed to endanger the institutions of family and nation that Czechs saw as most crucial to their survival.

Looking at how attitudes toward women's rights in the Czech lands changed and mutated over the two decades between the two world wars shows us one of the mechanisms by which the enthusiastically democratic Czech public of 1918 could be transformed into the willing supporters of a rightist authoritarian regime in 1938. The key difference between these two regimes, both of which claimed to be "democratic," was in the way they approached the matter of rights. In 1918, although there was plenty of debate over the meaning of citizenship, many rights were considered to be universal and worthy of state protection. It was "self-evident" that women and men, Czechs and Germans, rich and poor, would all have the same access to politics and the public sphere. The "authoritarian democratic" regime had a different interpretation of the state's responsibility to protect its citizens' rights: essentially, such considerations were always secondary to national security. When it came to issues of women's civil rights, Czech politicians gradually became more comfortable ignoring the need to consider the constitution as the basis for their legal and political practice. Eventually, they would place "the nation" above even the most basic requirements of democratic government. Following the same logic that allowed politicians to vilify the double earners and attack their wages, Czech authoritarian democrats not only banned married women from the workplace, but also attacked the civil rights of Jews, banned the Communist Party, and sucked the life out of parliamentary government by passing an Enabling Act, which allowed rule by presidential decree. In each case, these politicians hoped to save the nation from threat—the same action that democracy itself was supposed to achieve. What they failed to realize, however, was that they were in fact in the process of hollowing out democracy itself.

The Second Republic was not the result of a sudden decision or of the machinations of the Western powers at Munich. It came from a growing consensus among Czechs about what they wanted from government and from democracy: not individual freedom or equality, but national security and a form of social justice that did not threaten the gendered nature of the family. Citizenship became subservient to the needs of the nation, and rights were based on a citizen's place within the national community. This was both how women could be denied rights on the basis of their womanhood and how Jews or Communists could be stripped of their right to equal treatment. Equality, in all of these cases, seemed damaging to the national whole.

For some Czech women, giving up a claim to equality was a welcome relief. It allowed them to feel more secure in their own chosen roles as women. However, as the women who led the Women's Center would discover, trading freedom for security was a risky bargain. While Czech women during the Second World War might have had their place in the family strengthened, their ability to choose their own role in life was limited more than they would have liked. Having given up their claim to equality, they were ill-equipped to resist such attacks. The end of the Second World War seemed to bring the cause of women's equality back to where it had been in 1918, but this was only an illusion. Even though the politicians of the Second Republic were banished from public life, the crucial break between democracy and rights remained. It was deepened by the Communists, who created a "people's democracy" that gave short shrift to individual rights, favoring material equality and an end to class privilege instead. In the people's democracy, Masaryk's idea of democracy as a community of equal individuals died a final death, replaced by a state where individual freedom was denied and "equality" was achieved through force. Under this regime, there was no place for those like Milada Horáková, who had different ideas about what democracy should mean. As the living legacy of a different democratic vision, she was seen as a threat to the new socialist nation, and, as such, condemned to die.

The story of the Czech struggle with democracy is at once specifically Czech and tied to the European experience with democracy in the first half of the twentieth century. Although the particular ways in which Czechs negotiated with democracy were intertwined with their beliefs about themselves as a nation, their struggle to come to terms with the messy reality of democracy is also indicative of the problematic experience many Europeans had with democracy during these decades. The Czechs who rejected the democratic system they had known in 1938 did so not only because they felt this form of government was incapable of solving social problems, but because they feared the kinds of solutions democracy might bring. Democracy made the future too open; it left nothing sacred. Like many other Europeans in this era, they thought they had found a way of making democracy safer by limiting the freedom it offered and fashioning the rights of citizenship to promote stability rather than change. But their efforts instead transformed democracy into authoritarianism

In this way, this chapter of the past also becomes a cautionary tale for all those who want to make democratic governments work. The threatening potential of democracy to transform social relations as well as political practice is still with us today, and it no less easier to manage. In developing democracies in the Middle East, for example, the prospect of women's equality has created enormous anxiety. But this is not only a phenomenon that bedevils the less industrialized nations of the world. The decision of the United States Supreme Court in *Lawrence v. Texas* has helped to make the issue of equal civil rights for gay men and women a defining one in American politics today. Here, as in the Czech lands of an earlier era, the problem rests on the belief that acknowledging the right of gays to have the same legal status and privileges as married heterosexual men and women might have a pernicious effect on the institutions of family and marriage, endangering what some see as the core of social stability. This is not to say that the United States is on the cusp of turning into an authoritarian democracy. But it should remind us that even in the world's most power-ful democracy, there is nothing we can take for granted. In the United States, just like in Afghanistan, or the new Czech Republic, or anywhere, democracy is still only a process, always becoming, always changing, and never stable. Democracy will never be easy, and it will always have the power to threaten us with the new and unexpected. This is the nature of democracy. Perhaps the only remedy is to simply acknowledge this fact, and never assume that we have democracy, but only admit that we are working toward it.

# NOTES

## Abbreviations

| | |
|---|---|
| AFS ČR | Archiv Federálního Shromáždění Československé Republiky |
| AMV | Archiv Ministerstvo Vnitra |
| ANM | Archiv Národního Musea |
| ČSNS | Československá Strana Národně Socialistické |
| MS | Ministerstvo Spravedlnosti |
| MSP | Ministerstvo Sociální Péče |
| MV | Ministerstvo Vnitra |
| NRČ | Národní Rada Česká |
| PMR | Presidium Ministerské Rady |
| SÚA | Státní Ústřední Archiv |
| SVVŽ | Sdružení Vysokoškolsky Vzdělaných Žen |
| SZ | *Sbírka zákonů a nařizení československého státu* |
| Tisky | *Tisky k těsnopiseckém zprávám o schůzích poslanecké sněmovny národního shromáždění československého* |
| TZ-PS | *Těsnopisecké zprávy o schůzích poslanecké sněmovny národního shromáždění československého* |
| TZ-S | *Těsnopisecké zprávy o schůzích senátu národního shromáždění československého* |
| ÚKŽ-KSČ | Ústřední Komise Žen KSČ |
| ŽNR | Ženská Národní Rada |

## Introduction

1. The phrase comes from Padraic Kenney, *Carnival of Revolution: Central Europe 1989* (Princeton: Princeton University Press, 2002).

2. Other critical reappraisals of the post-Communist transition include Katherine Verdery, *What Was Socialism and What Comes Next?* (Princeton: Princeton University Press, 1996), esp. 204–35; and Sorin Antohi and Vladimir Tismaneanu, eds., *Between Past and Future: The Revolutions and 1989 and Their Aftermath* (Budapest: Central European University Press, 2000).

3. Carole Pateman, *The Sexual Contract* (Stanford: Stanford University Press, 1988).

4. Mary Louise Roberts, *Civilization Without Sexes: Reconstructing Gender in Postwar France* (Chicago: University of Chicago Press, 1994). Also see Susan Kingsley Kent, *Making Peace: The Reconstruction of Gender in Interwar Britain* (Princeton: Princeton University Press, 1993); Birgitte Soland, *Becoming Modern: Young Women and the Reconstruction of Womanhood in the 1920's* (Princeton: Princeton University Press, 2000). On fascism, see Kevin Passmore, ed., *Women, Gender, and Fascism in Europe, 1919–1945* (New Brunswick: Rutgers University Press, 2003); Victoria de Grazia, *How Fascism Ruled Women* (Berkeley: University of California Press, 1992); Claudia Koonz, *Mothers in the Fatherland: Women, The Family, and Nazi Politics* (New York: St. Martin's, 1987); Miranda Pollard, *Reign of Virtue: Mobilizing Gender in Vichy France* (Chicago: University of Chicago Press, 1998).

5. Although it has become popular to use the term "Bohemian lands" instead of "Czech lands," I use the latter here simply to try and make the material more accessible to a nonspecialist audience.

6. Just a small sampling of the best research in this vein includes Jeremy King, *Budweisers into Czechs and Germans* (Princeton: Princeton University Press, 2002); Chad Bryant, "Either German or Czech: Fixing Nationality in Bohemia and Moravia, 1939–1946," *Slavic Review* 61, no. 4 (2002): 683–706; Tara Zahra, "Reclaiming Children for the Nation: Germanization, National Ascription, and Democracy in the Bohemian Lands, 1900–1945," *Central European History* 37, no. 4 (2004): 501–43; and Eagle Glassheim, *Noble Nationalists: The Transformation of the Bohemian Aristocracy* (Cambridge, MA: Harvard University Press, 2005).

7. Bonnie Honig, "Difference, Dilemmas, and the Problems of Home," in *Democracy and Difference*, ed. Seyla Benhabib (Princeton: Princeton University Press, 1996), 258.

8. The magazine is *Vlasta*, which began life as *Rada Žen*, published by the Council of Czechoslovak Women, the leading Czech feminist organization after 1945 (for more on this, see chapter 7). On women in Communist Czechoslovakia, see Alena Heitlinger, *Women and State Socialism: Sex Inequality in the Soviet Union and Czechoslovakia* (Montreal: McGill-Queen's University Press, 1979).

9. A few recent books have begun to examine the history of Czech women, but have done little to link women's lives or organizations to Czech politics more broadly. Examples include: Jana Burešová, *Proměny společenského postavení českých žen v první polovině 20. století* (Olomouc: Universita Palackého, 2001); Milena Lenderová, *K hříchu i k modlitbě: žena v minulém století* (Prague: Mladá Fronta, 1999); and Lenderová, *Chytla patrola aneb prostituce za Rakouska i Republiky* (Prague: Univerzita Karlova, 2002).

## Chapter 1: Masaryk, Feminism, and Democracy in the Czech Lands

1. Jane Purvis, "'Deeds, Not Words,' Daily Life in the Women's Social and Political Union," in *Votes for Women*, eds. Jane Purvis and Sandra Stanley Holton, 135–40 (New York: Routledge, 2000). On the idea of "sex war," see Susan Kingsley Kent, *Sex and Suffrage in Britain 1860–1914* (Princeton: Princeton University Press, 1987).

2. Jiří Kořalka, "Zvolení ženy do českého zemského sněmu roku 1912," in *Žena v dějinách prahy, Documenta Pragensia*, ed. Václav Ledvinka and Jiří Pešek, 307–20 (Prague: Scriptorium, 1996).

3. T. G. Masaryk, "Moderní názor na ženu," in *Masaryk a ženy* (Prague: Ženská Národní Rada, 1930).

4. On the rise of Czech nationalism, see J. F. N. Bradley, *Czech Nationalism in the Nineteenth Century* (Boulder, CO: East European Monographs, 1984). A look at the earlier roots of the movement can be found in Hugh Agnew, *The Origins of the Czech National Renascence* (University Park: Pennsylvania State University Press, 1993).

5. Otto Urban, "Czech Society, 1848–1918," in *Bohemia in History*, ed. Mikuláš Teich (Cambridge: Cambridge University Press, 1998); Milan Znoj, Jan Havránek, and Martin Sekera, eds., *Český liberalismus* (Prague: Torst, 1995); Gary Cohen, "Neither Absolutism Nor Anarchy: New Narratives on Society and Government in Late Imperial Austria," *Austrian History Yearbook* 29, no. 1 (1998): 37–61.

6. Marie Neudorfl, "Masaryk's Understanding of Democracy Before 1914," Carl Beck Papers in Russian and East European Studies 708 (Pittsburgh: University of Pittsburgh Center for Russian and East European Studies, 1989), 10; Karel Čapek, *Masaryk on Thought and Life*, trans. M. and R. Weatherall (London: Allen and Unwin, 1938), 190–91. Of course, this doesn't mean that Masaryk himself always lived up to these ideals, as a few of his statements about German "immigrants and colonists" in the Czech lands attest.

7. T. G. Masaryk, *Tomáš Garrigue Masaryk o demokracii*, ed. Koloman Gajan, (Prague: Melantrich, 1991), 48, 108.

8. Čapek, *Masaryk on Thought and Life*, 204–6,194.

9. William Preston-Warren, *Masaryk's Democracy: A Philosophy of Scientific and Moral Culture* (Chapel Hill: University of North Carolina Press, 1941), 34.

10. Marie Neudorfl, "Masaryk and the Women's Question," in *T. G. Masaryk (1850–1937): Vol. 1, Thinker and Politician*, ed. Stanley B. Winters (London: Macmillan, 1990), 259.

11. When they married, Tomáš took her name as part of his own and became Tomáš Garrigue Masaryk.

12. Masaryk, "Moderní názor na ženu," 64–65. Mill makes similar statements in *The Subjection of Women* (Buffalo: Prometheus, 1986). See also his "Essay on Marriage and Divorce," in Alice Rossi, ed., *Essays on Sex Equality* (Chicago: University of Chicago Press, 1970).

13. T. G. Masaryk, *Mnohoženství a jednoženství,* 2nd ed. (Prague: Čin, 1925), 18–19.

14. Masaryk's definition of monogamy was very strict; he believed not just that people should have one sexual partner at a time, but that they should have only one sexual partner throughout their entire life. Masaryk, *Mnohoženství a jednoženství,* 21.

15. Masaryk, "Moderní názor na ženu," 65.

16. T. G. Masaryk, "Dodatek k Několika poznámkám o práci československých žen," in *Masaryk a ženy,* 22–23.

17. Linda Vonková, "Vzpomínka na jednu přednášku," in *Masaryk a ženy,* 199.

18. Olga Stranská, quoted in "Význam prof. Masaryka pro ženské hnutí," in *Masaryk a ženy,* 130.

19. T. G. Masaryk, "Postavení ženy v rodině a ve veřejném životě," in *Masaryk a ženy,* 71.

20. Masaryk, "Dodatek k Několika poznámkám o práci československých žen."

21. Masaryk, "Postavení ženy," 69–70.

22. R. T. S., "T. G. Masaryk jako otec," *Pražanka* 7, no. 331 (1931): 3. Many of his contemporaries extolled Masaryk's marriage and family life as a model of domestic happiness. See Jan Herben, *Masarykův rodinný život* (Brno: Fr. Borový, 1937).

23. On the early history of the Czech women's movement, see Marie Neudorfl, *České ženy v 19. století* (Prague: Janua, 1999); Milena Lenderová, *K hříchu i k modlitbě* (Prague: Mladá Fronta, 1999); and Katharine David, "Czech Feminists and Nationalism in the Late Habsburg Monarchy," *Journal of Women's History* 3, no. 2 (1991): 26–45.

24. Ludmila Mužíková-Nosilová, *Naše ženy v historii a ve vystavbě státu* (Prague: Ministerstvo Informací, 1946), 16–18. Also see Jana Brabencová, "Pražské ženy v procesu vývoje českého dívčího vzdělávání ve 2. polovině 19. století," in *Žena v dějinách prahy,* 203–12.

25. Gary Cohen, *Education and Middle Class Society in Imperial Austria* (West Lafayette: Purdue University Press, 1996), 73–74.

26. Brabencová, "Pražské ženy," 209–10.

27. David, "Czech Feminists," 28–30; Albina Honzaková, ed., *Československé studentky let 1890–1930* (Prague: Ženská Národní Rada a Minerva, 1930).

28. On the links between Czech feminism and nationalism, see Jitka Malečková, "Nationalizing Women and Engendering the Nation: The Czech

National Movement," in *Gendered Nations: Nationalisms and Gender Order in the Long Nineteenth Century*, ed. Ida Blom, Karen Hagemann, and Catherine Hall, 293–310 (New York: Berg, 2000).

29. David, "Czech Feminists," 40.

30. Mužíková-Nosilová, *Naše ženy*, 20.

31. Albina Honzáková, "Práce F. F. Plamínkové v ženským klubu českém," in *Kniha života: práce a osobnost F.F. Plamínkové* (Prague: Melantrich, 1935), 72–73.

32. Zdenka Wiedermannová-Motyčková, "Prof. Masaryk a ženské hnutí v Čechách," in *Masaryk a ženy*, 123; H. Gordon Skilling, *T. G. Masaryk Against the Current, 1882-1914* (University Park: Pennsylvania State University Press, 1994), 8–9. For individual memories of Masaryk, see the section entitled "Vzpomínky a úvahy" in *Masaryk a ženy*, 184–296.

33. Marie Vitková, "Masarykův vliv na generaci let devatdesátých," in *Masaryk a ženy*, 257; Ludmila Nosilová-Zlesáková, untitled, in *Masaryk a ženy*, 320; Albina Honzáková, "V předvečer osmdesátých narozenín T. G. Masaryka," in *Masaryk a ženy*, 273.

34. F. F. Plamínková, "Říjen 1918–1928," *Ženská Rada* 4, no. 9 (1928): 128.

35. The quotes are from a survey conducted in 1940 by the feminist journal *Ženská Rada* (Women's Council), in which prominent women activists were asked how they became feminists. "Anketa—Jak jsem se stala feministkou?" *Ženská Rada* 16, no. 2 (1940): 30–41.

36. There were, of course, both Germans and Austrians who adopted such an egalitarian stance, but they were at the outside rather than the center of their respective women's movements. And even many of these changed their attitudes toward an espousal of difference in the years after the First World War. This was certainly the case of the German radicals Anita Augsburg and Lida Gustava Heymann. See Leila Rupp, *Worlds of Women: The Making of an International Women's Movement* (Princeton: Princeton University Press, 1997). For a critique of German maternalism during the Weimar era, see Young-Sun Hong, "Gender, Citizenship and the Welfare State: Social Work and the Politics of Femininity in the Weimar Republic," *Central European History* 30, no. 1 (1997): 1–24.

37. On maternalism in Europe generally, see Sonya Michel and Seth Koven, eds., *Mothers of a New World: Maternalist Politics and the Origins of Welfare States* (New York: Routledge, 1993).

38. Plamínková quoted in Honzáková, "Osobnost F. F. Plamínkové," in *Kniha života*, 41.

39. The Austrian electoral system was quite complex and there were some women who already had the right to vote in some elections. Female estate owners in Bohemia were allowed to vote for Reichsrat delegates, but only by proxy. In addition, women who lived in Bohemia (but not in the cities of Prague or

Liberec) and met the tax threshold were able to vote for representatives to the Bohemian Diet. See David, "Czech Feminists," 36.

40. Albina Honzáková, "30 let práce Plamínkové za volební právo žen a občanskou rovnoprávnost žěn" (talk given on Czech radio, February 5, 1935), in *Kniha života*, 63.

41. Pavla Vošahlíková, "Česká žena v politice a veřejné činnosti na přelomu 19. a 20. století," in *Žena v dějinách prahy*, 295.

42. Although the Czech Social Democratic Party was not the only Social Democratic Party in what would become Czechoslovakia, it is the one I will mention most frequently, and so, for ease, I will call it simply the "Social Democratic Party." Its German-language counterpart will be the "German Social Democratic Party." I do not mean to imply that the Czech Social Democratic Party was in any way less nationally oriented or somehow superior to the German Social Democratic Party. My goal is merely to simplify the nomenclature.

43. T. Mills Kelly, "Feminist or Pragmatist or Both? Czech Radical Nationalism and the Woman Question, 1898–1914," *Nationalities Papers* 30, no. 4 (2002): 537–52.

44. Vošahlíková, "Česká žena," 297.

45. Kořalka, "Zvolení ženy."

46. For Masaryk's own reminiscences on his sudden rise to international prominence, see Karel Čapek, *Talks With T. G. Masaryk*, trans. Dora Round and Michael Heim (New Haven: Catbird Press, 1995).

47. Louis Rees, *The Czechs during World War One* (Boulder: East European Monographs, 1992).

48. T. G. Masaryk, Milan Štefánik, and Edvard Beneš, *Washingtonská deklarace* (Brno: Moravský Legionář, 1925). It was called the Washington Declaration because it was released by Masaryk in Washington DC.

49. See questionnaires collected by the Committee for Women's Voting Rights in preparation for a report for the International Women's Alliance, 1936, SÚA, ŽNR, box 16.

50. F. F. Plamínková, "Rok 1918," *Ženská Rada* 7, no. 8 (1931): 177.

51. There is no study of everyday life during the war to help illuminate this claim, although Maureen Healy's work on Vienna offers some potentially intriguing parallels. See Maureen Healy, *Vienna and the Fall of the Habsburg Empire: Total War and Everyday Life in World War I* (New York: Cambridge University Press, 2004).

52. F. V. Krejčí, *Naše osvobození* (Prague: A. Svěcený, 1919), 143; "Ženské hnutí—Jak žijeme: Filosoficky—politicky," *Naše Doba* 26, no. 6 (1919): 467–72.

53. Tisk 26/1918, http://www.psp.cz/eknih/1918ns/ps/tisky/t0026_00.htm.

54. Alfréd Meissner, January 22, 1919, meeting of the Czechoslovak National Assembly, http://www.psp.cz/eknih/1918ns/ps/stenprot/019schuz/s019001.htm.

55. Tisk 302/1919 ("Zpráva ústavního výboru o předloze řádu volení do obcí"), http://www.psp.cz/eknih/1918ns/ps/tisky/t0302-01.htm.

56. Bohuslav Franta, January 22, 1919, meeting of the Czechoslovak National Assembly, http://www.psp.cz/eknih/1918ns/ps/stenprot/019schuz/s019002.htm.

57. Antonín Němec, January 22, 1919, meeting of the Czechoslovak National Assembly, http://www.psp.cz/eknih/1918ns/ps/stenprot/019schuz/s019003.htm.

58. Plamínková, "Rok 1918."

59. Cyril Horáček, January 22, 1919, meeting of the Czechoslovak National Assembly, http://www.psp.cz/eknih/1918ns/ps/stenprot/019schuz/s019004.htm.

60. Bedřich Pospíšil, January 22, 1919, meeting of the Czechoslovak National Assembly, http://www.psp.cz/eknih/1918ns/ps/stenprot/019schuz/s019001.htm; and Jan Šrámek, January 23, 1919, meeting of the Czechoslovak National Assembly, http://www.psp.cz/eknih/1918ns/ps/stenprot/020schuz/s020003.htm.

61. Božena Ecksteinová, January 23, 1919, meeting of the Czechoslovak National Assembly, http://www.psp.cz/eknih/1918ns/ps/stenprot/020schuz/s5020002.htm

62. "Ženy v naší české republice nabývají nových oprávnění," *Ženský Obzor* 17, no. 1 (1919): 25.

63. Marie Tippmanová, "Vdaná žena ve veřejném povolání," *Žvěstování* 1, no. 35 (1919): 2.

64. Plamínková quoted in Mužiková-Nosilová, *Naše ženy*, 25.

65. Krista Nevšimalová, "Žena ve státě československém," *Ženský Obzor* 17, no. 3 (1919): 66.

66. There is no word for "gender" in Czech that captures the contemporary meaning of this word in English. Czech scholars today tend to simply use the English term. The word used in the constitution (*pohlaví*) denotes biological sex.

67. Drucilla Cornell calls this the "freedom of the imaginary domain": the freedom to live out one's own definitions of gender, family, and so on. See her *At the Heart of Freedom: Feminism, Sex and Equality* (Princeton: Princeton University Press, 1998).

68. Stenograph from 110th meeting of the Constitutional Committee (January 14, 1920), AFS ČR, box 31, 67.

69. Stenograph from 110th meeting, 67.

70. Stenograph from 110th meeting, 68.

71. Stenograph from 110th meeting, 68–69.

72. Stenograph from 112th meeting of the Constitutional Committee (January 14, 1920), AFS ČR, box 31, 34–37.

73. Masaryk quoted in F. F. Plamínková, "Masaryk-president a ženy," in *Masaryk a ženy*, 11.

74. Věra Babáková, "Masaryk a mravní základ ženského hnutí," in *Masaryk a ženy*, 261.

75. Karen Offen, *European Feminisms 1700–1950* (Stanford: Stanford University Press, 2000), 277–310.

76. Kumari Jayawardena, *Feminism and Nationalism in the Third World* (London: Zed Press, 1986).

77. Offen, *European Feminisms*, 277–310; Renate Bridenthal and Claudia Koonz, "Introduction: Women in Weimar and Nazi Germany," in *When Biology Became Destiny: Women in Weimar and Nazi Germany*, eds. Renate Bridenthal, Atina Grossmann, and Marion Kaplan, 1–29 (New York: Monthly Review Press, 1984); Paul Hanebrink, "Linking Anti-feminism and Antisemitism: Gender and the 'Christian' Nation in post-WWI Hungary," (unpublished paper presented at the Berkshires Conference on the History of Women, June 9, 2002).

## Chapter 2: The Fight over the Czechoslovak Civil Code

1. Steve Hause and Anne Kenney, *Women's Suffrage and Social Politics in the French Third Republic* (Princeton: Princeton University Press, 1984); Ellen Du Bois, *Woman Suffrage and Women's Rights* (New York: New York University Press, 1998); Jane Purvis and Sandra Stanley Holton, eds., *Votes for Women* (New York: Routledge, 2000).

2. "Žena a politika," *Moravská Žena* 1, no. 1 (May 1919): 5. This magazine later metamorphosed into *Křest'anská Žena*, the official publication of the Federation of Catholic Women and Girls.

3. This kind of analysis originated with Carole Pateman, *The Sexual Contract* (Stanford, Stanford University Press, 1988).

4. Mary Shanley, *Feminism, Marriage and the Law in Victorian England 1850–1895* (Princeton: Princeton University Press, 1989); Ute Gerhard, *Debating Women's Equality*, trans. Alison Brown and Belinda Cooper (New Brunswick: Rutgers University Press, 2001), 69–74.

5. Alois Hajn, "K reformě práva manželského," *Nová Síla* 1, no. 2, (1919): 2–3.

6. Emil Sobota, "Reforma práva manželského," *Ženský Svět* 23, no. 1 (1919): 1–3. Also see speech of Václav Bouček, May 20, 1919, 51st meeting of the Czechoslovak National Assembly, *TZ-PS*, 1413.

7. B. N., "Mravní význam nové úpravy manželského práva," *Zvěstování* 1, no. 23 (1919): 1–2.

8. "Oprava manželského práva," *Lidové Noviny*, May 16, 1919. See also Law 320 from May 22, 1919, *SZ*.

9. Jan Rýpar, May 22, 1919, 53rd meeting of the Czechoslovak National Assembly, *TZ-PS*, 1505.

10. Min. Dr. Soukup, 52nd meeting of the Czechoslovak National Assembly, May 21, 1919, *TZ-PS*, 1450.

11. Theodor Bartošek, 53rd meeting of the Czechoslovak National Assembly, May 22, 1919, *TZ-PS*, 1497.

12. "První den rokování o reformě manželského práva," *Národní Politika*, May 21, 1919.

13. Bartošek, May 22, 1919, *TZ-PS*, 1499.

14. Bouček, May 20, 1919, *TZ-PS*, 1412–13.

15. Dr. Černý, 52nd meeting of the Czechoslovak National Assembly, May 21, 1919, *TZ-PS*, 1472.

16. Dr. Kadlčák, 51st meeting of the Czechoslovak National Assembly, May 20, 1919, *TZ-PS*, 1432.

17. Karel Novotný, 51st meeting of the Czechoslovak National Assembly, May 20, 1919, *TZ-PS*, 1423.

18. Ludvík Aust, 53rd meeting of the Czechoslovak National Assembly, May 22, 1919, *TZ-PS*, 1502.

19. Luisa Landová-Štychová, 52nd meeting of the Czechoslovak National Assembly, May 21, 1919, *TZ-PS*, 1460–65.

20. Josef Matoušek, 52nd meeting of the Czechoslovak National Assembly, May 21, 1919, *TZ-PS*, 1484–85.

21. "Pro rozluku manželství a proti kněžskému bezženství," *Lidové Noviny*, May 21, 1919.

22. Protocols from meetings of commission, March 6, 1920, and June 16, 1920, SÚA, MS, box 302.

23. Protocols from meetings of the family law subcommission (1920–1923), SÚA, MS, box 303.

24. Bruno Kafka, *Právo rodinné (návrh subkomitétu pro revisi občanského zákoníka)* (Prague: Ministry of Justice, 1924), 14.

25. Marie Mikulova, *Žena v právním řádě československém* (Prague: self published, 1936), 40–47.

26. On German bourgeois feminism, see Richard Evans, *The Feminist Movement in Germany 1894–1933* (London: Sage, 1976); Elizabeth Harvey, "The Failure of Feminism? Young Women and the Bourgeois Feminist Movement in Weimar Germany, 1918–1933," *Central European History* 28, no. 1 (1995): 1–28. On Austria, see Harriet Anderson, *Utopian Feminism: Women's Movements in Fin de Siècle Vienna* (New Haven: Yale University Press, 1992).

27. For a detailed description of the WNC, see Jana Burešová, *Proměny společenského postavení českých žen v první polovině 20. století* (Olomouc: Universita Palackého, 2001).

28. For an overview of such conflicts, see Gary Cohen, *The Politics of Ethnic Survival: Germans in Prague, 1861–1914* (Princeton: Princeton University Press, 1981); and Jan Křen, *Konfliktní společenství* (Toronto: 68 Publishers, 1989).

29. Here the Czech WNC differed substantially from the German Bund

Deutscher Frauvereine, where housewives' associations had a major influence after 1918. See Evans, *Feminist Movement in Germany*, 250–53.

30. Minutes of the WNC committee on the "position of women in the law," 1923, SÚA, ŽNR, box 22.

31. "Občanský zákoník a jeho novelisace," SÚA, ŽNR, box 32.

32. "Subkomitétu pro revisi občanského zákoníka," *Ženská Rada* 1, no. 6 (1925): 5–7.

33. Letter from Ministry of Justice to WNC, March 30, 1927, SÚA, ŽNR, box 23.

34. "Ze ženské národní rady—valná schůze ŽNR," *Ženská Rada* 5, no. 4–5 (1929): 59.

35. B. Smolařová-Čapková, "Reforma občanského zákona," *Nová Síla* 7, no. 14–15 and 16–17 (1927): 81–82, 94, 105–6; B. Novotná, "Rodinné právo," *Zvěstování* 9, no. 7 (1927): 1–2; and suggestions sent by representatives of Agrarian, People's, and National Democratic women to the Ministry of Justice, SÚA, MS, box 1962.

36. In the 1919–1920 school year there were only 608 women in medical school and 196 women in law school in Czechoslovakia. By the 1929–1930 school year these numbers had risen to 925 in medical school and 517 in law. Anděla Kozáková, ed., *Čeho jsme docílily- deset let práce SVVŽ* (Prague: Sdružení Vysokoškolsky Vzdělaných Žen, 1932).

37. Betty Karpíšková, "Rozvody a rozluky ve světle statistických čísel," *Ženské Noviny* 16, no. 14 (1934): 1.

38. The Federation of Catholic Women and Girls claimed 250,000 members in 1930 and over 300,000 in 1936. "Rozmach a síla—Svazu katolických žen a dívek," *Křest'anská Žena* 19, no. 17 (1937): 1–5; Burešová, *Proměny společenského*, 237–64.

39. "Život rodiny," *Křest'anská Žena* 17, no. 33 (1935): 2–3. The Federation's vision of a women's domestic realm meant barring them from the working world, but did not include giving up political rights. Indeed, the Federation often exhorted its members to be politically active in the Catholic-led People's Party.

40. Bohumila Wiererová, "O pravé a nepravé emancipaci," *Křest'anská Žena*, 19, no. 25 (1937): 1–2.

41. Superrevisní Komise, *Zákon, kterým se vydává všeobecný zákoník občanský* (Prague: Ministerstvo Spravedlnosti, 1931), 32–33; Marie Mikulová, *Žena v právním řadě*, 47–48.

42. Superrevisní Komise quoted in Mikulová, *Žena v právním řádě*, 43.

43. DK. "Z chystaného nového čs. občanského práva," *Lidové Noviny*, January 1, 1932.

44. Requests for changes to family law statutes from women's groups to the super-revisory committee (1934–1935), SÚA, MS, box 1963.

45. Alfréd Meissner quoted in ald, "Min. Dr. Meissner o osnově občanského zákoníka," *Národní Osvobození*, March 26, 1932.

46. "Velká manifestace katolíků proti chystaným povinným laickým sňatkům," *Lidové Listy*, March 16, 1932.

47. "Občanský sňatek," *Křest'anská Žena* 14, no. 4 (1932): 1–2.

48. —lup. "Krise manželství zkázou rodiny," *Křest'anská Žena* 17, no. 9 (1935): 1–2.

49. F.N., "Zkáza rodiny," *Národní Politika*, January 12, 1935.

50. "K nové revisi občanského zákoníka," *Ženská Rada* 7, no. 7 (1931): 152.

51. M. Košková, "Řídí se veřejní činitelé naší republikánskou ústavou," *Ženská Rada* 10, no. 7 (1934): 128–30.

52. Like many professional Czech women in the interwar period, Milada Králová-Horáková hyphenated her name after her marriage. Since this was the name she used at the time of these events, I have used it here. In later years, she stopped using the hyphenated form of her name in print. In this book, I have followed her usage, so in the last chapters of the book, she is referred to as Milada Horáková.

53. Minutes of the WNC legal committee, March 15, 1932, and minutes of the WNC executive committee, May 24, 1932, SÚA, ŽNR, box 22.

54. WNC secretary's report for November 1934, SÚA, ŽNR, box 6.

55. WNC to Minister Dérer, November 30, 1934, SÚA, ŽNR, box 13.

56. WNC notes from meetings of Králová-Horáková and Srb on September 20, 25, and 27, 1935, also minutes of the WNC legal committee, November 1, 1935, SÚA, ŽNR, box 6; Srb's file notes on the meetings (dated October 1, 1935), SÚA, MS, box 1963.

57. This occasion marked the first use of a new parliamentary procedure, which allowed the government to present legislation to the entire Assembly and Senate for a brief preliminary debate before it was sent to committee. See "Předběžná rozprava o občanském zákoníku," *Národní Listy*, April 16, 1937.

58. Dr. Ladislav Rašín, 92nd meeting of the Czechoslovak National Assembly, April 15, 1937, *TZ-PS*, 32.

59. Rep. Oldřich Suchý, 93rd meeting of the Czechoslovak National Assembly, April 16, 1937, *TZ-PS*, 13.

60. Min. Ivan Dérer, 67th meeting of the Czechoslovak Senate, April 20, 1937, *TZ-S*, 18.

61. "Řeč Senátorky F.F. Plamínkové v plénu senátu 11 prosince 1937," *Ženská Rada* 14, no. 1 (1938): 18–21.

62. An interesting counterpoint to this trend is early Soviet Russia, though even there substantial resistance to civil equality for women existed. See Wendy Goldman, *Women, the State and Revolution: Soviet Family Policy and Social Life 1917–1936* (Cambridge: Cambridge University Press, 1993).

## Chapter 3: One Family, One Nation

1. Jan Zachoval, *Rodinná výchova* (Prague: Státní Nakladatelství, 1923), 16–17.
2. Ibid.
3. Waldo Emerson Waltz, *The Nationality of Married Women* (Urbana: University of Illinois Press, 1937), 79–84.
4. Hannah Arendt, *The Origins of Totalitarianism* (New York: Harcourt Brace, 1973), 267–302; Carolyn Seckler-Hudson, *Statelessness: With Special Reference to the United States* (Washington DC: Digest Press, 1934).
5. Alicia Cozine, "A Member of the State: Citizenship Law and Its Application in Czechoslovakia" (PhD diss., University of Chicago, 1996), 33–37.
6. This offer did not extend to Czechs and Slovaks who had acquired citizenship in other nations, such as the United States. See Law (*ústavní zákon*) 236/1920 (April 9, 1920), SZ.
7. Cozine, "Member of the State," 45–50.
8. Luisa Landová-Štychová, "Právní postavení československých občanek v manželství a rodině," *Ženská Rada* 1, no. 5 (1925): 10–12.
9. For a full discussion of the Cable Act, see Candice Lewis Bredbenner, *A Nationality of Her Own: Women, Marriage and the Law of Citizenship* (Berkeley: University of California Press, 1998), chap. 3; Nancy F. Cott, "Marriage and Women's Citizenship in the United States," *American Historical Review* 103, no. 5 (1998): 1440–74.
10. Waltz, *Nationality of Married Women*, 85.
11. The same was true in many other European countries, such as Germany. See Eli Nathans, *The Politics of Citizenship in Germany: Ethnicity, Utility and Nationalism* (New York: Berg, 2004), 209–11.
12. Bredbenner, *Nationality of Her Own*, 113–30; Seckler-Hudson, *Statelessness*, 76–99; Waltz, *Nationality of Married Women*, 85–96.
13. Cozine, "Member of the State," 17–19; Arendt, *Origins of Totalitarianism*, 278–85.
14. "Attachment B—1930," SÚA, ŽNR, box 52.
15. Františka Plamínková was on the boards of both the International Alliance for Women's Suffrage and Equal Citizenship and the International Women's Council. For an institutional history of the Alliance, see Arnold Whittick, *Woman into Citizen* (London: Athenaeum, 1979). On the international feminist movement generally, see Leila J. Rupp, *Worlds of Women: The Making of an International Women's Movement* (Princeton: Princeton University Press, 1997).
16. Chrystal MacMillan, "Nationality of Married Women: Present Tendencies," *Journal of Comparative Legislation and International Law* 7 (3rd series), no. 4 (1925): 142–54.
17. The Provisional Draft Convention on Nationality composed by the Al-

liance is reprinted in Cyril Hill, "Citizenship of Married Women," *American Journal of International Law* 18, no. 4 (1924): 720–36. Also MacMillan, "Nationality of Married Women: Present Tendencies," 152–54.

18. Chrystal MacMillan, "Committee on the Nationality of Married Women," (Status Report) *International Women's Suffrage News* 17, no. 1 (1923): 179–80.

19. "League of Nations Committee Report," *International Women's Suffrage News* 20, no. 9 (1926): 134.

20. League of Nations (Committee of Experts for the Progressive Codification of International Law), *Report on the Questions Which Appear Ripe for International Regulation (Questionnaires 1–7)* (Geneva: League of Nations, 1927), 9–17.

21. "League of Nations Committee Report."

22. Although the conference at The Hague was largely organized by the League of Nations, its participants were not limited to League members, hence the United States could be among them. Bredbenner, *Nationality of Her Own*, 206–7.

23. "Zpráva z konference o kodifikaci mezinárodního práva z Haagu," *Ženská Rada* 6, no. 3 (1930): 46.

24. Czechoslovak letter of January 21, 1929, printed in League of Nations, *Conference for the Codification of International Law—Bases for Discussion*, vol. 1 (Nationality) (Geneva: League of Nations, 1929), 209.

25. Milada Králová-Horáková, "Státní příslušnost vdaných žen na kodifikační konferenci v Haagu," *Ženská Rada* 6, no. 4 (1930): 64.

26. "The Board Meets in Holland," *International Women's Suffrage News* 24, no. 7 (1930); Králová-Horáková, "Státní příslušnost," Bredbenner, *Nationality of Her Own*, 210–11.

27. Milada Králová-Horáková, "Státní příslušnost vdaných žen na kodifikační konferenci v Haagu (dokončení)," *Ženská Rada* 6, no. 5 (1930): 75–77.

28. Ibid.

29. "The Nationality of Married Women—Recommendations of the Conference for the Codification of International Law," *International Women's Suffrage News* 24, no. 9 (June 1930): 138–39; Králová-Horáková, "Státní příslušnost . . . (dokončení)."

30. Bredbenner, *Nationality of Her Own*, 212–15.

31. Králová-Horáková, "Státní příslušnost . . . (dokončení)."

32. "Návrh o nabývání a pozbývání československého státního občanství," print number 1491/1931, *Tisky*.

33. Ibid.

34. Františka Plamínková to Milada Králová-Horáková, December 28, 1931, SÚA, ŽNR, box 52.

35. Ibid.

36. Cozine, "Member of the State," 154.

37. Minutes of the WNC legal committee, June 4, 1935, SÚA, ŽNR, box 6.

38. WNC to the Minister of Unification, April 6, 1936, SÚA, ŽNR, box 31.

39. Milada Králová-Horáková, "Zákon o státní příslušnosti a ženy," *Ženská Rada* 13, no. 5 (1937): 76.

40. Dr. Kvičera, "Státní občanství," *Brázda* 18, no. 6 (1937): 9–12. This kind of argument was also prominent in Germany. See Nathans, *The Politics of Citizenship in Germany*, 211.

41. "Vládní návrh o nabývání a pozbývání státního občanství československého," March 25, 1938, print number 1294/1938, *Tisky*.

42. Minutes of the Legal-Constitutional Committee of the National Assembly, May 11, 1938. AFS ČR, PS IV.

43. Waltz, *Nationality of Married Women*, 62–63. The other fourteen countries to unconditionally deprive a woman of citizenship if she married a foreigner were Afghanistan, Bolivia, Germany, Haiti, Honduras, Hungary, Iraq, Jordan, Liechtenstein, Liberia, the Netherlands, the Dutch Colonies, Spain, and Switzerland.

## Chapter 4: Women in the Civil Service

1. Out of a total female population of about 8,000,000, 1,969,436 were gainfully employed. Their wages, however, averaged only about 65 percent of men's. This number does not include women's unpaid work on family farms or in family businesses. Ludmilla Mužíková-Nosilová, *Naše ženy v historii a ve vystavbě státu* (Prague: Ministerstvo Informací, 1946), 30–31.

2. In 1921 there were only 81,105 women employed by the state. These numbers did not change radically over the interwar period. Nosilová, *Naše ženy*, 30.

3. Harriet Anderson, *Utopian Feminism: Women's Movements in Fin de Siècle Vienna* (New Haven: Yale University Press, 1992), 79–80.

4. Law 455/1919 (July 24, 1919), *SZ*.

5. Marie Loucká-Čepová, "Vdaná žena ve veřejném povolání," *Zvěstování* 1, no. 35 (1919): 2. Similar sentiments were voiced by Krista Nevšímalová in "Žena ve státě československém," *Ženský Obzor* 17, no. 3 (1919): 66–67.

6. Marie Tippmanová, "Ženina občanská práva a povinnosti," *Nová Síla* 1, no. 34 (1920): 1–2.

7. Interpellation of Reps. Landová-Štychová, Malá, Sychravová, et al. (October 27, 1920), print number 624/1920, *Tisky*.

8. Answer to interpellation of Landová-Štychová et al. (February 27, 1921), print number 1728/1921, *Tisky*.

9. Anna Vettrová-Bečvářová, "Přijímání žen do státních úřadů," *Nová Síla* 2, no. 10 (1922): 155–56.

10. Božena Novotná, "Ženy ve státních úřadech," *Zvěstování* 4, no. 22 (1922): 1–2.

11. Minutes of the WNC executive board, June 29, 1924, and October 19, 1924, SÚA, ŽNR, box 8.

12. Jiří Beneš, "Nesnáze celibátu a nesnáze necelibátu," *Přítomnost* 1, no. 36 (1924): 576.

13. Minutes of the WNC teachers' group, December 3, 1924, SÚA, ŽNR, box 33.

14. Law 103/1926, nicknamed the "salary law" and Law 104/1926, often called the "teachers' law" (July 7, 1926), *SZ*.

15. Law 103/1926, §144, paragraph 7; Law 104/1926, §24, paragraph 7, *SZ*. The few women who got benefits never received the same amounts as men. See M. R. Kubičková, "Právní nároky učitelů a učitelek," *List Říšského Svazu Československých Učitelek* 9, no. 4–5 (1930): 54–59.

16. M. R. Kubičková, "Propouštění vdaných zaměstnankyň (učitelek) ve veřejných službách," *List Říšského Svazu Československých Učitelek* 11, no. 11 (1932): 133–37,

17. Law 113/1926 (July 10, 1926), *SZ*.

18. Law 113/1926, §8, paragraph 6, *SZ*. This limitation was also applied to criminals, people who had been fired by the state for disciplinary reasons, and applicants over forty years of age.

19. Interpellation of Plamínková, Pánka, et al. (July 7, 1926), print number 253/1926, *Tisky*.

20. In fact, a woman's work might be likely to suffer after her wedding, since marriage for women meant assuming responsibility for many time-consuming domestic chores. The opinion that women could not be counted on to perform quality work after they married was common in the civil service. See, for example, Jan Řípa, "Žena a její účast ve státní službě," *Sociální Revue* 5, no. 3 (1924): 220–27. This journal was an official publication of the Ministry of Social Welfare.

21. Dr. Jan Šrámek, answer to interpellation of Plamínková et al. (April 18, 1928), print number 632/II-1928, *Tisky*.

22. Min. Udržal, answer to interpellation of Zemínová et al. (May 26, 1930), print number 491/XXII-1930, *Tisky*; Min. Trapl, answer to interpellation of Seidl, Jurnečková-Vorlová, Blatná, Kirpalová, et al. (April 29, 1932), print number 1781/II-1932, *Tisky*.

23. Jarmila Krejčí-Ambrožová wrote about how civil servants and their families depended on these bonuses for their livelihood in a letter to the editor of *Přítomnost*, printed as "O situaci státních zamestnanců," *Přítomnost* 8, no. 51 (1931): 815–16.

24. "13. služné státních zaměstnanců," *Ženská Rada* 6, no. 6 (1930): 106–8.

25. F. F. Plamínková, "Obrana žen ve veřejné službě," *Ženská Rada* 6, no. 7 (1930): 126–30.

26. "Czechoslovakia—news about women's work in the Women's National Council from 1930–33" (prepared for the International Women's Council), SÚA,

ŽNR, box 51. See also minutes from the meetings of the WNC executive committee, September 1930, SÚA, ŽNR, box 4.

27. "Objections to the employment of married women and rebuttals to them," SÚA, ŽNR, box 32.

28. Parliamentary club of the National Socialist party to the WNC, September 19, 1930, SÚA, ŽNR, box 29.

29. Minutes of the WNC executive committee, September 25, 1930, SÚA, ŽNR, box 4.

30. Ibid.

31. F. F. Plamínková, "Obrana žen ve veřejné službě," *Ženská Rada* 6, no. 7 (1930): 127.

32. This article was later published as "Krise a ceny" in Karel Engliš, *Světová a naše hospodářské krise* (Prague: Fr. Borový, 1934), 1–15.

33. The play was Martin Sekerka, *Dvojí příjem* (Prague: A. Neubert, 1936). For a sense of how working women were treated in fiction, see Vlasta Šternová, *Rozvodová advokátka* (Prague: Rodina, 1933), first serialized in the magazine *Pražanka* 7–8, no. 364–81 (1931–32).

34. V.G., "Vedlější zaměstnání," *Přítomnost* 9, no. 40 (1932): 626.

35. Mila Grimmichová, printed as "Pracující manželky," *Přítomnost* 9, no. 41 (1932): 656.

36. Ing. Josef Kremer, letter to the editor, *Přítomnost* 9, no. 42 (1932): 687.

37. Helena Neswedová, letter to the editor, *Přítomnost* 9, no. 42 (1932): 688.

38. A.B., letter to the editor, *Přítomnost* 9, no. 43 (1932): 701–2.

39. Albin Šušlík, letter to the editor, *Přítomnost* 9, no. 43 (1932): 703–4.

40. A. K. Emanov, letter to the editor, *Přítomnost* 9, no. 43 (1932): 703.

41. Dr. H., letter to the editor, *Přítomnost* 9, no. 44 (1932): 719.

42. I. Malinská, letter to the editor, *Přítomnost* 9, no. 45 (1932): 751–52.

43. Many women and women's groups took part in these attacks on working wives as well. For example, the Federation of Catholic Women and Girls frequently sent petitions to the government demanding that married women be released from their jobs in the civil service and unemployed college graduates (of either sex) hired in their place. For years 1929–1933 see SÚA, PMR, box 3137; for 1938–1939 see SÚA, MSP, box 217.

44. Unlike the base salary, the *činovné* did not grow with an employee's years of service but remained constant for as long as the employee held that particular job. It therefore mattered most to younger and poorer workers, since it formed a larger percentage of their monthly paycheck than it did for those in the higher pay grades. Under the government's proposal, if both spouses had the same salary, it was the wife whose salary would be cut.

45. M. R. Kubičkova, "Návrh zákona o sociálních a úsporných opatřeních personálních ve veřejné správě," *List Říšského Svazu Československých Učitelek*

11, no. 13 (1932): 165–68; O. Malá, "K sociálním a úsporným opatřením personálním ve veřejné správě," *Ženská Rada* 8, no. 9 (1932): 130–32.

46. The pension projections were based on household income. Women residing in households that collectively earned over 24,000 Czechoslovak crowns per year would have their benefits cut in half. If the household earned over 36,000 crowns after this cut, a woman's pension benefits would be reduced even more, and possibly eliminated.

47. Notes of WNC clerical worker's group from 1932, SÚA, ŽNR, box 29.

48. O. Malá, "A zase veřejné zaměstnankyně—rozhodný boj," *Ženská Rada* 8, no. 9 (1932): 166–71; O. Malá, "Veřejné zaměstnankyně—zákon o úsporách," *Ženská Rada* 8, no. 10 (1932): 181. See also minutes from the meetings of the WNC executive committee, June–December 1932, SÚA, ŽNR, box 5.

49. The austerity package became Law 204/1932 (December 31, 1932), *SZ.*

50. O. Malá, "Dobrý boj vybojován," *Ženská Rada* 9, no. 2 (1933): 22–24.

51. Věra Olivová marks the winter of 1932–1933 as the high point of unemployment in Czechoslovakia, with estimates of between 920,000 and 1,300,000 unemployed persons. See Olivová, *Czechoslovakia's Doomed Democracy* (London: Sidgwick and Jackson, 1972). The Czechoslovak Finance Ministry steadfastly resisted taking out foreign loans to balance its budget, preferring to hold to a very strict monetary policy. See Alice Teichová, *Wirtschaftsgeschichte des Tschechoslowakei 1918–1980* (Vienna: Böhlau, 1989).

52. Věra Urbanová, "A zase zaměstnané ženy!" *Ženská Rada* 9, no. 7 (1933): 153–54.

53. "Memorandum," *Ženská Rada* 9, no. 5 (1933): 121–22.

54. Many of the ministers did not seem to be well-informed about the proposal and were surprised at the detailed information possessed by the WNC representatives. "Results of Negotiations by Deputations Sent to Individual Ministries, October 10, 1933," SÚA, ŽNR, box 5.

55. Minutes of the WNC executive committee, November 16, 1933, account of meeting between Plamínková and Malypetr, SÚA, ŽNR, box 30.

56. F. F. Plamínková, "Vláda proti ženám," *Ženská Rada* 10, no. 1–2 (1934): 3–11.

57. Law 252/1933, *SZ.*

58. "Vládě, Národnímu Shromáždění a celé veřejnosti československé!" *Ženská Rada* 10, no. 1 (1934): 2.

59. This conclusion is convincingly illustrated by a collection of letters sent by private citizens to the Cabinet on this issue, in which even those who said they did not believe that married women should be fired from the civil service en masse expressed that women whose husbands could provide for them should stay at home. The view that women had both a right to work and to the personal benefits of work was quite rare. See SÚA, PMR, box 3137.

60. O. Rádl, "Dnešní ženská otázka," *Přítomnost* 11, no. 40 (1934): 634–37.

61. "Report from the married women's section," SÚA, ŽNR, box 33.

62. WNC to Karl Engliš, October 25, 1935, SÚA, ŽNR, box 33.

63. Minutes of the WNC executive committee, 1936, SÚA, ŽNR, box 6.

64. WNC to Engliš, October 25, 1935.

65. This meeting was apparently attended by 641 people. "Resolution Adopted by Protest Meeting of June 6, 1936," SÚA, ŽNR, box 32.

66. Elizabeth Heinemann, *What Difference Does a Husband Make? Women and Marital Status in Nazi and Postwar Germany* (Berkeley: University of California Press, 1999), 42; Renate Bridenthal and Claudia Koonz, "Beyond Kinder, Küche, Kirche: Weimar Women in Politics and Work," in *When Biology Became Destiny: Women in Weimar and Nazi Germany,* ed. Renate Bridenthal, Atina Grossman, and Marion Kaplan (New York: Monthly Review Press, 1984).

67. Victoria de Grazia, *How Fascism Ruled Women, Italy 1922–1945* (Berkeley: University of California Press, 1992), 193–200.

68. Miranda Pollard, *Reign of Virtue: Mobilizing Gender in Vichy France* (Chicago: University of Chicago Press, 1998), 145–73.

69. Alice Kessler-Harris, *In Pursuit of Equity: Women, Men and the Quest for Economic Citizenship in 20th Century America* (New York: Oxford University Press, 2001), 56–63.

70. Kessler-Harris makes a similar argument throughout *In Pursuit of Equity.*

71. Cameralis, "Ještě ke snižování platů statního úřednictva," *Hospodařská Politika* 8, no. 1 (1934): 12–13.

72. F. "Zase celibát v státní službě?" *Přítomnost* 21, no. 41 (1935): 644–65.

## Chapter 5: Abortion Politics in Interwar Czechoslovakia

1. Jan Scheinost, "Paragraf 144," *Lidové Listy*, June 29, 1932.

2. For an analysis of abortion in Czechoslovakia from a different perspective, see Teresa J. Balkenende, "Protecting the National Inheritance: Nation-state Formation and the Transformation of Birth Culture in the Czech Lands, 1880–1938," (PhD diss., University of Washington, 2004), 192–256.

3. Landová-Štychová left the Czech Socialist Party in 1922 and in 1923 was deprived of her seat in the National Assembly as a result. She was reelected to the Assembly in 1925 as a member of the Communist Party.

4. Print number 694/1920 (October 26, 1920), *Tisky*.

5. Luisa Landová-Štychová, "Pro právo matek, živých děti a proti pokoutnímu provádnění potratů," *České Slovo*, February 20, 1921.

6. Betty Karpíšková, "Palčivá otázka," *Ženské Noviny* 3, no. 2 (1921): 2.

7. Božena Novotná, "Kde je lék proti nemoci, jež ohrozila lidstvo," *Zvěstování* 3, no. 3 (1921): 1.

8. Anna Honzáková. Reprinted in "O vyhnání plodu—K diskusí," *Ženský List* 2, no. 17 (1921): 2–3. See also Landová-Štychová, "Pro právo matek."

9. Landová-Štychová, "Pro právo matek." See also "Spolek českých lékařů v Praze: schůze ze dne 21. XI. 1921 (Přednáška Dra Wassermanna)," *Časopis Lékařův Českých* 60, no. 52 (1921): 874.

10. Milan Janů, "Otázka potratová," *Ženská Rada* 1, no. 5 (1925): 2; "Ženská hlídka," *Ženský Obzor* 18, no. 3–4 (1921): 59–61.

11. Janů, "Otázka potratová," 5–8.

12. Janů, "Otázka potratová," 8; "Spolek českých lékařů," 875–79.

13. "Spolek českých lékařů," 875.

14. Ibid., 875–79.

15. Jiří Trapl, "Umělé přerušení těhotenství," *Přítomnost* 2, no. 25 (1925): 392–94.

16. "Zápis jednání sekce III, otákza 3 a—Otázka trestnosti vyhnání plodu," *Druhý sjezd československých právníků r. 1925* Sekce III, Otázka 3. a), 29. See also Balkenende, "Protecting the National Inheritance," 225–27.

17. Antonín Kissich, "Otázka trestnosti vyhnání plodu," *Druhý sjezd československých právníků r. 1925* Sekce III, Otázka 3. a), Práce 3, 9.

18. "Zápis jednání sekce III," 33–34.

19. Dr. Svozilová, "Trestnost přerušeného těhotenství," *Ženská Rada* 1, no. 3 (1925): 5–7.

20. Print number 535/1926, *Tisky*.

21. Print number 219/1926, *Tisky*. For more on all three abortion bills, see Balkenende, "Protecting the National Inheritance," 229–40.

22. For example, the otherwise very detailed reports given at the 1925 lawyer's congress in Brno only mention Landová-Štychová's 1920 bill, not her 1922 revision of it.

23. "Paragraf 144 (Anketa)," *Právo Lidu*, March 16, 1930.

24. "Paragraf 144 (Letter from Karel Ježek)," *Právo Lidu*, May 11, 1930.

25. "Paragraf 144 (Letter from G. Braun)," *Právo Lidu*, March 23, 1930.

26. "Paragraf 144 (Letter from Josef Vištein)," *Právo Lidu*, April 13, 1930.

27. "Paragraf 144 (Letter from František Šlégl)," *Právo Lidu*, April 20, 1930.

28. "Paragraf 144 (Letter from MUDr Kamil Neumann)," *Právo Lidu*, March 30, 1930. Similar claims were made by MUDr Augustin Turek from Prague in his letter from "Paragraf 144," *Právo Lidu*, April 13, 1930.

29. "Paragraf 144 (Letter from X.Y.)," *Právo Lidu*, March 30, 1930.

30. "Paragraf 144 (Letter from FR. H.N.)," *Právo Lidu*, April 6, 1930. Also see Milena Illová, "Hradby padly," *Právo Lidu*, April 20, 1930.

31. "Paragraf 144 (Letter from Marie Hanusová)," *Právo Lidu*, March 23, 1930.

32. "Paragraf 144 (Letter from Božena L.)," *Právo Lidu*, May 4, 1930.

33. "Paragraf 144 (Letter from A. Pychovám)," *Právo Lidu*, May 4, 1930.

34. "Paragraf 144 (Letter from J. Srbová)," *Právo Lidu*, March 23, 1930.

35. "Paragraf 144 (Letter from Marcela K.)," *Právo Lidu*, March 30, 1930.

36. "Paragraf 144 (Letter from M. ST)," *Právo Lidu*, May 4, 1930.

37. "Paragraf 144 (Letter from Božena Janoušková)," *Právo Lidu*, May 11, 1930.

38. "Paragraf 144 (Letter from Ed. Štorch)," *Právo Lidu*, April 6, 1930.

39. "Paragraf 144 (Letter from Božena Janoušková)," *Právo Lidu*, May 11, 1930.

40. "Paragraf 144 (Letter from Mila Grimmichová)," *Právo Lidu*, April 27, 1930.

41. "Paragraf 144 (Letter from Marie Roslková)," *Právo Lidu*, April 13, 1930.

42. "Paragraf 144 (Letter from J. Kocman)," *Právo Lidu*, May 4, 1930.

43. "Paragraf 144 (Letter from AL. PL.)," *Právo Lidu*, May 4, 1930.

44. "Paragraf 144 (Letter from Dr. Max Popper)," *Právo Lidu*, March 23, 1930.

45. Betty Karpíšková, "Mateřství a potrarství," *Právo Lidu*, April 13, 1930.

46. "Důvodová zpráva (k osnově zákonu o vyhnání plodu)," SÚA, MS, box 2070; additional commentary and complete statistics for 1930 in SÚA, MS, box 536.

47. Ibid.

48. "Zákon, zmírňující tresty za vyhnání plodu," *České Slovo*, June 19, 1932.

49. "Meissnerova sociální indikace nejpalčivější otázkou chudých žen," *Právo Lidu*, October 23, 1932.

50. "Přehled přípominek k osnově zákonu o výhnání plodu," SÚA, MS, box 2070.

51. Betty Karpíšková (Kar.), "Co říkají strany Meissnerově osnově o vyhnání plodu," *Ženské Noviny* 14, no. 26 (1932): 1.

52. Betty Karpíšková (Kar.), "Soudr. dr Meissner na obranu za práva chudých žen," *Ženské Noviny* 14, no. 25 (1932): 1.

53. Betty Karpíšková, *Kontrola porodů a Meissnerova osnova* (Prague: Ústřední Výbor Žen Sociálních Demokratických, 1932), 14.

54. "Ministr dr. Meissner připravuje pro náš stát recepci sovětského zákonodárství o vyhnání plodu," *Lidové Listy*, June 19, 1932.

55. Dr. J. Richter, "§144," *Lidové Listy*, August 30, 1932.

56. Emanuel Rádl, "Právo na potrat," *Křesťanská Revue* 6, no. 1 (1932): 7–11.

57. Emanuel Rádl, *Proti tak zvané sociální indikaci (námitky proti návrhu nového zákona o umělém potratu)* (Prague: YMCA v Praze, 1932), 20–23.

58. Ibid., 38–39. Also see Balkenende, "Protecting the National Inheritance," 244–53.

59. "Vražda cestou zákona," *Křesťanská Žena* 14, no. 28 (1932): 2–3.

60. A.Kr., "Několik poznámek k par. 144," *Československá Žena* 9, no. 15 (1932): 227–28.

61. L.T., "Nešťasná dvojí moralka," *Lidové Listy*, June 29, 1932.

62. Ml., "Arcibiskupové, biskupové, preláti a jiné hlavy katolíků o potrat-ech," *Ženské Noviny* 15, no. 1 (1933): 1.

63. Božena Trávníčková, "O §144," *Ženský Obzor* 26, no. 3–4: 33–38.

64. Trávníčková, "O §144"; see also Rádl, *Proti tak zvané*, 28–29.

65. Report of the WNC legal commission, August 8, 1932, SÚA, ŽNR, box 23.

66. Ibid.

67. Minutes of the WNC presidium, September 1, 1932, SÚA, ŽNR, box 5.

68. Report of the WNC legal committee, August 8, 1932, SÚA, ŽNR, box 23.

69. WNC to Justice Ministry, September 15, 1932, SÚA, MS, box 2070; "Paragraf 144," *Ženská Rada* 8, no. 7: 133.

70. Statistics on socio-economic status of those prosecuted from Božena Pátková, *Umělé přerušení těhotenství ve světle spravedlnosti a práva* (Prague: Ústřední Sekretariátu Žen pro Činnost Pracovních Komisí Žen Československé Strany Národně Socialistické, 1934), 7–8.

71. Atina Grossman, *Reforming Sex: The German Movement for Birth Control and Abortion Reform 1920–1950* (New York: Oxford University Press, 1995).

## Chapter 6: Women and Politics in the Czech Lands after Munich

1. Bedřich Pilč, "Ženy v třetí říše vyprávějí," *Přítomnost* 14, no. 13 (1937): 203–5.

2. Voting statistics taken from Zdeněk Kárník, *České země v éře první republiky (1918–1938), Díl druhý: Československo a české země v krizi a v ohrožení (1930–1935)* (Prague: Libri, 2002), 496–97.

3. Igor Lukes, *Czechoslovakia Between Stalin and Hitler: The Diplomacy of Edvard Benes in the 1930's* (Oxford: Oxford University Press, 1996).

4. Lukes, *Czechoslovakia Between Stalin and Hitler*, 56.

5. George F. Kennan, *From Prague After Munich: Diplomatic Papers, 1938–1940* (Princeton: Princeton University Press, 1968), 7.

6. František Kutnar, "Naše nynější krise," *Brázda* 19: 40–41 (1938): 630–31.

7. Rudolf Halík, "Do nového života," *Venkov*, October 2, 1938.

8. Whether the Second Republic was defending Czechs, Czechoslovaks, or Czechs *and* Slovaks was always a little ambiguous. On the (exclusionary) Czech nationalist mentality of the Second Republic, see Jan Rataj, *O autorativní národní stát* (Prague: Karolinium, 1997), 93–119.

9. Antonín Pelaček, "Demokracie autorativní," *Brázda* 19, no. 50–51 (1938): 781–83; Rudolf Halík, "Jdeme k zjednodušení politických poměrů," *Venkov*, October 22, 1938; Petr Němec, "České pravicové skupiny v životě protektorátní

společnosti," in *Sborník k dějinám 19. a 20. století*, ed. Vlastislav Lacina (Prague: Historický Ústav, 1993), 331–56.

10. Němec, "České pravicové skupiny."

11. The young intellectuals behind *Brázda* were perhaps a bit more radical than the Agrarian rank and file. See "Jak budovat druhou republiku," *Brázda* 19, no. 44 (1938): 1–16. The article was reprinted in the historian František Kutnar's memoir of his work with the *Brázda* group, *Generace brázdy* (Prague: Historický Klub, 1992).

12. A rare exception was the extensive critique by Jan Slavík, "Kritika návrhu týdeníku 'Brázdy' na vybudování druhé republiky," *Sobota* 9, no. 41–44 (1938): 482–83, 498–99, 520–21, 530–31.

13. "Jak budovat druhou republiku." All quotations in the next three paragraphs are from this source.

14. Their explicit intellectual debt to Germany in this area was acknowledged by Antonín Peláček, "K novému nacionalismu," *Brázda* 19, no. 43 (1938): 666–67. The family policies in the *Brázda* program have analogues all over Europe, however. See Kevin Passmore, ed., *Women, Gender and Fascism in Europe, 1919–1945* (New Brunswick: Rutgers University Press, 2003).

15. These suggestions were criticized by Czech feminists who defended women's right to work and choose their occupations, and questioned the wisdom of encouraging the birth rate in a country swollen with refugees and the financial efficacy of using loans instead of earnings to establish young couples in life. Zdeňka Patschová and Vilma Součková, "Několik poznámek o úkolech žen v novém státě," *Ženská Rada* 14, no. 9–10 (1938): 186–88 and 199–200.

16. The founding platform of the new National Unity Party mimicked the *Brázda* program in many respects. "Národě če–ské," *Venkov*, November 18, 1938.

17. Jan Gebhart and Jan Kuklík, "Pomnichovská krise a vznik strany Národní Jednoty," *Český Časopis Historický* 90, no. 3 (1992): 365–92.

18. For an insider's account of this process of "cultural fusion," see the memoirs of left-wing literary critic Václav Černý, *Křik koruny české* (Prague: Atlantis, 1992).

19. Rataj, O *autorativní národní stát*, 112–19. In his memoir of this period, Václav Černý asserts that the government was forced by the tabloid press to attack the Jews, and that it refused to confiscate Jewish property, adopt Aryan laws, or do anything more than make a pretense of harshness. The Czech government rather hoped, he said, that all the Jews would convert to Christianity and the problem of what to do with them would go away. See Černý, *Křik koruny české*, 68–69.

20. "Národě če" ské."

21. Jaromír Sedláček to the Ministry of Justice, January 31, 1939, SÚA, MS, box 1963.

22. Government resolution 379/1938, SZ. Because of the powers given to it by the Enabling Act of 1938, the government did not have to submit these resolutions to a vote in the National Assembly.

23. The amount depended upon the former salary level of the woman, but was between 12,000–18,000 crowns (take-home pay) per year.

24. Government resolution 380/1938, SZ.

25. Fr. Tretera, "Jak se zaměstnat," *Přítomnost* 15, no. 43 (1938): 693–94; Ferdinand Peroutka, "Pryč s humanitou— a co potom?" *Přítomnost* 15, no. 44: 690–91.

26. "Vdané ženy (okolo dneska)," *Sobota* 9, no. 40 (1938): 480.

27. Anonymous to Ministerial Council, November 10, 1938, SÚA, PMR, box 3137.

28. Letters found in SÚA, PMR, box 3137.

29. Milena Jesenská, "Vdané ženy z práce," *Nad naše síly* (Olomouc: Votobia, 1997): 134. For some of her work in English, see Kathleen Hayes, ed., *The Journalism of Milena Jesenská: A Critical Voice in Interwar Central Europe* (New York: Berghahn, 2003).

30. Minutes of the plenary meetings of the Czechoslovak Association of University Women, 1926–1935, ANM, SVVŽ, box 1. On Czech rightist women, also see Melissa Feinberg, "Gender and the Politics of Difference in the Czech Lands After Munich," *East European Politics and Societies* 17, no. 2 (May 2003): 202–30.

31. Marie Tumlířová, "Mé první setkání s paní Senátorkou Plamínkovou," in *Kniha života: Práce a osobnost F. F. Plamínkové*, ed. Albina Honzáková (Prague: Melantrich, 1935), 279–80.

32. Minutes of the clubs' session of the WNC plenary meeting, March 11, 1939, SÚA, ŽNR, box 21.

33. Letter from members of the Czechoslovak Association of University Women to Prime Minister Beran, October 25, 1938, SÚA, NRČ, box 288.

34. Women's Center presidium to Jan Kapras, February 10, 1939, SÚA, NRČ, box 288.

35. Program of the cultural division of the Women's Center, SÚA, NRČ, box 288.

36. The maternalist ideology espoused by the Women's Center was, of course, commonly used by women's groups in interwar Europe. The Women's Center was, therefore, more in step with broader European feminist trends than the egalitarian WNC had been.

37. Women's Center presidium to Jan Kapras, February 10, 1939.

38. Minutes of the Women's Center founding committee, February 17, 1939, SÚA, NRČ, box 288.

39. Women's Center presidium to Jan Kapras, February 10, 1939.

40. Program of the social division of the Women's Center, 1939, SÚA, NRČ, box 288.

41. Like their male compatriots on the Czech right, these women rejected fascism, seeing themselves as "conservative" or "rightist." However, their hopes and plans (and tactics) for a sort of equality in a separate sphere certainly bear a resemblance to those of the Nazi women described by Claudia Koonz in *Mothers in the Fatherland* (New York: St. Martin's, 1987).

42. WNC "working notes" from April 27, 1939, SÚA, ŽNR, box 7. Formal meetings were not permitted during the first months of the occupation.

43. Minutes of the WNC executive committee, August 3, 1939, SÚA, ŽNR, box 7.

44. In late 1940, the Women's Center was forced to prepare a "standpoint" on the WNC, in which it claimed the two groups performed different functions and therefore should both be allowed to exist. Minutes of the Women's Center presidium, November 28, 1940, SÚA, NRČ, box 289.

45. Theodore Procházka, *The Second Republic* (Boulder: East European Monographs, 1981), 85–146.

46. Emil Sobota, *Co to byl protektorát* (Prague: Hampl, 1946).

47. The phrases come from Hácha's advisors J. Havelka and J. Kliment, quoted in Jan Gebhart and Jan Kuklík, "Počatky národního souručenství v roce 1939," *Český Časopis Historický* 91, no. 3 (1993): 419.

48. The National Partnership never really lived up to the dreams of its creators. It was considered suspect by the Germans from the start, and its activities were highly scrutinized by occupying forces. Vojtech Mastný, *The Czechs Under Nazi Rule* (Princeton: Princeton University Press, 1971).

49. The initial committee was announced by Hácha on March 21, 1939. Gebhart and Kuklík, "Počatky národního souručenství," 421.

50. There does not seem to be any reason to doubt these figures. All evidence indicates that people did want to join the National Partnership, though they might have had varying ideas about what this meant, i.e., some may have seen it as resistance to the occupiers, some as an expression of national solidarity, some as a way to have some sort of voice in public life, etc.

51. These objections to women's participation were not issued publicly, but came out in a much later private conversation between WNC functionary Irene Malínská and Dr. Mrazík, the general secretary of the National Partnership on April 27, 1940. See Malínská's report to the WNC office, SÚA, ŽNR, box 1.

52. Women's section of the National Unity Party to the National Partnership (copy), April 14, 1939, SÚA, NRČ, box 297.

53. Františka Plamínková to President Hácha, March 23, 1939, SÚA, ŽNR, box 1.

54. Anna Mrskošová to President Hácha (copy), April 10, 1939. She apparently sent the same letter to Hrubý, and gave a copy to the WNC. See SÚA, ŽNR, box 1.

55. Minutes of the WNC executive committee, October 19, 1939, SÚA, ŽNR, box 7. A number of women's groups, including not only the Women's Center but also the still extant (and still influential) Women's National Council, tried to negotiate with the National Partnership leadership on this issue. None were successful in persuading the NP to change its policy.

56. Antonie Maxová to Milena Šmejcová, March 16, 1940, SÚA, ŽNR, box 7.

57. Minutes of the Women's Center executive committee, February 8, 1940, SÚA, NRČ, box 289.

58. Minutes of the Women's Center executive committee, April 11, 1940, SÚA, NRČ, box 289.

59. Ibid. All quotes in this paragraph are also from this source.

60. The incident apparently convinced Marie Provazníková that she no longer wanted to be part of the Women's Center. She did not attend any meetings after the argument over the NP, although her name continued to be listed on the sign-in sheets.

61. Minutes of the Women's Center executive committee, 1939–1943, SÚA, NRČ, boxes 288 and 290. Also Melissa Feinberg, "Dumplings and Domesticity: Collaboration and Resistance in the Protectorate of Bohemia and Moravia," in *Women and War in Central and Eastern Europe*, ed. Nancy Wingfield and Maria Bucur (Bloomington: Indiana University Press, 2006).

62. Minutes of the WNC executive committee, April 25, 1940, SÚA, ŽNR, box 7. In particular, the issue of how to deal with the NP had strained the WNC's relationship with the Organization of Progressive Moravian Women (ZOPŽM), the most prominent women's rights group in Moravia.

63. This meeting is outlined in the WNC secretary's report from May 1940, SÚA, ŽNR, box 7.

64. Minutes of the WNC presidium, May 16, 1941, SÚA, ŽNR, box 7.

65. Karel Werner, "Hradu sloužila ráda Ženská Národní Rada," *Polední List*, February 6, 1942.

66. "Paní předsedkyně nečte noviny," *Polední List*, February 14, 1942.

67. "Paní předsedkyně to nečetla," *Večerní České Slovo*, February 17, 1942.

68. "Nár. Souručenství odmítá tvrzení paní Plamínkové," *Polední List*, February 20, 1942.

69. Minutes of the WNC board, October 19, 1939, SÚA, ŽNR, box 7.

70. da, "Ženy bez politiky," *České Slovo*, August 28, 1941.

71. Minutes of the members' session during the WNC 18th annual plenary meeting, March 2, 1941, SÚA, ŽNR, box 21.

72. It is not clear from this report how many of these attempts succeeded, though it is apparent that at least some did. Minutes of the members' session during the WNC 17th annual plenary meeting, March 3, 1940, SÚA, ŽNR, box 21; "Dnešní stav organisování žen," January 29, 1940, SÚA, ŽNR, box 32.

73. See, for example, F. F. Plamínková, "Literatura pro ženy," *Ženská Rada*, 16, no. 7 (1940): 114–18; and Manča Uhrová, "Četba pro ženy," *Ženský Obzor* 32, no. 4 (1941): 49–50.

74. Circular to WNC clubs, October 9, 1940, SÚA, ŽNR, box 7.

75. Zora Dvořáková and Jiří Doležal, *O Miladě Horákové a Milada Horáková o sobě* (Prague: Klub Dr. Milady Horákové, 2001), 34–37.

76. It is Vojtech Mastný's contention that after this experience, Czechs basically lost all will to resist. Mastný, *Czechs Under Nazi Rule*, 220–25.

## Chapter 7: The Limits of Citizenship in the People's Democracy

1. Milada Horáková, "Poslední setkání," *Rada Žen* 2, no. 5 (1946): 3; Miroslav Ivanov, *Justiční vražda, aneb smrt Milady Horákové* (Prague: Betty, 1991); *Milada Horáková, k 10. výročí její popravy* (Washington DC: Rada Svobodného Československa, 1960); Zora Dvořáková and Jiří Doležal, *O Miladě Horákové a Milada Horáková o sobě* (Prague: Klub Milady Horákové, 2001); Zora Dvořáková, *Milada Horáková* (Prague: Středočeské Nakladatelství, 1991).

2. Edvard Beneš, *Democracy Today and Tomorrow* (New York: Macmillan, 1939), 214–17.

3. Beneš expounded on these ideas in late 1945 in "Světová krise, kontinuita práva, a nové právo revoluční" in *Přednášky na univerzitě karlově 1913–1948* (Prague: Společnost Edvarda Beneše, 1998), 85–95. See also M. R. Myant, *Socialism and Democracy in Czechoslovakia 1945–1948* (London: Cambridge University Press, 1981), 30–32.

4. Paul Zinner, *Communist Strategy and Tactics in Czechoslovakia* (Westport, CT: Greenwood Press, 1975), 63–67.

5. Bradley F. Abrams, *The Struggle for the Soul of the Nation: Czech Culture and the Rise of Communism* (Lanham: Rowan and Littlefield, 2004), 9–38; Mynant, *Socialism and Democracy*, 46–52; Zinner, *Communist Strategy*, 83–96.

6. Rudolf Kučera, "Totalitní demokracie v Československu 1945–1948," *Střední Evropa* 14 (1998): 72–81.

7. *Košický vládní program* (Prague: Nakladatelství Svoboda, 1984); Myant, *Socialism and Democracy*, 46–52.

8. On the trials, see Benjamin Frommer, *National Cleansing: Retribution Against Nazi Collaborators in Postwar Czechoslovakia* (Cambridge: Cambridge University Press, 2004).

9. Emanuel Mandler, *Benešovy dekrety: proč vznikaly a vo jsou* (Prague: Nakl. Libri, 2002); Myant, *Socialism and Democracy*, 53–90.

10. Abrams, *Struggle for the Soul of the Nation*, 89–103.

11. Myant, *Socialism and Democracy*, 106.

12. "Národ zhodnotí ve volbách strany nikoliv podle slov, ale podle činů," *Rudé Právo*, May 19, 1946; "S komunisty do lepších časů," *Rudé Právo*, May 26, 1946.

13. Ladislav Štoll, "O naši národní ideologii," *Rudé Právo*, March 10, 1946; Abrams, *Struggle for the Soul of the Nation*, 118–38.

14. This argument is also made by Abrams in *Struggle for the Soul of the Nation*, especially 199–274.

15. "Volební bitva—a co potom?" *Právo Lidu*, May 22, 1946.

16. Cartoon in *Svobodné Slovo*, May 19, 1946.

17. Election results from Zinner, *Communist Strategy*, 258.

18. *Košický vládní program*, 18, 31.

19. Marie Hořinová, "Nedělní volby do parlamentu rozhodnou ženy," *Lidová Demokracie*, May 24, 1946; Mila Grimmichová, "Ženy rozhodnou ve volbách svou většinou," *Právo Lidu*, May 22, 1946

20. "České ženy budujte s námi šťastný domov!" *Rudé Právo*, May 18, 1946; "Ženy jsou vstříc lepšímu životu," *Rudé Právo*, May 19, 1946; "Ženy stojí v popředí," *Právo Lidu*, April 30, 1946; "Ženy sociální demokratky—bojovnice pro boku mužů," *Právo Lidu*, May 1, 1946.

21. "O zrovnoprávnění žen-hospodyň," *Svobodné Slovo*, May 19, 1946; "Naše práce pro zrovnoprávnění žen," *Svobodné Slovo*, May 23, 1946.

22. National Socialist election flyer ("Ženy Československé!"), SÚA, ČSNS, box 75.

23. Hořinová, "Nedělní volby do parlamentu rozhodnou ženy"; M. Dvořáková, "Dívky a volby," *Lidová Demokracie*, May 19, 1946; Marie Trojanová, "Slovo k českým ženám," *Lidová Demokracie*, May 21, 1946; "První sjezd československé strany lidové," *Lidová Demokracie*, April 2, 1946.

24. Minutes of the National Women's Front, September 25, 1945, SÚA, ÚKŽ-KSČ, folder 48.

25. Zděnka Patschová, "Reaktivace provdaných žen ve veřejné službách," *Rada Žen* 1, no. 11 (1945): 9.

26. Minutes of the National Women's Front, February 26 and March 4, 1946, SÚA, UKŽ-KSČ, folder 48.

27. Minutes of the KSČ Central Women's Commission, November 11, 1946, SÚA, ÚKŽ-KSČ, folder 1; "Zpráva o činnosti Rady čsl. žen," SÚA, ÚKŽ-KSČ, folder 67.

28. Minutes of the National Women's Front, October 10, 1946, SÚA, UKŽ-KSČ, folder 48; *Protokol celostátního manifestačního sjezdu žen konaného ve dnech 26–28. října 1946* (Prague: Národní Fronta Žen, 1946), 23–32.

29. *Protokol celostátního manifestačního sjezdu žen*, 45–55. On the debates over the constitution, see Karel Kaplan, ed. *Příprava ústavy ČSR v letech 1946–1948* (Prague: Ústav pro Soudobé Dějiny, 1993).

30. Fraňa Zemínová to Smetanová, March 28, 1947, SÚA, ČSNS, box 454.

31. "Projev pro nábor žen," and "Pracovní plan—1947," SÚA, ČSNS, box 453.

32. Fraňa Zemínová to Marie Srmšová, October 2, 1947, SÚA, ČSNS, box 453.

33. Fraňa Zemínová to Marie Kostlivá, February 13, 1948, SÚA, ČSNS, box 453.

34. "Úkoly a činnosti (1947)," SÚA, UKŽ-KSČ, folder 4.

35. Rudolf Slanský, "Bez získání většiny žen nezískáme většinu národa," *Rádkyně* 2, no. 5 (1947): 49–50.

36. "Jak plníme plán," *Rádkyně* 3, no. 2 (1948): 29–30; Jiří Kocian, *Československá strana národně socialistická v letech 1945–1948* (Brno: Doplňek, 2002), 143.

37. Minutes of the KSČ Central Women's Commission, December 11, 1947, SÚA, UKŽ-KSČ, folder 1.

38. Vilma Součková, "Rada československých žen," *Rada Žen* 1, no. 1 (1945): 2.

39. Minutes of the CCW presidium, May 29, 1945, SÚA, UKŽ-KSČ, folder 65.

40. CCW Secretary's Report for 1945–1946, SÚA, ČSNS, box 454; CCW Secretary's Report for 1946–1947, SÚA, ČSNS, box 454.

41. "Zpráva o činnosti Rady Československých Žen za dobu od 7.1947–02.1948," SÚA, UKŽ-KSČ, folder 67.

42. Minutes of the KSČ Central Women's Commission, November 11, 1946, UKŽ-KSČ, folder 1.

43. Součková, "Rada československých žen."

44. Quoted in Mila Lewis, "Milada's Living Heroism," in *Milada Horáková*. See also Betka Panpanek, "Milada Horáková," in ibid., 89–93.

45. Dvořáková and Doležal, *O Miladě Horákové*, 57.

46. Myant, *Socialism and Democracy*, 160–95.

47. The standard work on February 1948 is still Karel Kaplan, *Nekrvavá revoluce* (Toronto: 68 Publishers, 1985). Also see Myant, *Socialism and Democracy*, 195–200; Zinner, *Communist Strategy*, 196–205.

48. Myant, *Socialism and Democracy*, 200–218.

49. Kaplan, *Nekrvavá revoluce*.

50. Transcript from meeting of the Committee of the Council of Czechoslovak Women, February 25, 1948, SÚA, UKŽ-KSČ, folder 65, 1–4; transcript from meeting of extended KSČ Central Women's Commission, February 26, 1948, SÚA, UKŽ-KSČ, folder 1.

51. Transcript from meeting of the Committee of the Council of Czechoslovak Women, February 25, 1948, 5–7.

52. Transcript from meeting of the Committee of the Council of Czechoslovak Women, February 25, 1948, 8–14.

53. Transcript from meeting of the Committee of the Council of Czechoslovak Women, February 25, 1948, 14–17.

54. Transcript from meeting of the Committee of the Council of Czechoslovak Women, February 25, 1948, 17–19.

55. "Akční výbor rady čsl žen a národní fronty," *Vlasta* 2, no. 10 (1948): 15; "Vždy k lidem a národem a socialismu," *Vlasta* 2, no. 10 (1948): 15; Julie Prokopová, "Za mír a lepší zítřek," *Vlasta* 2, no. 9 (1948): 2.

56. Transcript from meeting of extended KSČ Central Women's Commission, February 26, 1948.

57. Ibid.; "Vždy k lidem a národem a socialismu."

58. Dvořáková and Doležal, *O Miladě Horákové*, 63–66; Ivanov, *Justiční vražda*, 131.

59. Dvořáková and Doležal, *O Miladě Horákové*, 67–68.

60. Ibid., 69, 66–77.

61. This work was very similar to the kinds of activities Horáková had been involved with during the German occupation a few years previously. Dvořáková and Doležal, *O Miladě Horákové*, 67–75; Karel Kaplan, *Největší politický proces: Milada Horáková a spol* (Prague: Doplněk, 1995), 86–89.

62. Dvořáková and Doležal, *O Miladě Horákové*, 78–91; Kaplan, *Největší politický proces*, 112–13.

63. Kaplan, *Největší politický proces*, 132; Dvořáková and Doležal, *O Miladě Horákové*, 209–13.

64. Dvořáková and Doležal, *O Miladě Horákové*, 210.

65. Protocols from interrogations of Milada Horáková, January 27, 1950, AMV, Akce Střed, sign. 6301/2, 108–9. Most, though not all, of her interrogation records have now been published in Dvořáková and Doležal, *O Miladě Horákové*, 95–207.

66. Jiří Radotínský, *Rozsudek, který otřásel světem* (Prague: ČTK Pressfoto, 1990).

67. Protocols from interrogations of Milada Horáková, April 29, 1950, AMV, Akce Střed, sign. 6301/2, 129–30.

68. The accused represented 42 percent of all female National Socialists elected to the National Assembly in the 1946 elections, making this the most persecuted political group by far.

69. "Obžaloba proti pučistům a špionům usilujícím o válku proti republice," *Mladá Fronta*, May 31, 1950; Miroslav Dvořák and Jaroslav Černý, *Žoldnéři války: soudní proces s dr. Horákovou a spol.* (Prague: Mír, 1950), 5–8.

70. Radotínský, *Rozsudek, který otřásel světem*, 46.

71. Dvořáková and Doležal, *O Miladě Horákové*, 214; Kaplan, *Největší politický proces*, 157.

72. Dvořák and Černý, *Žoldnéři války*, 16–18; "Špionka Horaková doznává své zločiny proti republice a míru," *Mladá Fronta*, June 1, 1950.

73. Dvořák and Černý, *Žoldnéři války*, 9–10; Vlasta Urbanová, "Zrádci lidu,"

*Vlasta* 4, no. 20 (1950): 2; Karel Beran, *Před soudem lidu* (Prague: Melantrich, 1950), 108; Julie Prokopová, "Zločin a trest," *Rádkyně* no. 7 (1950): 105–6.

74. Dvořák and Černý, *Žoldnéři války*, 17.

75. "Slučovací sjezd našich žen zahájen," *Mladá Fronta*, April 1, 1950; Karel Marek, "Náš lid bojuje za mír," *Tvorba* 14, no. 7 (1950): 162; "Lid ozsuzuje rozvratníky a zrádce našeho národa," *Svobodné Slovo*, June 6, 1950.

76. Urbanová, "Zrádci lidu"; Prokopová, "Zločin a trest."

77. Radotínský, *Rozsudek, který otřásel světem*, 79–80; Dvořáková and Doležal, *O Miladě Horákové*, 215; Lewis, "Milada's Living Heroism," 97.

78. "Nejpřísnější tresty bandě rozvratníků," *Mladá Fronta*, June 4, 1950; "Týden údernických směn odpovídají stavaři na zločinné plány zrádců," *Mladá Fronta*, June 7, 1950. Many of these resolutions are published in Kaplan, *Největší politický proces*, 300–315.

79. Radotínský, *Rozsudek, který otřásel světem*, 74–84.

80. Milada Horáková, *Dopisy Milady Horákové, Pankrác 24–27.6.1950* (Prague: Lidové Noviny, 1990), 18.

81. Ibid., 67.

82. Marie Mikulová, "Právní poradna," *Vlasta* 2, no. 12 (1948): 10.

83. *Ústava československé republiky ze dne 9. května 1948* (Prague: Státní Pedagogické Nakladatelství, 1958), chap. 1.

84. Alexej Čepička, *Šťastná rodina, šťastný národ* (Prague: Ministerstvo Informací a Osvěty a Ministerstvo Spravedlnosti, 1949).

85. Jan Jerie, *Uvolnění potratů v našem státě* (Prague: Ústřední Ústav Zdravotnické Osvěty, 1958), 8.

86. Radotínský, *Rozsudek, který otřásel světem*, 87.

87. Zdeněk Urbánek, introduction, *Dopisy Milady Horákové*.

## Conclusion

1. Mark Mazower, *Dark Continent: Europe's Twentieth Century* (New York: Vintage, 1998), 3–6.

2. František Soukup, *28. Říjen 1918, díl I* (Prague: Orbis, 1928), 18.

3. Marie Tippmanová, "Ženina občanská práva a povinnosti," *Nová Síla* 1, no. 34 (1920): 1–2.

# SELECTED BIBLIOGRAPHY

*Archival Sources*

Státní Ústřední Archiv, Prague
    Československá Strana Národně Socialistické
    Ministerstvo Sociální Péče
    Ministerstvo Spravedlnosti
    Ministerstvo Vnitra
    Ministerstvo Zahraničních Věci, Výstřižkový Archiv
    Národní Rada Česká, 1918–1945
    Presidium Ministerské Rady
    Úřad Říšského Protektora, 1939–1945
    Ústřední Komise Žen KSČ
    Ženská Národní Rada

Archiv Kanceláře Prezidenta Republiky, Prague
    Papers from Masaryk, Beneš, and Hácha Administrations, Signatury D and T

Archiv Federálního Shromáždění Československé Republiky, Prague
    Papers from Committee Meetings of the National Assembly
        RNS (1919–1920)
        PS I (1920–1925)
        PS II (1925–1929)
        PS III (1929–1935)
        PS IV (1935–1939)

Archiv Ministerstvo Vnitra, Prague
    Fond Akce Střed

Archiv Národního Musea, Prague
    Feministické Hnutí
    Pozůstalost Františky Plamínkové
    Sdružení Vysokoškolsky Vzdělaných Žen

*Published Czechoslovak Government Papers*

*Sbírka zákonů a nařizení československého státu*
*Těsnopisecké zprávy o schůzích poslanecké sněmovny národního shromáždění*
*československého*

*Těsnopisecké zprávy o schůzích senátu národního shromáždění československého*

*Tisky k těsnopiseckém zprávám o schůzích poslanecké sněmovny národního shromáždění československého*

## Periodicals 1918–1945

| Daily Newspapers | Journals/Weeklies | Women's Periodicals |
|---|---|---|
| *České Slovo* | *Akademie* | *Československá Žena* |
| *Lidové Listy* | *Brázda* | *Eva* |
| *Lidové Noviny* | *Člověk* | *Křesťanská Žena* |
| *Národní Osvobození* | *Dělnická Osvěta* | *List Říšského Svazu* |
| *Národní Politika* | *Hospodářská Politika* | *Československých Učitelek* |
| *Polední List* | *Křesťanská Revue* | *Módní List* |
| *Právo Lidu* | *Modrá Revue* | *Nová Síla* |
| *Venkov* | *Naše Doba* | *Pražanka (List Paní a* |
| | *Nová Evropa* | *Dívek)* |
| | *Přítomnost* | *Věstník ZOPŽM* |
| | *Sobota* | *Zvěstování* |
| | *Sociální Problémy* | *Žena v Povolání* |
| | *Sociologická Revue* | *Ženská Rada* |
| | *Die Wahrheit* | *Ženské Noviny* |
| | | *Ženský Obzor* |
| | | *Ženský Svět* |

## Periodicals 1945–1950

| | | |
|---|---|---|
| *Lidová Demokracie* | *Masarykův Lid* | *Rada Žen* |
| *Mladá Fronta* | *Tvorba* | *Rádkyně* |
| *Právo Lidu* | | *Vlasta* |
| *Rudé Právo* | | |
| *Svobodné Slovo* | | |

## Published Primary Sources

Beneš, Edvard. *Democracy Today and Tomorrow*. New York: Macmillan, 1939.

———. *Přednášky na univerzitě karlově 1913–1948*. Prague: Společnost Edvarda Beneše, 1998.

Beran, Karel. *Před soudem lidu*. Prague: Melantrich, 1950.

Blahá, Arnošt. *Dnešní krise rodinného života*. Brno: Nakladem Vlastním, 1933.

———. "Problém ženského hnutí." *Sociologická Revue* 5, no. 4 (1934): 345–65.

Buzková, Pavla. *Krise ženskostí—úvahy*. Prague: Melantrich, 1925.

———. *Pokrokový názor na ženskou otázku*. Prague: Pokrok, 1909.

Čapek, Karel. *Masaryk on Thought and Life. Conversations with Karel Čapek*. Translated by M. and R. Weatherall. London: Allen and Unwin, 1938.

Čepička, Alexej. *Šťastná rodina, šťastný národ*. Prague: Ministerstvo Informací a Osvěty a Ministerstvo Spravedlnosti, 1949.

Černý, Václav. *Křik koruny české*. Brno: Atlantis, 1992.

*Deset let čsl. ochrany ženských zájmů, 1919–1929*. Prague: Žsl. Ochrana Ženských Žájmů, 1930.

Franta, Bohuslav. *Parlamentní právo žen*. Prague: Český Čtenář, 1916.

Fuss, Henri. *Nezaměstnanost a umístění žen*. Prague: Ženská Národní Rada, 1935.

Halík, Ivo. "Přerušení těhotenství." In *Druhý sjezd československých právníků* 18. Brno: Sjezdový Výbor, 1925.

Herben, Jan. *Masarykův rodinný život*. Brno: Fr. Borový, 1937.

Hill, Cyril. "Citizenship of Married Women." *American Journal of International Law* 18, no. 4 (1924): 720–36.

Honzáková, Albina, ed. *Československé studentky let 1890–1930*. Prague: Ženská Národní Rada a Minerva, 1930.

———, ed. *Kniha života: Práce a osobnost F. F. Plamínkové*. Prague: Melantrich, 1935.

———. *T. G. Masaryk a ženy*. Prague: Ženská Národní Rada, 1938.

Horáková, Milada. *Dopisy Milady Horákové. Pankrác 24.6—27.6.1950*. Prague: Lidové Noviny, 1990.

Hubáček, G. "K otázce vyhnání plodů." In *Druhý sjezd československých právníků* 23. Brno: Sjezdový Výbor, 1925.

Jesenská, Milena. *Cesta k jednoduchostí*. Prague: Barrister and Principal, 1992.

———. *Nad naše síly*. Olomouc: Votobia, 1997.

Jungwirtha, Anna. *Péče o matka a dítě*. Prague: Czechoslovak Social Democratic Propaganda Section, 1946.

Kafka, Bruno. *Právo rodinné: návrh subkomitétu pro revisi občanského zákoníka pro československou republiku*. Prague: Minsterstvo Spravedlnosti, 1924.

Karpíšková, Betty. *Kontrola porodů a Meissnerova osnova*. Prague: Ústřední Výbor Žen Sociálních Demokratických, 1932.

Kissich, Antonín. "Otázka trestnost vyhnání plodů." In *Druhý sjezd československých právníků*, 11. Brno: Sjezdový Výbor, 1925.

*Košický vládní program*. Prague: Nakladatelství Svoboda, 1984.

Kozáková, Anděla, ed. *Čeho jsme docílily- deset let práce SVVŽ*. Prague: Sdružení Vysokoškolsky Vzdělaných Žen, 1932.

———. *Právní postavení ženy v českém právu zemském*. Prague: Seminář Českého Pravá na Karlově Universitě, 1926.

Krčmar, Jan. *Právo manželské*. Prague: Všehrd, 1920.

Krejčí, F. V. *Naše osvobození.* Prague: A. Svěcený, 1919.

Kučerová, Vlasta. *K historie ženského hnutí v čechách.* Brno: Ženské Revue, 1914.

League of Nations. *Conference for the Codification of International Law—Bases for Discussion,* vol. 1 (Nationality). Geneva: League of Nations, 1929.

League of Nations (Committee of Experts for the Progressive Codification of International Law). *Report on the Questions Which Appear Ripe for International Regulation (Questionnaires 1–7).* Geneva: League of Nations, 1927.

Machotka, Otakar. *K sociologii rodiny.* Prague: Knihova Statistického Obzoru, 1932.

MacMillan, Chrystal. "Nationality of Married Women: Present Tendencies," *Journal of Comparative Legislation and International Law* 7 (3rd series), no. 4 (1925): 142–54.

Mandl, Vladimír. *Rozluka manželství (podle §13–24 zák. ze dne 22. května 1919, čís. 320 Sb z. a n.).* Prague: Československý Kompas, 1933.

Masaryk, Tomáš. *Česká otázka.* 2nd ed. Prague: Pokrok, 1908.

———. *The Ideals of Humanity.* London: Allen and Unwin, 1931.

———. *The Making of a State.* London: Allen and Unwin, 1927.

———. *Mnohoženství a jednoženství.* 2nd ed. Prague: Čin, 1925.

———. *O ženě.* Prague: Čin, 1930.

Masaryk, Tomáš G., Milan Štefánik, and Edvard Beneš. *Washingtonská declarace.* Brno: Moravský Legionář, 1925.

Masaryková, Alice G. *Dětství a mládí.* Pittsburgh: Masaryk Publications Trust, 1960.

Maxová, Antonie. *Proč je rovnoprávnost žen ohrozena a jak ji nutno hájit.* Prague: Říšský Svaz Československých Učitelek, 1934.

Mayer, Jiří. *Ochrana ženy ve věcech právních.* Prague: Československý Kompas, 1935.

Mikulová, Marie. *Žena v právním řadě československé.* Prague: self-published, 1936.

Mužíková-Nosilová, Ludmila. *Naše ženy v historii a ve vystavbě státu.* Prague: Ministerstvo Informací, 1946.

Neumann, Stanslav. *Dějiny ženy. Populární kapitoly sociologické, ethnologické, a kulturně historické.* Vol. 4. Prague: Melantrich, 1932.

Nováková, Tereza. *Ze ženského hnutí.* Prague: J. R. Velímek, 1912.

*Obecný zákoník občanský pro republiku československou.* Translated by František Joklík. 3rd ed. Prague: Hejda a Tuček, 1922.

Opočenský, Jan. *Nacism a naše státní a národní tradice.* London: Čechoslovák, 1942.

Plamínková, F. F. *O právu vdaných žen na výdělečnou práci.* Prague: Ženská Národní Rada, 1934.

———. *Občanská rovnoprávnost žen.* Prague: Státní Školní Knihosklad, 1920.

———. *The Political Rights of Women in the Czechoslovak Republic*. Prague: Gazette de Prague, 1920.

———. *Žena v demokracii*. Prague: Svaz Národní Osvobození, 1924.

*Protokol celostátního manifestačního sjezdu žen konaného ve dnech 26–28. října 1946*. Prague: Národní Fronta Žen, 1946.

Rádl, Emanuel. *O ženském hnutí*. Prague: Čin, 1933.

———. *Proti tak zvané sociální indikaci (námitky proti návrhu nového zákona o umělém potratu)*. Prague: YMCA v Praze, 1932.

Rys, Vladimír. *Je potrat vraždou?* Prague: Volné Myšlenky, 1933.

Seckler-Hudson, Carolyn. *Statelessness: With Special Reference to the United States*. Washington DC: Digest Press, 1934.

Sedláček, Jaromír. *Reforma manželského práva*. Prague: V. Linhart, 1938.

———. *Rodinné právo*. Brno: Československý Akademický Spolek "Právník," 1934.

Sobota, Emil. *Co to byl protektorát*. Prague: Hampl, 1946.

Stránská-Absolonová, Olga. *Za novou ženu*. Prague: B. Kočí, 1920.

Superrevisní Komise. *Zákon, kterým se vydává všeobecný zákoník občanský*. Prague: Ministerstvo Spravedlnosti, 1931.

Úřad Lidové Osvěty. *Tři roky v říši*. Prague: Orbis, 1942.

Vacek, Josef. *Naše revoluce a manželství*. Prague: Nakladatelské Družstvo Maje, 1920.

Waltz, Waldo Emerson. *The Nationality of Married Women*. Urbana: University of Illinois Press, 1937.

Zachoval, Jan. *Rodinná výchova*. Prague: Státní Nakladatelství, 1923.

Záhoř, Zdeněk. *Pohlaví, láska, otcovství*. Prague: Odkaz, 1920.

Zavadil, Jaroslav. *Manželské právo*. Prague: V. Linhart, 1938.

Ženská Národní Rada. *Masaryk a ženy*. Prague: Ženská Národní Rada, 1930.

Žlábek, Josef, and Vladímir Verner. *Státní občanství a domovské právo v republice československé*. Prague: Československý Kompas, 1923.

## Selected Secondary Sources

Abrams, Bradley F. *The Struggle for the Soul of the Nation: Czech Culture and the Rise of Communism*. Lanham: Rowman and Littlefield, 2004.

Anderson, Harriet. *Utopian Feminism: Women's Movements in Fin de Siècle Vienna*. New Haven: Yale University Press, 1992.

Arendt, Hannah. *The Origins of Totalitarianism*. New York: Harcourt Brace, 1973.

Balkenende, Teresa. "Protecting the National Inheritance: Nation-state Formation and the Transformation of Birth Culture in the Czech Lands, 1880–1938." PhD diss., University of Washington, 2004.

Bednářová, Věra. "České ženské hnutí do roku 1948." *Český Časopis Historický* 89, no. 2 (1991): 232–37.

Benhabib, Seyla, ed. *Democracy and Difference*. Princeton: Princeton University Press, 1996.

Bredbenner, Candace Lewis. *A Nationality of Her Own: Women, Marriage and the Law of Citizenship*. Berkeley: University of California Press, 1998.

Bridenthal, Renate, Atina Grossman, and Marion Kaplan, eds. *When Biology Became Destiny: Women in Weimar and Nazi Germany*. New York: Monthly Review Press, 1984.

Broklová, Eva. *Československá demokracie: politický systém ČSR, 1918–1938*. Prague: Sociologické Nakladatelství, 1992.

Burešová, Jana. *Proměny společenského postavení českých žen v první polovině 20. století*. Olomouc: Universita Palackého, 2001.

Canning, Kathleen. "Class vs. Citizenship: Keywords in German Gender History." *Central European History* 37, no. 2 (2004): 225–44.

Canning, Kathleen, and Sonya O. Rose, eds. *Gender, Citizenships, and Subjectivities*. Oxford: Blackwell, 2002.

Cott, Nancy F. "Marriage and Women's Citizenship in the United States" *American Historical Review* 103, no. 5 (1998): 1440–74.

Cozine, Alicia K. "A Member of the State: Citizenship Law and Its Application in Czechoslovakia." PhD diss., University of Chicago, 1996.

Daley, Caroline, and Melanie Nolan, eds. *Suffrage and Beyond: International Feminist Perspectives*. New York: New York University Press, 1994.

David, Katharine. "Czech Feminists and Nationalism in the Late Habsburg Monarchy." *Journal of Women's History* 3, no. 2 (Fall 1991): 26–45.

de Grazia, Victoria. *How Fascism Ruled Women*. Berkeley: University of California Press, 1992.

Dvořáková, Zora. *Milada Horáková*. Prague: Středočeské Nakladatelství, 1991.

Dvořáková, Zora, and Jiří Doležal. *O Miladě Horákové a Milada Horáková o sobě*. Prague: Klub Milady Horákové, 2001.

Evans, Richard. *The Feminist Movement in Germany, 1894–1933*. London: Sage, 1976.

Feinberg, Melissa. "Democracy and Its Limits: Gender and Rights in the Czech Lands, 1918–1938," *Nationalities Papers* 30, no. 4 (December 2002): 553–70.

———. "Gender and the Politics of Difference in the Czech Lands After Munich," *East European Politics and Societies* 17, no. 2 (May 2003): 202–30.

Frommer, Benjamin. "Expulsion or Integration: Unmixing Interethnic Marriage in Postwar Czechoslovakia." *East European Politics and Societies* 14, no. 2 (2000): 381–410.

Gajan, Koloman, ed. *Tomáš Garrigue Masaryk o demokracii*. Prague: Melantrich, 1991.

Gebhart, Jan, and Jan Kuklík. *Dramatické a všední dny protektorátu.* Prague: Themis, 1995.

——. "Počatky národního souručenství v roce 1939." *Český Časopis Historický* 91, no. 3 (1993): 417–39.

——. "Pomnichovská krize a vznik strany Národní Jednoty." *Český Časopis Historický* 90, no. 3 (1992): 365–93.

Gerhard, Ute. *Debating Women's Equality*, trans. Alison Brown and Belinda Cooper. New Brunswick: Rutgers University Press, 2001.

Glendon, Mary Ann. *Abortion and Divorce in Western Law.* Cambridge: Harvard University Press, 1987.

Goldman, Wendy. *Women, the State and Revolution: Soviet Family Policy and Social Life, 1917–1936.* Cambridge: Cambridge University Press, 1993.

Grossman, Atina. *Reforming Sex: The German Movement for Birth Control and Abortion Reform 1920–1950.* New York: Oxford University Press, 1995.

Hause, Steven, and Anne Kenney. *Women's Suffrage and Social Politics in the French Third Republic.* Princeton: Princeton University Press, 1984.

Havelková, Hana, ed. *Lidská práva, ženy a společnost, člověk a jeho práva.* Prague: ESVLP, 1992.

Hayes, Kathleen, ed. *The Journalism of Milena Jesenská: A Critical Voice in Interwar Central Europe.* New York: Berghahn, 2003.

Healy, Maureen. *Vienna and the Fall of the Habsburg Empire: Total War and Everyday Life in World War I.* New York: Cambridge University Press, 2004.

Heinemann, Elizabeth. *What Difference Does a Husband Make? Women and Marital Status in Nazi and Postwar Germany.* Berkeley: University of California Press, 1999.

Heitlinger, Alena. *Women and State Socialism: Sex Inequality in the Soviet Union and Czechoslovakia.* Montreal: McGill-Queen's University Press, 1979.

Honzajzer, Jiří. *Vznik a rozpad vládních koalic v Československu v letech 1918–1938.* Prague: Orbis, 1995.

Horská, Pavla. "Za práva žen." *Dějiny a Současnost* 14, no. 1 (1992): 27–33.

Ivanov, Miroslav. *Justiční vražda, aneb smrt Milady Horákové.* Prague: Betty, 1991.

Jayawardena, Kumari. *Feminism and Nationalism in the Third World.* London: Zed Press, 1986.

Jerie, Jan. *Uvolnění potratů v našem státě.* Prague: Ústřední Ústav Zdravotnické Osvěty, 1958.

Kaplan, Karel. *Největší politický proces: Milada Horáková a spol.* Prague: Doplňek, 1995.

——. *Nekrvavá revoluce.* Toronto: 68 Publishers, 1985.

——, ed. *Příprava ústavy ČSR v letech 1946–1948.* Prague: Ústav pro Soudobé Dějiny, 1993.

Kárník, Zdeněk. *České země v éře první republiky (1918–1938)*. 3 vols. Prague: Libri, 2000–2003.

Kelly, Mills T. "Feminism, Pragmatism or Both? Czech Radical Nationalism and the Woman Question." *Nationalities Papers* 30, no. 4 (2002): 537–52.

Kent, Susan Kingsley. *Making Peace: The Reconstruction of Gender in Interwar Britain*. Princeton: Princeton University Press, 1993.

———. *Sex and Suffrage in Britain 1860–1914*. Princeton: Princeton University Press, 1987.

Kerber, Linda K. *No Constitutional Right to Be Ladies*. New York: Hill and Wang, 1998.

Kessler-Harris, Alice. *In Pursuit of Equity: Women, Men and the Quest for Economic Citizenship in 20th Century America*, New York: Oxford University Press, 2001.

King, Jeremy. *Budweisers into Czechs and Germans*. Princeton: Princeton University Press, 2002.

Klimek, Antonín. *Boj o hrad*. Prague: Panevropa, 1996.

Kocian, Jiří. *Československá strana národně socialistická v letech 1945–1948*. Brno: Doplněk, 2002.

Koonz, Claudia. *Mothers in the Fatherland: Women, The Family, and Nazi Politics*. New York: St. Martin's, 1987.

Kovtun, George. *The Spirit of Masaryk*. New York: St. Martin's, 1990.

Kučera, Rudolf. "Totalitní demokracie v Československu 1945–1948." *Střední Evropa* 14 (1998): 72–81.

Kutnar, František. *Generace brázdy*. Prague: Historický Klub, 1992.

Lacina, Vlastislav, ed. *Sborník k dějinám 19. a 20. století*. Prague: Historický Ústav, 1993.

Ledvinka, Václav, ed. *Žena v dějinách Prahy, Documenta Pragensia*. Prague: Scriptorium, 1996.

Lenderová, Milena. *K hříchu i k modlitbě: žena v minulém století*. Prague: Mladá Fronta, 1999.

Lister, Ruth. *Citizenship: Feminist Perspectives*. New York: New York University Press, 1997.

Malečková, Jitka. "Nationalizing Women and Engendering the Nation: The Czech National Movement." In *Gendered Nations: Nationalisms and Gender Order in the Long Nineteenth Century*, edited by Ida Blom, Karen Hagemann, and Catherine Hall, 293–310. New York: Berg, 2000.

Mandler, Emanuel. *Benešovy dekrety: proč vznikaly a co jsou*. Prague: Nakl. Libri, 2002.

Mastný, Vojtech. *The Czechs Under Nazi Rule*. Princeton: Princeton University Press, 1971.

Mazower, Mark. *Dark Continent: Europe's Twentieth Century*. New York: Vintage, 1998.

Myant, M. R. *Socialism and Democracy in Czechoslovakia 1945–1948.* London: Cambridge University Press, 1981.

Nathans, Eli. *The Politics of Citizenship in Germany: Ethnicity, Utility and Nationalism.* New York: Berg, 2004.

Neudorfl, Marie. *České ženy v 19. století.* Prague: Janua, 1999.

———. "Masaryk's Understanding of Democracy Before 1914." In *The Carl Beck Papers in Russian and East European Studies*, 51. Pittsburgh: University of Pittsburgh Center for Russian and East European Studies, 1989.

Nussbaum, Martha. *Sex and Social Justice.* New York: Oxford University Press, 1999.

Odložilik, Otakar. *Masaryk's Idea of Democracy.* New York: Masaryk Institute, 1952.

Offen, Karen. *European Feminisms 1700–1950.* Stanford: Stanford University Press, 2000.

Olivová, Věra. *Czechoslovakia's Doomed Democracy.* London: Sidgwick and Jackson, 1972.

Orzoff, Andrea. "Battle for the Castle: The Friday Men and the Czechoslovak Republic, 1918–1938." PhD diss., Stanford University, 1999.

Passmore, Kevin, ed. *Women, Gender, and Fascism in Europe, 1919–1945.* New Brunswick: Rutgers University Press, 2003.

Pateman, Carole. *The Sexual Contract.* Stanford: Stanford University Press, 1988.

Phillips, Anne. *Engendering Democracy.* University Park: Pennsylvania State University Press, 1991.

Polák, Stanlislav. *Charlotte Garrigue Masaryková.* Prague: Mladá Fronta, 1992.

Pollard, Miranda. *Reign of Virtue: Mobilizing Gender in Vichy France.* Chicago: University of Chicago Press, 1998.

Preston-Warren, W. *Masaryk's Democracy: A Philosophy of Scientific and Moral Culture.* Chapel Hill: University of North Carolina Press, 1941.

Procházka, Theodore. *The Second Republic.* Boulder: East European Monographs, 1981.

Rada Svobodného Československa, ed. *Milada Horáková—k 10. výročí její popravy.* Washington DC: Rada Svobodného Československa, 1960.

Radotínský, Jiří. *Rozsudek, který otřásel světem.* Prague: ČTK Pressfoto, 1990.

Rataj, Jan. *O autoritativní národní stát.* Prague: Karolinium, 1997.

Reinfeld, Barbara. "Františka Plamínková, Czech Feminist and Patriot." *Nationalities Papers* 25, no. 1 (1997): 13–33.

Roberts, Mary Louise. *Civilization Without Sexes: Reconstructing Gender in Postwar France.* Chicago: University of Chicago Press, 1994.

Rupp, Leila J. *Worlds of Women: The Making of an International Women's Movement.* Princeton: Princeton University Press, 1997.

Sayer, Derek. *The Coasts of Bohemia.* Princeton: Princeton University Press, 1998.

Schellová, Illona, and Karel Schelle. *Vývoj kodifikace občanského práva.* Brno: Masarykova Univerzita, 1993.

Scott, Joan. *Only Paradoxes to Offer: French Feminists and the Rights of Man.* Cambridge, MA: Harvard University Press, 1996.

Shanley, Mary. *Feminism, Marriage and the Law in Victorian England, 1850–1895.* Princeton: Princeton University Press, 1989.

Skilling, H. Gordon. *T. G. Masaryk, Against the Current 1882–1914.* University Park: Pennsylvania State University Press, 1994.

Soland, Birgitte. *Becoming Modern: Young Women and the Reconstruction of Womanhood in the 1920's.* Princeton: Princeton University Press, 2000.

Steenbergen, Bart van, ed. *The Conditions of Citizenship.* London: Sage, 1994.

Teich, Mikuláš, ed. *Bohemia in History.* Cambridge: Cambridge University Press, 1998.

Veselá, Renata. *Vývoj rodinného práva do roku 1938.* Brno: Masarykova Univerzita, 1993.

Vlček, Eduard, and Karel Schelle. *Vybrané kapitoly z právních dějin.* Brno: Masarkyova Univerzita, 1993.

Werbner, Pnina, and Nira Yuval-Davis, eds. *Women, Citizenship, and Difference.* New York: Zed Press, 1999.

Whittick, Arnold. *Woman into Citizen.* London: Athenaeum, 1979.

Winters, Stanley B., ed. *T. G. Masaryk (1850–1937): Volume 1, Thinker and Politician.* London: Macmillan, 1990.

Zahra, Tara. "Reclaiming Children for the Nation: Germanization, National Ascription, and Democracy in the Bohemian Lands, 1900–1945," *Central European History* 37, no. 4 (2004): 501–43.

Zinner, Paul. *Communist Strategy and Tactics in Czechoslovakia.* Westport, CT: Greenwood Press, 1975.

# INDEX

abortion: attitudes of medical professionals toward, 134–36, 158; debates over,
130–31, 155–58; frequency of, 134–35,
146–47; illegally performed, 132, 135,
141–42, 146–48; laws prohibiting,
131; moral objections to, 130, 133–36,
144–45, 148, 151–53, 155; proposals to
legalize, 131–32, 135, 137–39, 147–48,
154; public opinions of, 132–33, 137,
139–46; "socially indicated," 135–38,
140, 147–48, 152; and the working
class, 132, 140–46, 151, 158
Agrarian Party, 94, 163, 193, 212; on abortion reform, 149, 151, 154; on civil
marriage, 45; views on women's suffrage, 21, 39, 41
Austria, 31, 76, 80–81. *See also* Habsburg
Monarchy
Austrian Civil Code of 1811, 42–44, 50, 59
authoritarian democracy, 3, 163, 174, 223,
226–27, 229

Bartošek, Theodor, 37, 46–47
Bednáříková-Tunwaldová, Růžena, 170,
180
Beneš, Edvard, 29, 125, 161–62, 199, 202,
218; activities during the Second World
War, 191–92; decrees, 193–94; during
February 1948, 206; relationship to the
WNC, 169
Beran, Rudolf, 162–63, 165–67, 170,
174–75

Cable Act, 77–78
Catholic Church, 158; and abortion, 131,
144, 149–52, 158; and civil marriage,
44–46, 48, 52, 61–63, 67, 93; women in,
54, 59–60, 63, 153, 198, 201. *See also*
Federation of Catholic Women and
Girls
*celibát*, 34, 102–9, 117, 167
Central Action Committee, 206–10
Christmas bonus, 109–13, 119
citizenship, 99–101, 225, 227; after 1945,

193, 196, 228; after Munich, 165; egalitarian conception of, 3–4, 35–36, 88,
125–27, 157; gendered view of, 4–5, 42,
73, 108–9, 128, 156, 165, 176–77, 179,
184–85. *See also* Czechoslovak citizenship law; women's citizenship
civil marriage, 44–45, 52, 61–62, 67
civil service: Jews excluded from, 165;
pay cuts in, 110–12, 119–23; public
attitudes toward, 101–2, 110, 114–18;
regulations, 103, 105–8, 117, 166
Committee for Women's Voting Rights,
26–27, 30
Council of Czechoslovak Women (CCW),
191, 198, 203–5, 207–10, 217
Czech feminists: in 1918, 34; and abortion,
131, 154–56; attacks on, 182–86; campaigns for civil code, 43, 52–53, 76–77;
ideology, 3–4, 10, 24–25, 225; influence,
89; and maternalism, 25–26, 168–70;
relationship to Tomáš Masaryk, 13,
23–24, 38–40. *See also* Women's
National Council
Czech National Council, 170, 174, 181
Czech nationalism, 14–16, 74–76, 93–95,
97–98
Czechoslovak Association of University
Women, 23, 119, 156, 169–70, 211
Czechoslovak citizenship law, 73–74,
83–84, 226; of 1920, 75–76; revisions
to, 88, 91–93, 94–97, 163, 203, 220
Czechoslovak civil law code, 42–42, 90,
93; National Assembly debates on,
66–68; revisions to, 50–52, 60–62,
69, 166
Czechoslovak Communist Party: banned,
164; Central Women's Commission of,
202–4, 210–11, 221; in February 1948,
205–7; history, 192; legacy, 10; program,
194, 219–20; tactics, 193–95, 199; views
on abortion, 149, 151, 220; views on
family law, 56, 220; views on women's
rights, 196–97, 219–20; women in,
202–3, 220